CREATIVE

DESTRUCTION

CREATIVE DESTRUCTION

Business Survival Strategies in the Global Internet Economy

WITHDRAWN

LEE W. MCKNIGHT

PAUL M. VAALER

RAUL L. KATZ

Editors

The MIT Press
Cambridge, Massachusetts
London, England

Printed and bound in the United States of America.

Library of Congress Cataloging-in-Publication Data

Creative destruction : business survival strategies in the global Internet economy / Lee W. McKnight, Paul M. Vaaler, Raul L. Katz, editors.
    p. cm.
    A collection of 12 papers which grew out of a March 1999 symposium held at the Fletcher School of Law and Diplomacy, Tufts University. 'Creative Destruction or Just Destruction? Telecoms in Transition: Survival and Success in the Global Internet Economy' was co-sponsored by the Fletcher School's Hitachi Center for Technology and International Affairs, the Fletcher School's Edward R. Murrow Center for International Information and Communication, and Booz-Allen & Hamilton.
    Includes bibliographical references and index.
    ISBN 0-262-13389-X (hc. : alk. paper)
    1. Technological innovations—Economic aspects—Congresses. 2. Evolutionary economics—Congresses. 3. Organizational change—Congresses. 4. Internet—Congresses. 5. Globalization—Congresses. I. Title: Business survival strategies in the global Internet economy. II. McKnight, Lee W. III. Vaaler, Paul M. IV. Katz, Raul Luciano.
    HC79.T4 .C74 2001
    658.4'062 dc21   00-053708

Text design and composition: Paperwork
Cover design: Three Fish Design

For our wives and families

CONTENTS

A C K N O W L E D G M E N T S

This book would never have been completed without the support and guidance of many people and organizations. Our first and deepest expression of gratitude is for the original work and timely insights of the diverse group of authors who contributed to this book: William Baumol of New York University, Jean Camp of Harvard University, Leslie Helm of Glocom University (Japan), Jill Hills and Maria Michalis of the University of Westminster (UK), Marty Hyman and Peter Pekar of Booz·Allen & Hamilton, William Lehr of Columbia University and the Massachusetts Institute of Technology, Terry McGarty of Zephyr Communications, and Walter Molano of BCP Securities. They shared our enthusiasm for developing a deeper understanding of "creative destruction" and its relevance to Internet-related industries, firms, and political and social policies. The contributing authors combined that enthusiasm with insight and analysis specific to their own backgrounds, research interests, and experience.

We also are grateful to all of the participants in the symposium that brought many of these authors together for the first time to begin to explore these issues. *Creative Destruction* was stimulated by a symposium held at the Fletcher School of Law and Diplomacy, Tufts University, "Creative Destruction —or Just Destruction? Telecoms in Transition: Survival and Success in the Global Internet Economy." The symposium was co-sponsored by the Fletcher School's Hitachi Center for Technology and International Affairs, the Fletcher School's Edward R. Murrow Center for International Information and Communication, and Booz·Allen & Hamilton. The symposium brought together leading academic and professional commentators on the key technological, regulatory, organizational, and competitive dynamics compelling change in the way firms and their stakeholders do business in an increasingly global and Internet-centric society.

The symposium panels, papers, and presentations sparked a lively debate among the participants, which was ably moderated by panel chairs from the Fletcher School faculty, including Carsten Kowalczyk, Lisa Lynch, and Joel Trachtman. There were excellent panelist and paper presentations from the invited participants. We single out for special recognition chief executives Frank Blount of Telstra (Australia); Steven Chrust, founder of Winstar Communications and SGC Advisory Services; Juan Carlos Masjoan of Telecom Argentina; Terrence McGarty of Zephyr Communications; Hitachi America's chief technologist, Kenji Takeda; corporate strategist Takashi Hatchoji of Hitachi Ltd (Japan); executive vice presidents Randall Battat of Motorola Corporation and Andrew Morley of Level 3 Communications; Bill Griffin, formerly of GTE; Richard J. Solomon of the University of Pennsylvania; and Robert Pepper, chief of the U.S. Federal Communications Commission, Office of Plans and Policy. These panelists and others stirred the pot of ideas for all of us striving to link Joseph Schumpeter's concept of creative destruction to the dynamics reshaping firms, industries, and regulatory policies worldwide. We thank all of the panelists for their contributions. We also thank the Fletcher School, Booz·Allen & Hamilton, and John Wylie of Credit Suisse-First Boston (Australia) for their financial sponsorship and support of the symposium.

The flood of positive feedback after the spring 1999 symposium encouraged us to take the next step and begin the writing and editing for this volume. Robert Prior, Victoria Richardson-Warneck, Elizabeth Murry, and many others at the MIT Press have guided and supported our work over the last year. Anne Kilgore of Paperwork coordinated manuscript preparation, and designed and produced the text. Caroline Vaaler of Three Fish Design put together the wonderful cover and dust-jacket art for the book. We appreciate their guidance, competence, and patience.

We also have received substantial assistance from various individuals at our respective institutions. At the Fletcher School several faculty and staff members and students assisted us during the writing and editing process. We single out Greg Czarnecki, Annalee Babb, and most of all, Peter Cukor, for special recognition. At different times they cheerfully took on many tasks, which contributed substantially to this volume. Peter Cukor's energy, insight, and resolve were crucial to the success of the symposium and to the timely completion of this book. Warm thanks go to him and to others at the Fletcher School. Consistent support for this project from the Fletcher School's Hitachi Center for Technology and International Affairs was also a function of the encouragement and organizational support given by Hitachi Ltd in Japan. Dr. Katsushige Mita, Asahiko Isobe, and many individuals at Hitachi Ltd's public policy research arm, the Hitachi Research Institute, coordinated their efforts with ours to help realize the symposium and book projects. They also have our gratitude. Support for this project from the Fletcher School's Edward R. Murrow Center for International Communication was also unstinting. The Murrow Center's involvement was made possible in part by the MIT Internet and Telecoms Convergence Consortium (ITC) and its sponsors. Special thanks go to David Clark, Sharon Gillett, and John Wroclawski, and to our ITC friends from the telecommunications, computing, and Internet industries, too numerous to mention, who provided critical feedback and were an early sounding board for some of the research results that have been elaborated for a broader audience in this book.

Booz·Allen & Hamilton contributed generous organizational, intellectual, and financial support for this edited volume. Their support confirms Booz·Allen & Hamilton's belief in and commitment to maintaining intellectual leadership in academic and professional communities dealing with the complex business and policy implications associated with the emergence of new technologies in telecommunications and other Internet-related industries. Several individuals at Booz·Allen & Hamilton merit special recognition for this commitment. In addition to contributing author Marty Hyman, Bill Michels and Ragu Gurumurthy in Booz·Allen's New York office and Richard Buenneke in the McLean office were participants in the symposium and active supporters of the book project. Melissa Rosen, from Booz·Allen's marketing department, was invaluable in putting together the proceedings of the symposium.

Throughout the editorial process, Betty Doheny kept the three editors in touch, no matter where in the world our other work took us. We thank all of these individuals for their contributions.

We reserve our last acknowledgment for those whose help we too often fail to recognize and thank. Our wives and families provided us a comfortable haven to which we could retreat after days of writing, editing, and completing the numerous other tasks related to the book. Our wives, Elaine McKnight, Barbara Christie Samuels, and Katherine Vaaler, and our families provided constant support and encouragement and made it all worthwhile. To all of you, our thanks and love.

LEE W. MCKNIGHT
PAUL M. VAALER
RAUL L. KATZ

PART1

INTRODUCTION

1 | INTRODUCTION TO CREATIVE DESTRUCTION

Lee W. McKnight, Paul M. Vaaler, and Raul L. Katz

More than half a century ago, economist Joseph Schumpeter explained that processes intrinsic to any capitalist society engendered a "creative destruction" whereby innovations would destroy existing technologies and methods of production only to be assaulted themselves by imitative rival products with newer, more efficient configurations. In the telecommunications and information industries alone in the past 150 years, we have seen the displacement of the telegraph by the telephone; black-and-white by color television; mechanical calculators, typewriters, and other office machines by computers; and so on. But such orderly, incremental transitions from older to newer technologies seem inappropriate comparisons for today's telecommunications field. The rate of transition away from older technologies is accelerating, and the transition processes are discontinuous and uncertain. Think, for instance, of circuit-switched copper-terminated networks run by incumbent telecommunications carriers. Currently, they are under simultaneous assault from optical networks, wireless, and cable-based technologies, tied together by the Internet protocol. These platforms, while coexisting at the moment, are all fighting for a dominant share of the market and a claim to future technological preeminence. This situation is characteristic not only of industrialized countries but can be observed in most emerging economies. Furthermore, this process of "anarchic" technological substitution is also accompanied by mergers, acquisitions, bankruptcies, investment, and divestments in worldwide markets.

Is the current chaotic state of the telecommunications industry evidence of a process of "creative destruction"—or just destruction? Can Schumpeter's ideas be used to explain the process? Or do they provide ex post facto rationalizations for an industry engaged in activities that waste valuable societal resources while offering limited benefits to consumers and society as a whole?

These questions are important in understanding the dynamics of the telecommunications, media, entertainment, and a host of other industries, and in analyzing the implications for firms and social policies.

This book is a result of our continuing search for answers to these questions. As a first step in our explorations, an interdisciplinary symposium cochaired by this book's editors, was convened at the Fletcher School of Law and Diplomacy at Tufts University. [1]

This volume builds on themes addressed at the March 1999 symposium and broadens their application to industrial and policy realms beyond the telecommunications field. The book includes significant new contributions, such as William Baumol's chapter "Innovation and Creative Destruction," Lee McKnight's "Internet Business Models: Creative Destruction as Usual," and Leslie Helm's "Social Communications Innovation and Destruction in Japan." All other chapters, while based on work first presented at the symposium, have been substantially revised. This book is not a proceedings volume—it is a new initiative based on a novel application of the creative destruction concept. It provides a comprehensive view of the relevance of Schumpeter's framework to explain ongoing dynamics and discontinuities across a range of Internet-related industries, firms, and policies.

While Schumpeter's concept provided the impetus for this book, the topic's importance is accentuated by the rapidly accelerating pace of regulatory, technical, and business innovation, which is "destroying" old regimes and creating in their place more exciting though less predictable scenarios for executives and policymakers. Four points consistent with the theme of creative destruction frame this book:

The Destruction of Traditional Industry Structures: Clearly defined industry boundaries, entry barriers, and market positions within the telecommunications industry have been replaced, perhaps permanently, by blurred and fluid industry borders, rapidly shifting interfirm alliances, and the unrelenting introduction of cost-reducing product and process innovations.

The Destruction of Traditional Regulatory Approaches: Regulatory frameworks limiting competitive entry and defining the specific prices, products, and services of "natural" monopolist incumbent telecommunications firms have given way to lighter-handed schemes that promote competitive entry for domestic startups and grant greater latitude to both start-ups and incumbents to reprice existing products and services, create new offerings, and reconfigure their organizations through privatization, mergers and acquisitions, and strategic alliances.

The Destruction of Traditional Competitive Positioning Strategies: Strategies that rely on persistently profitable, protected market positions have been replaced by "hypercompetitive" strategies. Telecommunications firms must frequently change their market positions, partners, products, and pricing to meet competitive challenges from other traditional telecommunications firms, as well as firms whose experience in transport, media, computers and/or software has given them some cost or quality advantage in providing substitute products and services.

The Destruction of Traditional Technological Assumptions: The historical dominance of analog, narrow bandwidth, circuit-switched fixed-line technologies designed primarily for voice telephony has been challenged—if not displaced—by digital, wide-bandwidth, wireless and IP-based platforms capable of providing voice, video, and data transmission at higher speeds and lower costs to consumers and businesses worldwide.

These points certainly confirm the destruction of telecommunications, media, and other fields as we knew them even five or ten years ago. This book is intended to stimulate continued discussion and debate on the primary challenge now facing firms, governments, and other players—how to exploit the new opportunities created by such destructive dynamics. For public policy-makers, this book underscores the importance of national regulations, promoting competition and contestable (not monopolistic) market structures, and the importance of harmonizing such regulatory frameworks internationally. For business executives, it highlights the centrality of new technologies such as the Internet in driving down prices, and in allowing new entrants to circumvent traditional channels for product and service supply, marketing, and distribution. For everyone, this book reveals how quickly industry landscapes are changing through forces of creative destruction—or merely destruction.

CREATIVE DESTRUCTION OR JUST DESTRUCTION?

As mentioned above, Schumpeter's theory of "creative destruction" argues that innovation and growth lead to the replacement of obsolete products, processes, and firms by more up-to-date and superior successors. In "The Creative Response in Economic History," Schumpeter opposes adaptive to creative responses of the economic systems, whereby the latter result in changes that are "outside of the range of existing practice." More specifically, creative responses "cannot be predicted by applying the ordinary rules of inference from the pre-existing facts," for they "shape the whole course of subsequent events and their "'long-run' outcome," and "have . . . something . . . to do . . . with individuals' decisions, actions, and patterns of behavior."[2]

In *Capitalism, Socialism and Democracy,* Schumpeter further specifies the concept of creative response by arguing that capitalism "is incessantly being revolutionized from within by new enterprise, i.e., by the intrusion of new commodities or new methods of production or new commercial opportunities into the industrial structure as it exists at any moment."[3] Think of how this concept applies to the current state of industries such as telecommunications. Its current stage of technological development mandates transition from circuit switched to IP-centric networks, and many analysts conclude that Schumpeter's theory has found its proper paradigmatic evidence. In effect, throughout this book the reader will be exposed to the general argument that the network (r)evolution caused by the introduction of IP-based platforms will result in natural benefits to consumers and society at large in terms of improved economics (lower prices), faster innovation (new products and services), and improved customer service quality. When extended to deregulation and privatization, both processes resulting from compelling economic forces and political circumstances, the argument for creative destruction as a source of increased welfare benefits gains further strength.

By almost any measure, telecommunications has changed dramatically over the past two decades. Consider the recent U.S. experience with telecommunications. At the beginning of the 1980s, the American Telephone and Telegraph Company (AT&T), along with the 22 local Bell companies it owned, dominated U.S. telecommunications. AT&T and the Bell companies sold local, domestic U.S., and international long-distance services, as well as customer-premise telephone hardware, providing both private and business customers with a single point of contact for all of their telecommunications requirements. AT&T and its Bell system formed a regulated, end-to-end monopoly serving more than 95 percent of all Americans. Demand for telecommunications services and products grew modestly, predictably, and profitably.

At the dawn of the new millennium, however, the industry is quite different. Legal challenges and regulatory change in the 1980s divested AT&T of its 22 Bell operating companies (BOCs), and the 1996 Telecommunications Act has allowed, upon FCC certification, the former BOCs to compete with AT&T for long-distance customers. The advent of fiber-optics, wireless, and Internet-based voice, data, and video telecommunications technology has opened the competition to players with previous industry experience in such diverse fields as oil pipeline construction and management, cable TV, film, and computer software. Demand for telecommunications services has exploded, market share has fragmented among AT&T's new competitors, industry productivity has shot up, industry prices have dropped, and customer product and service offerings have expanded.

AT&T now shares the long-distance markets with MCI, Sprint, and hundreds of re-sellers, and the former BOCs now share local markets with a variety of local service providers. Through mergers and acquisitions, as well as restructuring, the number of BOCs has shrunk from twenty-two to four at the time of this writing. Their partners and competitors in Internet services, wireless, and cable come from not only the United States but around the world. Yet amidst this competitive hurly-burly, AT&T has not disappeared. Indeed, through investments in Internet services firms, wireless firms like McCaw Cellular, and cable companies such as Media One and TCI, AT&T is struggling to regain its preeminent position in the industry. But AT&T's strategy, as well as the strategies of other U.S. telecommunications competitors, are far from assured of success. Old telecommunications regimes have been destroyed with rapid speed, replaced over the last two decades by regimes based on regulatory, technological, organizational, and competitive assumptions for which evidence—supporting and contrary—is only now beginning to emerge.

The global changes are perhaps even more profound. Over the last two decades, many developed countries in Europe and Asia and many developing countries around the world have witnessed the transformation of their state-owned and state-run telecommunications operations: France Telecom, Telstra (Australia), Telecom Argentina, and South Africa Telecom, for example, have evolved in a matter of a few years from government departments into "corporatized" state-owned enterprises, public-private joint-ventures, or fully privatized and deregulated firms with individual and institutional shareholders from around the world. The end of old telecommunications regimes outside the United States has implications far beyond the competitive strategies of incumbents and new entrants. The added element of privatization and deregulation represents a fundamental redefinition of the role of the state in providing national security, guiding economic development, and furthering social justice.

Yet, after decades of fundamental restructuring, room exists to wonder about the "creative" nature of the discontinuities affecting the telecommunications industry. What is the rate of decrease of average prices for telecommunications services? How is that rate evolving over time? What is the rate of technological substitution?

In this process of industry transformation, consumers have benefited in a number of dimensions. However, we have witnessed evidence to the effect that destruction might not always have been creative, even after accounting for spillover effects. Average prices for services have declined dramatically in aggregate, even if, at some points in time, we have witnessed tariff increases driven by firms' needs to increase revenues to recover from the loss of cross-subsidies. Technological innovation has enabled a wide array of new services, even though a number of product introductions represented substantial wasted investment. The waves of mergers, acquisitions, and divestitures might have contributed to significant "value destruction" driven by nonproductive investments.

Whereas in the past, telecommunications was considered a distinct industry, it is now of greatest interest as an enabler of a wide variety of Internet industries. The new Internet economy encompasses Internet service providers of many varieties, as well as a wide variety of hardware, software service, and "content" providers. Many of the most interesting firms provide a mix of products and services that cross these broad categories. What then, can be said about the Internet-engendered forces of creative destruction? Quite a bit, as this book demonstrates. Readers must weigh from their own perspectives the analyses and suggested business survival strategies offered by the authors brought together in this book. Some of the strategies may ensure survival—others may hasten your firms' destruction—caveat emptor.

STRUCTURE OF THE BOOK

The book is divided into five parts. The first part is this introduction and provides an overview of the issues to be addressed in subsequent chapters. Here we introduce the reader to the alternatives at stake and describe the structure of, and motivation for, this book. Part 2, "Theory and Practice of Creative Destruction," reviews the applicability of the framework to the analysis of telecommunications and Internet-based businesses. Part 3, "The Global Context for Creative Destruction," explores the institutional context within which creative destruction is achieved by presenting case studies in Latin America, Europe, and Asia. Part 4 of the book, "Business Destruction Strategies in the Global Internet Economy," presents alternative strategies for redefining firms and markets coping with the process of creative destruction. Authors explore the creation of strategic alliances, cross-border acquisitions, technological innovation, and value-chain redefinition. Part 5, "Creative Business Survival Strategies," explores the result of the destruction processes in terms of redefinition of firm boundaries and new intercorporate business models. This part concludes by outlining possible future industry scenarios. Together, the five parts lay out the central issues, responses, and prospective trajectories wrought by creative destruction.

THEORY AND PRACTICE OF CREATIVE DESTRUCTION

Part 2 of the volume reviews the concept of creative destruction and its applicability to the discontinuities currently shaking a range of industries, including telecommunications and media. In "Innovation and Creative Destruction," William Baumol examines the relevance of the concept to the telecommunications industry. He argues that with its intrinsic rate of productivity growth and its record of product innovation, creative destruction is a justifiable process. He raises the issue, however, that the most value-destructive challenge faced by the industry is that of the high sunk costs of duplication of networks, for which he suggests an access fee structure that is competitively neutral.

In "Internet Business Models: Creative Destruction as Usual," Lee Mc-Knight responds to Baumol's conceptual discussion of creative destruction with an application of the concept to Internet-related industries and generic Internet business models. He examines different organizational structures, pricing strategies, and management policies consistent with Internet-based provision of products and services. McKnight details how the Internet is becoming integrated into all businesses, so that it is now business as usual. But McKnight argues that most Internet-based businesses existing today will fail, as competitive forces and market reality demand that economic value be proven, for supposed Internet innovations to displace alternative (technologies and industries) creative destruction as usual.

THE GLOBAL CONTEXT FOR CREATIVE DESTRUCTION

In Part 3, the authors explore a dialectic between markets and governments facilitating technological innovation. In "Creative Destruction in Latin American Telecommunications Privatization," Walter Molano examines changes in the telecommunications sector of the Southern Cone of Latin America. He argues, following Schumpeter, that to facilitate "a creative response" by the supply side of the economy, governments need to relinquish control of the telecommunications sector—that is, they must allow privatization. He forecasts, however, that once the technology stabilizes and the industry enters a period of consolidation, governments will redefine their mechanisms of control.

Consistent with Molano, in "Creative Destruction in European Internet Industries and Policies," Jill Hills and Maria Michalis examine recent national and Pan-European legislative and regulatory changes in the media and communications industries and their implications for competing firms. In 1998, the European Commission opened local telecommunications service markets throughout the European Union to full competition. The "magic" of the market was expected to spur innovation and productivity, both in the telecommunications industry and across related industries, and to foster capital creation, new business start-ups, and higher employment across European labor markets, some of which have stubbornly high unemployment rates. As Hills and Michalis note, the European regulatory initiative also implied the rollback of many industry incumbents from dominant market positions. Their rollback, however, sometimes prodded by regulation, has curtailed many incumbent capital expenditure projects, led to the shutdown of less profitable divisions, and resulted in job losses.

A process of "creative destruction" in European telecommunications might work more smoothly if capital, technology, and, most important, people could move quickly from shrinking incumbents to growing entrants. But this transition is slower than in the United States, and the creation of new regional institutions, such as a Euro-FCC to assess and manage the transition, is un-likely to help much in the near term. Hills and Michalis caution that regulatory reform in telecommunications would more likely destroy old jobs before creating new ones, or create new ones only in distant geographic locales. If labor mobility is low, as is the case throughout much of Europe and in many emerging market countries, then regulatory reform is, indeed, a venture meriting careful, deliberate formulation and implementation. In the light of the hesitation of some European governments to adopt a framework to regulate the emerging Internet industries, the authors argue their case for adaptation of existing rules governing the content industries. Hills and Michalis conclude by evaluating the institutional fitness of various national and Pan-European communications regulatory bodies.

In "Social Communications Innovation and Destruction in Japan," Leslie Helm endorses Schumpeter's claims but determines that Japan's framework of regulation and social rules aimed at promoting industrial development is in fact unable to deal with the anarchic "creative gales of destruction" entailed by the introduction of the Internet. He forecasts that unless Japan reexamines its approach to managing innovation and promoting "organizational continuity," the consequences might be the opposite of "catching up" with the global trend.

As the reader will see, while focusing their analyses on distinct geographies—Latin America, Europe, and Japan—all three chapters in this section validate Schumpeter's theory. They confirm the need for governments to withdraw from active intervention to enable creative responses from within the economic system. Two chapters, however, predict the reemergence and redefinition of regulatory frameworks, either when some technological stability is achieved (Molano) or when needed to rein in otherwise anarchic regulatory approaches frequently accompanying the process of creative destruction (Hills and Michalis).

BUSINESS DESTRUCTION STRATEGIES IN THE GLOBAL INTERNET ECONOMY

Part 4 reviews various strategic approaches adopted by firms to cope with the rapid rate of change in the Internet economy. In "Alliance Enterprise Strategies Destroying Firm Boundaries," Peter Pekar examines the rise of interfirm alliances in many Internet-based industries (for example, telecommunications, computers, retailing), analyzes the motivations for alliance formation, and assesses firm performance in such cooperative arrangements. He argues, as figure 1 below illustrates, that the telecommunications industry appears well suited to the alliance model of organization, given the industry's rate of globalization and the relative ease with which capabilities can be shared among alliance members.

Pekar's fundamental thesis is that the "command and control" unified organizational model of earlier stages of capitalist development is inadequate

Figure 1

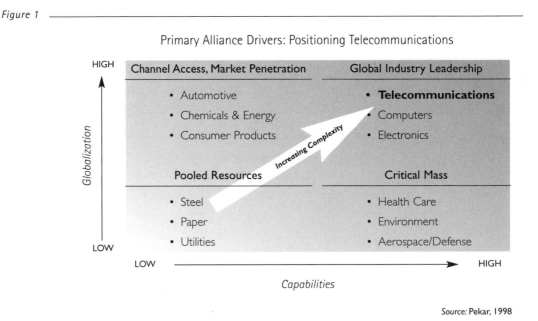

Primary Alliance Drivers: Positioning Telecommunications

Source: Pekar, 1998

to deal with creative destruction processes. He argues that a web of alliances is better prepared to deal with innovative dynamics that occur less within each company and more at the organizational interfaces. Indirectly, Pekar is validating Helm's theory regarding Japan's inability to deal with creative destruction processes.

In "Creating and Destroying Shareholder Value Across Borders," Paul Vaaler examines cross-border investments by recently privatized telecommunications enterprises to understand how shareholders in these newly created private firms react to management decisions to invest abroad. Vaaler finds evidence to support the contention that shareholder reactions to these decisions depend largely on the extent to which the shareholders are free of state interference. Shareholder reactions are also positively related to the length of time these new firms have spent in the private (not state) sector. Telecommunication firms with more experience in the private sector and less state ownership exhibit higher abnormal returns associated with their foreign investment announcements. And those higher abnormal returns seem particularly pronounced when they involve announcements of international alliances, empirical evidence consistent with Pekar's theoretical framework predicting an increasing popularity and centrality of alliances in international business.

Part 4 concludes with "The Internet Protocol and the Creative Destruction of Revenue," by Terry McGarty, who offers insight into the nature of IP-based telecommunications networks and strategy. These emerging technologies promote convergence among formerly proprietary communications networks. The use of IP and the ability to integrate with existing networks allows for the full global integration of multimedia, voice, data, and other similar services-based telecommunications facilities. It pushes the intelligence to the edge of the network and establishes a minimalist approach to network design and execution. The IP-based network of networks creates an essentially borderless open market, dramatically changing how transactions and tariffs are viewed and prices determined. Firms can choose the country in which a transaction will occur, under whose tax regimes, and with what protections for consumers. Promoting IP-based networks for Next Generation telecommunications will also broaden and deepen increasingly global markets for related goods and services that can be sold over the Internet. McGarty analyzes an Internet telephony pricing model based on the actual practice of a firm operating in the

New York local access and long-distance business market. The model illustrates the substantial cost advantage and likely pricing strategies of IP versus circuit switching telecommunications service providers. The analysis has implications for regulators overseeing such competitive dynamics, and for firms seeking to generate revenues from telecommunications services.

CREATIVE BUSINESS SURVIVAL STRATEGIES

The first four parts of the book describe many of the destructive tendencies engendered by the Schumpeterian process. Part 5 discusses new opportunities created by the same process. In "A New Theory of the Internet Firm," William Lehr presents an analytical framework to examine incentives of players operating at various stages of the Internet value chain to vertically integrate. He concludes that incentives to vertically integrate across the value chain are strong and widespread, although downstream integration, where wholesalers forward integrate into retail positions, appears to be a dominant trend. By contrast, Jean Camp's "Sustainable Open Source Software Business Models," considers the implications of the new technical and business relationships between innovators—in this case, software developers—and their peers and competitors in the software industry. Open source software business models explicitly depend upon firms giving away what were once considered trade secrets, and inviting others to destroy the value of the firms' products through further innovation. Can business models based on such a strong embrace of Schumpeterian principles succeed?

The final part, and this book, concludes with "Alternative Industry Futures in the Global Internet Economy," by Marty Hyman and Raul Katz. They present alternative industry configurations that will likely follow from the telecommunications industry's unprecedented restructuring. The authors identify two factors likely to reshape the future industry structure. The first factor is the proliferation of increasingly open, interoperable standards in voice, data, and video telecommunications technologies. Open standards, such as the Internet protocol, promote greater innovation in the various subfields of telecommunications and foster more frequent entry and exit of firms competing to provide these technologies. Hyman and Katz build upon McKnight's analysis of Internet Business Models and "IP Rules" to demonstrate that lower costs—a second factor driving change—will follow from keener competition and more frequent technology upgrades by both industry incumbents and new entrants. Based on these drivers of change, Hyman and Katz outline four alternative future scenarios.

The authors argue that it is too early to provide a definitive view of the ultimate industry configuration. Industry players will be forced to craft flexible business strategies capable of responding to alternative industry scenarios. Following Pekar, a web of alliances might be a better approach than more rigid

Figure 2

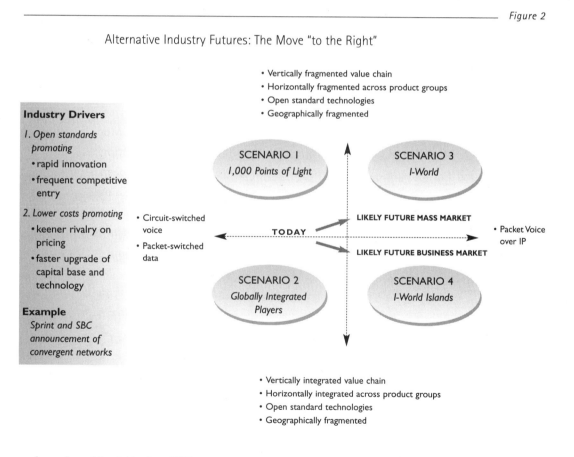

Alternative Industry Futures: The Move "to the Right"

Source: Booz•Allen & Hamilton, 1999

positional strategies. And following Baumol's updated treatment of Schumpeter, we should never expect a steady state, but rather continued technological change—and destruction.

CREATIVE OR DESTRUCTIVE?

What does the research contained in this book lead us to conclude? We remain soberly optimistic, recognizing the new opportunities for innovation and wealth creation stemming from the natural processes of capitalism so well articulated by Schumpeter 50 years ago—long before anyone heard of the Internet. How do individual authors of the book's chapters end up regarding this question? Baumol argues that because the beneficiaries of the innovation process are in part those whose older products are displaced—that is, the telecommunications service providers—creative destruction is partly justified. He also points out, however, the social costs and economic inefficiencies derived from the high sunk cost of duplication of networks. McKnight argues that few Internet business models have demonstrated their sustainability as yet. At the same time, however, McKnight illustrates how innovation is built into the Internet. Creative destruction, then, is amplified, in both its destructive and creative aspects, in a global Internet economy. In his exploration of the interaction between innovation and government intervention, Molano argues that regulation and state intervention emerge as a main factor in the telecommunications industry whenever the pace of technological change stabilizes. In other words, in periods of rapid innovation, governments tend to withdraw from participating in the telecommunications industry through either liberalization or privatization. In Molano's words, governments lack the flexibility to adapt to "creative destruction."

Hills and Michalis, on the other hand, argue for the creative destruction of the Internet in generating value by lowering barriers to entry and promoting the openness of networks—McGarty's argument. The authors, in this case, however, present the view that, by "converging" with traditional technologies—that is, broadcasting—the Internet might strengthen existing regulatory frameworks rather than contribute to their demise. McGarty implicitly argues for the value created by the diffusion of the Internet. The creative destruction that leads to the emergence of new networks, with its associated economics, allows for an increase in openness of networks and markets and a dramatic lowering of barriers to entry.

Implicitly, Lehr supports the creative destruction theory. He considers that the multiple moves along the value chain that result in acquisitions and alliances represent rational moves by firms seeking to reduce cost, promote innovation, and extend market power. Camp and Pekar support this perspective, arguing that alliances and new organization structures, and business and technology innovation processes are central features of the emerging economic model. Vaaler's study of shareholder reactions and abnormal returns associated with alliance announcements adds empirical support to these claims. Katz and Hyman conclude that while creative destruction forces are definitely at work, the industry discontinuities are still operative, with no end in sight.

CONCLUSION

Creative Destruction provides you, the reader, with new perspectives for thinking about changes currently sweeping through a range of industries worldwide. Whether the changes undermining industry regimes are institutional, organizational, or technological, the concept of creative destruction also implies new opportunities for nimble managers and policymakers in the global Internet economy.

This volume provides conceptual and analytic tools to understand and shape adroit business responses. The contributors propose new regulatory approaches, technology strategies, inter-organizational relationships, foreign investment approaches, customer marketing plans, and other ways to increase your ability to survive and prosper during this seemingly chaotic process of change. The book offers broader and deeper insight into how to recognize and manage the dynamics of creative destruction rather than simply destruction.

PART 2

THEORY AND PRACTICE OF CREATIVE DESTRUCTION

2 | INNOVATION AND CREATIVE DESTRUCTION

William J. Baumol

Joseph Schumpeter's felicitous term, "creative destruction," is useful both because of its clear message and because of its stimulating ambiguity. Its message is that innovation and growth force obsolete technical configurations to be swept away without hesitation or remorse. In their prescient discussion of the macroeconomics of industrial growth, Marx and Engels had asserted the same for social relationships: "The bourgeoisie . . . has put an end to all feudal, patriarchal, idyllic relations. It has pitilessly torn asunder all the motley feudal ties . . ." (*Manifesto of the Communist Party,* 1847). Schumpeter, an unapologetic admirer of Marxian growth analysis, then extended the idea to the related micro issue—the replacement of obsolete products, processes, and firms by more up-to-date and superior successors.

The phrase is ambiguous, however, to the extent that it avoids judgment on the desirability of this process of replacement of the old by the new, and by itself offers no basis on which to judge how far the process should go to serve the public interest most effectively. Schumpeter surely does imply that without creative destruction we would be condemned to stagnation and forced to forgo the improvements of living standards offered by technical progress. But even he must have recognized that there is value in some of the old ways, which progress nevertheless sweeps aside just as effectively as past procedures that are patently inferior. More important, both in terms of the current literature and probably for policy as well, are the associated quantitative issues. Does the economy engage in too much or too little creative destruction? How can one judge? Most economists who dealt with the subject held that the substantial spillovers of innovation probably lead to considerable underinvestment in innovation activities from the viewpoint of economic efficiency. But recent writers, notably Aghion and Howitt (1998), have raised the opposite possibility —that because the creators and those who suffer the resulting destruction are different individuals or groups, it entails an externality that will tend to induce overinvestment in innovation by the former.

I discuss this issue here and conclude that the one externality will tend to offset the other, producing on balance a result that is better for economic efficiency. I also argue that the beneficial spillovers from innovation that were the focus of the earlier discussions are the source of vast benefits for society that are counterbalanced by their disincentive for innovative activity. Thus, the externalities stemming from creative destruction may be doubly beneficial, not only offsetting some of the disincentive effects of the spillovers, but also permitting preservation of their beneficial consequences.

I end with a discussion on the application of the idea to the telecommunications industry, arguing that creative destruction is not the primary issue here. This industry, with its record as a leader in productivity growth, its interrelations with computer technology, and its abundance of new and improved products and processes, surely justifies the destruction of the obsolete by the novel substitutes it provides. Moreover, the industry's beneficiaries from the new technology are at least in part those whose older products are displaced. This clearly reduces the disparity between the private and social costs of the creative destruction. Rather, in my view, the most urgent problem for economic efficiency is the high sunk cost of duplication of the facilities required for operation and, in particular, for competitive entry. The problem is ultimately one of determining a proper (competitively neutral) fee for access to the extant facilities of incumbent monopolists. Along with this, there is the apparent incompatibility between competitive entry and the regulators' desire for continuation of the cross subsidies that underlie the "universal-service" goal. These are urgent problems not only in the United States but throughout the industrial world, and they will grow more serious as the World Trade Organization's 1997 Agreement on Basic Telecommunications is used to permit entry by foreign rivals into each country's formerly monopolized telecommunications market. I will end with a description of my proposal for dealing with these problems.

NET BENEFITS OF CREATIVE-DESTRUCTION EXTERNALITIES

Creative Destruction and Efficiency of Investment in Innovation

The standard view on efficiency in innovation is that externalities prevent the assignment of an adequate quantity of resources to this activity (see, for example, Nordhaus [1969, p. 39]). That is because the process is characterized by substantial spillovers that yield a large proportion of the benefits to others than those who participated in the innovation process. Those beneficiaries include not only the general consuming public but, often, direct competitors of the innovators. Because the rewards to the innovator are thereby reduced, perhaps severely, the resulting innovative activity can be expected to be less than optimal.

Recently, as theorists have sought to formalize more elements of the growth process, they have returned to Schumpeter's notion of creative destruction. In the process, they observed that this feature of innovation, too, generates externalities, but unlike the spillovers, these are "negative externalities"—that is, they are detrimental to those they affect. The implication is that innovation generates a social cost that is not borne by the innovator. Consequently, the innovator can be expected to disregard them and invest more in innovation than is justified by their social cost. In short, the innovation activity may be excessive, rather than inadequate, as previously believed.

What is common to both of these positions is the conclusion that innovation is a source of externalities, while optimality is possible only if these spillovers, beneficial or detrimental, are zero. I will take a very different position. First, I will argue that, contrary to accepted views, zero spillovers are not merely unnecessary for optimality but that the two are in fact incompatible. Moreover, I will suggest that the spillovers in the form of benefits to others than the innovators are surprisingly large, perhaps desirably so. If so, the externalities associated with creative destruction are a countervailing influence that may be socially beneficial in two ways. First, they may help to offset the depressing effect on innovation activity of the spillovers of their benefits. Second, they may nevertheless do so without weakening the desirable consequences of those spillovers.

The Benefits of Beneficial Innovation Spillovers

The reason a zero spillover level in innovation is not optimal is the trade-off between increased flow of invention and the distribution of some of the benefits to others—the resulting rise in *overall* living standards. Moreover, I will argue that there is no one level of spillovers that is unambiguously optimal. Instead, there is a range of values of what will be called the *spillover ratio,* that is, the share of the benefits of innovation that goes to persons other than the investors, within which *all values of the ratio are Pareto-optimal in the absence of any possibility of lump-sum transfers.* Thus, they are all what may be considered second-best Pareto optima, subject to a constraint that rules out hypothetical but totally infeasible redistributive arrangements.

Clearly, innovation leads to substantial gains in real wages and to higher standards of living, more generally. But all such gains that result from innovation must constitute spillovers, because they are social benefits that are not private benefits to the innovator. Because this must be so, it can be argued, further, that the bulk of the unprecedented rise in the developed world's living standards since the Industrial Revolution could not have occurred without the revolution's innovations.[1] Consequently, a substantial share of the benefits of innovation must have gone to persons other than the innovators in the form of spillovers.[2] This means that there is inevitably a trade-off between the number of innovations actually produced and the standard of living of the majority of the population. In this scenario, as overall GDP is raised by innovation, any increase in workers' standards of living constitutes a rise in the spillovers from innovation that depresses the flow of further innovation. Thus, the more the general public benefits from such growth in GDP, the slower that growth must be. This trade-off must be deemed to lie at the heart of the capitalist growth process: the private payoff to innovation and the speed with which new technology and new products become available.

Size of the Beneficial Spillovers

The resulting scenario is quite dramatic. Romer (1994) notes that if the innovators had not lost *any* of the benefits they generated—if spillovers had been zero—then real wages would hardly have risen from their levels before the Industrial Revolution.[3] It is almost impossible to imagine how great a difference that would have made. What are probably the best available estimates put U.S. per-capita GDP in 1820 at *less than one-seventeenth of what it is today,* and even as late as 1870 real per-capita GDP is estimated to have been less than one-ninth its current level (Maddison [1995, pp. 196–97]). If we assume the most extreme case—that the spillovers from innovation could somehow have been reduced to (anywhere near) zero—the living standards of the vast majority of the citizens of today's rich countries would have stalled at pre-Industrial Revolution levels. One can hardly accept the notion that it would be socially preferable to achieve a total GDP far higher than today's level through maximal incentives for innovation while, simultaneously, most of the population is condemned to near-medieval living standards. But that is the world that a zero-spillovers premise depicts.

This analysis suggests that the total size of the spillovers from innovation is surprisingly large. If we provisionally accept the conclusion that the bulk of the rise in per-capita GDP and the rise in productivity since the Industrial Revolution *ultimately* could not have occurred without innovation, it is possible to arrive at a very crudely estimated lower bound for the spillover ratio. For this purpose, we may note that since 1870 the U.S. per-capita GDP is estimated by Maddison (1995) to have increased almost ninefold. Such a rise in GDP per person implies that fully 8/9, or nearly 90 percent, of current GDP was contributed by innovation carried out since 1870. And this ignores the continuing contribution of pre-1870 innovations, such as the steam engine and the railroad.

At the same time, the share of total investment income in GDP during this period was certainly less than 30 percent. But in 1997, research and development expenditures made up only about 16 percent of total investment in the United States (*Statistical Abstract of the United States,* 1997). Thus, if the return on innovation investment were the same (after adjustment for risk) as the return to investment of other types, the return to innovation would have been less than $(30)(0.16) = 4.8$ percent of GDP. This makes it conservative to estimate that returns to innovators were less than 10 percent of GDP and that more than 80 percent of the benefits have gone to persons who made no direct contribution to innovation.

The very crude estimates offered here are not out of line with the available estimates of private and social returns to innovation (see, for example, Nadiri

[1991], Mohnen [1992], and Wolff [1997]). Wolff, for example, estimates the social rate of return to be 53 percent (in line with previous work on the subject) and the private rate of return to be between 10 percent and 12.5 percent or less (a figure slightly below earlier estimates) (Wolff [1997, p. 16]). These estimates yield a spillover ratio of about 80 percent. For the discussion here, the precise figure does not matter. What is noteworthy is that the beneficial spillovers of innovation are impressively large.

The Efficiency-Distribution Trade-off

Surely, few of us would be prepared to argue that it would be optimal to multiply the wealth of the world's richest innovators far above their current levels, while the rest of the population is condemned to the miserable living standards of the bulk of the seventeenth-century population. But that is just what zero spillovers would mean. It follows that beneficial spillovers of substantial size are necessary to achieve a distribution that most people would consider desirable, or even just acceptable. But such large spillovers surely exact a substantial efficiency cost in terms of their disincentive to innovative activity and investment. Thus, given that lump-sum transfers are impossible in reality, there is an unavoidable trade-off.

Once we recognize that a desired distribution cannot be achieved without some sacrifice in economic efficiency, we are led to study the nature of the trade-off and the means to minimize its cost to society. If, for this analysis, society is divided into different groups it can be expected that one group will prefer an efficiency-distribution combination different from that preferred by another. To simplify, let Y be some index of total net output of the community and E be an index of degree of equality of distribution (as measured, perhaps, by the reciprocal of variance) and assume that there are incentive compatibility constraints making Y decrease monotonically as E increases. Suppose that the maximum amount of Y the economy can produce, consistent with incentive compatibility constraints, is $Y = e$. Let society be divided into two groups: Group I most prefers the combination (Y_1, E_1), while group II's optimum is (Y_2, E_2). Then, if each group's valuation of an outcome decreases steadily as its distance from its preferred (Y, E) increases, every intermediate (Y, E) combination *must* be Pareto-optimal, though for many such combinations $Y < e$. That is, from any such point in (Y, E) space it will be impossible to make one group better off without harming the other. To emphasize that these are *constrained* Pareto optima, I will refer to any such outcome as *"NLS Pareto optimal,"* that is, optimal so long as *no lump-sum transfers* are possible.

The implication for our discussion of innovation is, first, that zero externalities of innovation cannot be NLS Pareto optimal because the bulk of the population—the noninnovators—would hardly be pleased to be returned to the living standards of the seventeenth century. Moreover, it is at least not implausible that the current level of innovation spillovers, enormous as they are, do not fall outside the range of NLS Pareto optimality.

The Benefits of the "Negative Externalities" of Creative Destruction

If creative destruction were the only source of externalities, it is indeed plausible that they would lead to an excess of investment in innovation over the amount required for economic efficiency. This is the conclusion to which the Aghion-Howitt analysis correctly leads. But, as we see, this is by no means the only source. Indeed, it is plausible that the sizes of their externalities are relatively modest in comparison with the enormous beneficial spillovers of innovation. The creative-destruction externalities, moreover, go in the opposite direction from the others in terms of their expected effect on innovative activity.

Three conclusions follow:

a) The creative-destruction externalities are an offset to the beneficial spillovers, and can be expected to bring the economy, on balance, closer to the requirements of efficiency and the incentives for the optimal quantity of innovation activity.

b) If the creative-destruction externalities are, indeed, the smaller of the two, their effect cannot be an *overcorrection.* That is, the net result will be an increase in innovative activity that still is insufficient to bring us to the efficient level.

c) The improvement in efficiency will have been achieved with no offsetting deterioration in distribution, for the distributive benefits we have been discussing do not depend on the *net* result after the one externality has partially offset the other. Rather, the distributive benefits depend exclusively on the benefit spillovers, whose absolute magnitude will, if anything, be increased by the expansion of innovative activity induced by the creative-destruction spillover.

IS (CREATIVE) DESTRUCTION THE PRIME TELECOMMUNICATIONS ISSUE?

On Technical Change and Productivity Growth in Telecommunications

It is generally accepted that most industries with a record of slow productivity growth are to be found in the services, but discussions of the subject usually point out that in this respect the services are extremely heterogeneous. Almost always, telecommunications is selected to illustrate the point. For many years it has been one of the economy's leaders in productivity growth, substantially outpacing the rate of growth of manufacturing productivity overall. In only a handful of industries, including computers and other electronic components, has productivity grown faster than in telecommunications. Indeed, the productivity achievements of the computer industry and telephone service in this arena are hardly unconnected, because the two activities are so highly and increasingly interrelated that it has even been asserted that the two industries are becoming one.

The point here is that some of the most spectacular innovations of recent years, those most likely to have major effects on the economy and society, have a fundamental involvement with telecommunications. These range from innovations in the instruments of communications themselves—wireless telephony for example—to what promises to be a revolutionary upheaval, the Internet. All of these innovations bring with them some amount of creative destruction. Wireless telephony may well, for instance, render obsolete some of the older telephone facilities, while the Internet is already threatening the existence of many marginal retailers.

I have seen no hard evidence from which to categorically judge the net benefits, or even definitively reject the possibility that the benefits are exceeded by the damage. Yet it is surely implausible that the gains for society have not been positive or that they have been negligible. Moreover, most observers would surely agree, though admittedly only from impressionistic observation, that these gains promise to be only the beginning of many vast benefits promised for the future. We cannot confidently say that the investment in product and process innovation has been somewhat excessive or somewhat insufficient relative to the unknown amount required for maximization of economic efficiency. But in a rough-and-ready evaluation, which is all one can reasonably expect here, surely there are reasons to believe that the magnitude of innovative activity in this field is not enormously far from the most desirable level.

Given that such a spectacular innovation record can hardly have been attained without some obsolescence of the older products and processes, it would seem to follow that creative destruction is hardly the most worrying development in the field of telecommunications.

Natural and Erected Impediments to Competition: The Primary Problem?

In my opinion, the major policy problem affecting the telecommunications industry is the slow progress of competition in the arena, particularly in parts of the industry where competition seems to be most urgently needed. There are two obvious foci of this concern: the local loop and international telecommunications. The local competition problem is sufficiently well known to require no recapitulation here. The international issue only calls for a few observations. The World Trade Organization's 1997 Agreement on Basic Telecommunications among some 70 countries was plainly expected to bring competition into national markets until then served predominantly by public-sector monopolies. These monopolies then been protected from entry both by legislation and by the scale economies generated by heavy sunk-capital requirements. Thus, there is exactly the same problem for competitive entry into both local domestic markets by domestic suppliers and national markets by foreign providers. It is simply too costly for the bulk of potential entrants to replicate the facilities of the incumbent monopoly supplier. This may be deemed the primary "natural barrier" to competition in the field. The way around this barrier is now universally recognized: an imposed access requirement, forcing the incumbent monopolist to rent access to its facilities to those who desire to compete. But this is a real solution only if something is done about the price of entry. Otherwise, the incumbent can still protect itself by erecting an artificial barrier in the form of excessive access fees. Of course, as with any price, an imposed access charge can also be damaging to welfare if it is set too low, because that only invites entry by inefficient competitors who then are, in effect, granted a suicidal subsidy by the incumbent.

Thus, to me the urgent problem for telecommunications, at least for the next few years, is the determination and adoption of "competitively neutral" access prices—that is, prices that permit entry and subsequent competition between entrants and incumbents exclusively on their efficiency merits. Access prices should be such as to permit the most efficient firms, whichever they may be, to earn profits with lower prices to users of the telecommunications services than less efficient competitors can afford to offer. In my view, then, the critical problem in the arena is the determination of a formula for such competitively neutral access fees. I shall presently describe what I believe to be such a formula. Moreover, I will argue that the same formula, properly applied, can solve the second urgent problem in the economics of telecommunications, described in the next section.

How Can Competition and the Cross Subsidies of "Universal Service" Coexist?

Regulators have long suffered from an apparently irreconcilable dilemma. Their own understandable predilections, supplemented by powerful political pressures, have led them to impose a set of cross subsidies in the prices of the firms they regulate. Cross subsidies systematically favor particular groups of customers, such as household customers or isolated farmers, at the expense of other groups, such as business customers or those near supply sources, by forcing the latter group to subsidize the former. At the same time, however, regulators have also sought to stimulate entry and competition in regulated industries. For example, in the United States the Telecommunications Act of 1996 requires a monopoly local telephone service provider to lease parts of its network to its competitors at cost-based rates, thereby allowing entrant firms to offer service without incurring the tremendous expense of building a duplicative network before beginning service. The dilemma is that the twin goals of imposing cross subsidies and promoting competition are ordinarily incompatible. Effective competition tends to eliminate the source of cross subsidies by driving down the prices of items that yield particularly large profits.

There is, I contend, a better solution: a regime of *non-uniform* and competitively neutral pricing of access to bottleneck services owned by an incumbent monopoly—the fixed facilities to which access is required for viable entry. I will show that the proposed arrangement is indeed *competitively neutral*. Moreover, I will prove that the arrangement is the only access pricing rule that can achieve neutrality in the presence of cross subsidy and price discrimination in final-product sales. Last, I will argue that all affected parties can gain from this arrangement, because it offers full access to efficient suppliers in each and every pertinent market. Both incumbents and entrants will gain by having access to all markets. The public will gain because competition will pervade the industry. Finally, regulators will gain because their apparently inconsistent goals will be reconciled: Pervasive competition will coexist with the cross subsidies they deem to be in the social interest.

Parity-Priced Access: Necessary Condition for Competitive Neutrality

The efficient solution to the problem of determining an efficient price for a bottleneck service is based on the result I call the "Level-Playing-Field Theorem." This theorem tells us that only by using the formula (1) below, can we *neutrally* price a monopoly-owned bottleneck service required by both the bottleneck owner and its final-product competitors. These formulas are widely known in the literature as the efficient component pricing rule (ECPR) or the *parity pricing* formula. According to the theory, a level playing field, and hence efficiency in the competition between the bottleneck owner and its competitors, can only arise if the bottleneck service in question is priced as follows:[4]

Bottleneck service price per unit = Bottleneck owner's final product price minus the incremental cost to the owner of all final-product inputs, other than bottleneck service,

or, in convenient symbols:

1. $P_b = P_{bf} - IC_{br}$

where the subscript *f* refers to *final* product, so that P_{bf} is the price of the bottleneck owner's final product, and *r* refers to the *remaining* inputs (other than the bottleneck input) that enter into the incremental cost of the final product.

I will demonstrate that, at any other price for the bottleneck service, a competitor's minimum viable final product price will not be equal to the bottleneck owner's price plus (or minus) the competitor's cost advantage (or disadvantage) in supplying the inputs other than the bottleneck service needed for the final product. In other words, at any other bottleneck service price, one of the suppliers will be unable to achieve the final product price advantage to which its own efficiency entitles it.

To derive the competitive neutrality formula (1), we define a *level playing field* in the pricing of access to require the following:

Suppose a firm's incremental cost (IC) per unit of output of supplying the non-bottleneck components of the final product is X dollars less than that of a bottleneck-owning competitor (or the reverse). Then, this more efficient firm should just be able (without losing money) to price the final product by X dollars less than the price charged by its less efficient competitor.

More formally, we have as the definition of a level playing field:

2. Bottleneck owner final-product price −
    minimum competitor final-product price =
    IC of owner-supplied remaining inputs −
    IC of competitor-supplied remaining inputs.

But we know that the competitor's minimum (financially viable) price is:

3. Minimum competitor final-product price =
    price of bottleneck service +
    IC of competitor-supplied remaining inputs.

Adding these two equations we immediately obtain the *competitive neutrality formula:*

4. The only price of bottleneck service that provides a
    level playing field =
    bottleneck owner final-product price −
    IC of owner-supplied remaining inputs.

This is clearly the same as formula (1), so that:

PROPOSITION 1. Any bottleneck service price that violates competitive-neutrality formula (4) or its equivalent (1) must tilt the playing field, favoring either the bottleneck owner at the expense of its competitors or the reverse.

Parity Pricing and Universal-Service Cross Subsidies Under Competition

An extension of the Level-Playing-Field Theorem demonstrates that it is possible to make competition and cross subsidies compatible. The theorem shows that where there is cross subsidy or price discrimination of any sort in final product prices, then any *uniform* price for access to a bottleneck service cannot be competitively neutral. Such a uniform price *must* tilt the playing field by favoring some of the rival suppliers of final products at the expense of the others.

The problem of incompatibility of competition and universal service persists because, in practice, bottleneck inputs are rarely used only to produce a single product. A railroad bridge that all competitors along a given route must use can carry coal and wheat and many other products. A local telecommunications loop carries business and household telephone messages, data and voice messages, and messages from California and Connecticut. I will argue that the price of a homogeneous bottleneck service should not be fixed and independent of the final product in whose production it is used. Rather, *differential pricing* of the bottleneck service should be permitted or even required, depending on the pricing of the final product for which it is employed.

Specifically, suppose there is discrimination in the bottleneck owner's prices of the final products, I and J, for which the bottleneck input is used. That is, the difference between the bottleneck owner's prices for I and J is not equal to the difference between the incremental costs for I and J (that is, $P_{fbi} - P_{fbj}$ is not equal to $IC_{rbi} - IC_{rbj}$). Then *uniform pricing* of the bottleneck service will force the bottleneck owner to end its discriminatory pricing of the final product. The only possible alternative is transformation of the market, in effect, into a cartel in which different suppliers specialize in the supply of different products and do not compete with one another.

In contrast, *differential pricing* of the bottleneck service permits the competitive neutrality formulas (1) to be satisfied for *each* product for which the bottleneck service is required. Then the differential pricing of the final product can be preserved, and effective competition can continue in the market for each of the final products. Specifically, such a differential pricing arrangement will be the only viable solution in a regulated market in which the regulator seeks to preserve effective competition and to impose some cross subsidy that is deemed to serve the public interest or is required by political pressures.

Interfirm Discrimination Through Uniformity of Access Price

I will first show that if differential prices are charged for final products that use the bottleneck service, but the bottleneck service is priced uniformly in all uses, then the playing field cannot be level.

To make this point clear, suppose that the bottleneck input is used to produce (at least) two final products, I and J. These products are sold by the bottleneck owner at discriminatory prices. That is, the price for product I minus the incremental cost for product I is greater than the price for product J minus the incremental cost for product J:

5. $\quad P_{fbi} - IC_{rbi} > P_{fbj} - IC_{rbj}$,

where the subscript r, again, refers to the cost of the *remaining* (non-bottleneck) inputs, assuming for simplicity that the incremental cost of bottleneck use is the same for both products. Suppose the price of the bottleneck service, P_b, is set at the average (perhaps weighted) of the difference between the final price and the incremental cost $(P_f - IC_r)$ for the two products. Then the price of bottleneck service is greater than the price for product J minus the incremental cost for J:

6. $\quad P_b > P_{fbj} - IC_{rbj}$.

So, if a competitor, C, has the same cost for the remaining inputs (that is, $IC_{rbj} = IC_{rcj}$), then

7. $\quad P_{fbj} < P_b + IC_{rcj} = \min P_{fcj}$

meaning that a competitor who is just as efficient as the bottleneck owner in supplying product J will be unable, without losing money on sales of J, to charge a final-product price, P_{fcj}, that is as low as that of the bottleneck owner. Clearly, the playing field for sale of J will not be level, and the competitor will find itself unable to compete in the product J market, even though it is an equally efficient producer of J. Of course, the problem is that the uniform price of the bottleneck service must exceed the competitively neutral price for that input when it is used to produce output J. The competitor will be saddled with what amounts to an excessive discriminatory price for the bottleneck service that handicaps or prevents its competition with the bottleneck owner in the supply of product J.

The same reasoning shows that the uniform averaged competitively neutral price for the bottleneck service will render the bottleneck service owner's price for product I greater than the competitor's minimum price for product I,

$$8. \quad P_{fbi} > \min P_{fci}$$

if the bottleneck owner and the competitor are equally efficient in supplying product I. Thus, the averaged uniform price for the bottleneck service must tilt the playing field in the competitor's favor in the supply of product I.

More generally, we have the Uniform Access-Price Theorem:

PROPOSITION 2. If the final-product prices for two goods that use a bottleneck service as an input are discriminatory in the sense of (5), then no uniform bottleneck-service price can satisfy the competitive neutrality requirement (4) for every final product. So for those products for which (4) is not satisfied, one of the suppliers of those products must be handicapped in a discriminatory manner.

The implications are clear. The competitor will be forced to supply those products in which the net yield to the bottleneck owner, $P_{fb} - IC_{rb}$, is greatest. This is another way of saying that the competitor will have no option but to engage in cream skimming.

There are two possible scenarios for the sequel:

a) The bottleneck owner will reduce its price for final-product I, and (particularly if it is losing money on J, meaning that a cross subsidy is involved) it may be forced to raise its price for final product J until the two sides of inequality (5) are made equal to one another. Then the discrimination in final-product prices will have been ended by competition—the expected sequel to cream-skimming competition.

b) Alternatively, either regulatory fiat or self-interest or some other exogenous force may keep the final-product prices of I and J at their discriminatory level. Then the bottleneck owner will find itself the sole supplier of product *J,* while the other firm (if there are only two firms) will become the sole supplier of *I.* In that case, the result will be, in effect, the establishment of a cartel in which each firm finds itself assigned an exclusive territory that is immune from direct competition. Some truncated competitive force will remain in the market, because each firm will have to keep the price of its final product below the level that will make entry into that field by the other firm financially feasible. But up to that limit each firm will be shielded from the constraint of effective competition. There will be more than one firm in the industry, but there will be no real competition.

Consequences of Differential Competitively Neutral Prices for Bottleneck Services

As an alternative, the regulator can impose strict compliance with competitive neutrality for a bottleneck service, final product by final product. By now, it should be evident that this requires the price charged by the bottleneck owner to vary with the use to which the bottleneck service is used by a competitor. It may require a bottleneck service fee of X dollars per minute when the bottleneck is used to carry calls from business customers and Y dollars per minute if it transmits calls from households. The competitive neutrality formula (4) tells us, ceteris paribus, that the bottleneck service price must vary from one bottleneck use to another precisely by the amount that the corresponding final product prices vary. For example, given two final products with equal incremental costs for which the price of one product is 0.2 dollars more than the other, the competitively neutral prices of bottleneck service for the two uses must also differ by exactly 0.2 dollars. Several consequences follow from such a pricing arrangement.

CONSEQUENCE 1: *Bottleneck-Owner Indifference Among Suppliers.* With these access prices, the bottleneck owner will be *indifferent,* so far as profits are concerned, between use of its facilities by itself and use of those facilities by its competitors. The competitive neutrality pricing formula guarantees that the bottleneck owner will obtain exactly the same profit, whichever of the two courses is taken. For with price set in accord with formula (4),

9. $P_{bi} = P_{fbi} - IC_{rbi} = IC$ of providing a unit of bottleneck service for product *I plus* profit from sale of a unit of *I* by the bottleneck owner.

Thus, for each product, *I*, the price charged by the bottleneck owner to competitors for bottleneck services will give the owner exactly the same profit as if it had used the services to supply product *I* itself. This result is well known in the literature on parity (ECPR) pricing.[5]

CONSEQUENCE 2: *Access Prices for Cross-Subsidized Products.* The second implication of differential and competitively neutral pricing is more surprising: The result deals with the case where the final-product J receives a cross subsidy and is therefore priced below incremental cost (its profit yield to the bottleneck owner is negative). Then (9) tells us that the competitively neutral price for bottleneck service to be used in the production of J *must also be less than the incremental cost* of supplying the bottleneck service for the purpose! That is, the bottleneck owner must subsidize access to its competitors.

Though this result may seem bizarre at first, its logic is straightforward. Cross subsidy by the bottleneck owner means that if rivals are to compete effectively with the bottleneck owner, replication of this cross subsidy must be available to them in some way. If the bottleneck owner sells product J to consumers at a price below cost, then it must provide its rivals with bottleneck service at a price that does not cover cost as well. In other words, if product J is the recipient of a cross subsidy when sold by the bottleneck proprietor, then competitive neutrality requires that the same cross subsidy be made available to rival suppliers of J through access pricing. Otherwise, rivals that have no other source of cross subsidy will not be able to compete in the supply of J because of their inability to match the bottleneck owner's final-product price of J. In these circumstances, if the bottleneck service price covers the entire incremental cost of providing the service for output J production, the playing field cannot be level.

CONSEQUENCE 3: *Open Competition in All Industry Products.* Differential and competitively neutral prices offer entrants and other rivals of the bottleneck owner the prospect that they will be able to compete in every market in which the bottleneck owner offers products. Thus, unless their entry or survival is threatened by the inefficiency of their *own* operations, they will not find themselves excluded from any branch of the regulated industry.

CONSEQUENCE 4: *Cream-Skimming Prevention—Competitor Indifference Among the Different Products That Are Supplied with the Aid of the Bottleneck.* The fourth consequence of differential and competitively neutral prices is that they eliminate any incentive for cream skimming by competitors. The differential bottleneck service price is adjusted so that when a final product price is relatively high, the bottleneck service price for use in making that product will be elevated by exactly the same amount, other things being equal. Consequently, the competitor will have no incentive to favor high-priced products over low-priced products.

CONSEQUENCE 5: *Preservation of Cross Subsidies Despite Effective Competition.* The final implication of differential and competitively neutral pricing should now be obvious. In contrast to what is normally expected, such a pricing arrangement is consistent with continued competition in each and every one of the bottleneck owner's products, along with preservation of any and all cross subsidies in the bottleneck owner's final-product prices. Thus, these access prices enable the regulator to have it both ways. They enable competition to survive, and even to permeate every branch of the regulated industry. And they permit retention of the cross subsidies so characteristically favored by regulators. They can require the impoverished or isolated farmers and other customers whom it is especially costly to serve to be granted subsidized prices. They can demand that prices favor household over business customers because of the external benefits to firms that derive from an increase in number of consumers connected to the network. In short, they can promote universal service by means of cross subsidy without having it undermined by the forces of competition.

3 INTERNET BUSINESS MODELS: CREATIVE DESTRUCTION AS USUAL

Lee W. McKnight

Most of these sites rode in on a wave of hype as excessive as those that herald Hollywood's bigger bombs. (On the Web, as in show business, the big hits are often sleepers.) . . . Now that these start-ups are in peril or ruin, their press is almost as apocalyptic as the initial buzz was celebratory. When Disney bought a 60 percent interest in Toysmart.com back in August, an expert at Forrester Research gushed to the Associated Press, "There's nothing bad in it for Disney." When Toysmart went belly-up last week, another Forrester analyst authoritatively told the A.P. it was "the wrong company selling the wrong product at the wrong time." Now you tell us!

Frank Rich, *New York Times*[1]

Widespread fascination with e-commerce, e-business, e-services, and e-whatever has nourished great expectations for the new economy of the information age. Wild swings in stock valuations, however, and sudden bankruptcies of Internet businesses that overlook the nontrivial matter of building a revenue stream and profits along with a website has led some to doubt that there is anything fundamentally new going on with the Internet. United States Federal Reserve Chairman Alan Greenspan warned of "irrational exuberance" in the stock market fueled in part by investors' Internet euphoria.[2] Market corrections as well as manias, panics, and crashes are ancient and continually recurring features of market economies. Indeed, the overheated Internet stock market of 1999–2000 displayed many classic characteristics of a collective mania (Kindleberger, 1989).

Amidst all the Internet hype, many are still dazzled by the real and paper fortunes of Internet millionaires and billionaires. But Cassandras warn that the end is near (Browning, 2000). In fact, the millennium is over, and the Internet stock bubble seemingly burst in the spring of 2000. But has the party ended or only just begun? Is it time to wake up and smell the tulips—as in the infamous Dutch tulip mania? This seventeenth-century prototypical financial market speculative craze led to an inevitable crash when "the last fool" realized that he was paying an excessive sum for what was, after all, just a flower.[3] Tulips are pretty, but of limited utility as a store of wealth. Sort of like bits on a network of networks? Might Internet business models be built from similarly misplaced conceptions of value?

Is the Internet economy simply a delusion? Or is there something fundamentally different in an Internet economy that warrants careful study and analysis by business leaders, policymakers, technologists, and the public? Are we witnessing collective mania or fundamental change? Both viewpoints on the Internet economy contain an element of truth, but neither adequately addresses the question of what specifically is different or new in Internet business models, if anything. Successful business strategies must be informed by the forces that drive Internet innovation—not by those fueling Internet hype (Shapiro and Varian, 1998).

This chapter analyzes the factors that enable innovation on and through the Internet, the likely long-term viability of selected innovative Internet business models, and the implications of these new models for the global economy and society.[4] Given the breadth of the analysis, individual business models and emerging Internet industry sectors are not explored in depth, but rather are discussed in comparison with other Internet markets. The most important insight emerging from this analysis is that the seeming chaos of rapid market rises to prominence of new firms, new technologies, and new business models is not a passing phenomenon, but rather is a permanent feature of an Internet economy. The parallel phenomenon of seemingly overnight collapses of apparently stable and established businesses and brands, as well as the rapid decline of new businesses, are similarly destined to be a recurring feature of the Internet economy. In short, the Internet enables creative destruction as usual.

The Internet has become a medium for commerce, marketing, advertising, and distribution, as well as invention, entertainment, and discussion. It is an innovation engine that enables creation of a remarkable range of new products and services (McKnight and Bailey, 1997). It also has been said that innovation in the Internet is occurring as much in business model development as in technology (Bronson, 1999). But that begs the question: Which, if any, Internet business innovations create sustainable competitive advantages?

Before examining Internet business models, it is important to be clear about what this chapter does not attempt to do. No new valuation methodology for virtual, cyber, pure play and/or click and mortar, or any other type of Internet-related businesses is introduced or used in this analysis. No advice on investment strategies is offered.[5] Here we attempt to be both more modest and more rigorous in developing an interdisciplinary framework for considering the technology and practical consequences of developing Internet businesses and Internet business models. We demonstrate why successful Internet businesses are predicated on creative destruction—as usual.

BUSINESSES IN THE INTERNET ECONOMY: IP RULES

Innovation is the key factor enabling growth and change in capitalist economies. The tendency for capitalism to foster new innovations and destroy old technologies, businesses, and business models was insightfully analyzed by Joseph Schumpeter many decades ago (Schumperter, 1989). These basic characteristics of capitalist economies are also, naturally, the principal forces driving the Internet economy and likely will continue to be dominant motivations for business innovation (Shapiro and Varian, 1998). The speed, reach, and effect of these destructive and creative economic forces is accentuated and accelerated by the worldwide interconnectivity of businesses, consumers, and societies through the Internet. Simply put, the Internet works its magic through rapid development and diffusion of innovations (Rogers, 1995). Not all Internet business models are equally viable, however. Not all innovations developed by Internet businesses will be found actually useful, and not all businesses that develop useful Internet technologies, products, and services will succeed in bringing them to market (Schwartz, 1999).

The business organization and cultural factors that enable successful business innovation apply to Internet businesses as well. That is, the Internet is a disruptive technology, undermining established business practices and markets at the same time that new markets are created.[6] Internet businesses, while potentially reaching a global marketplace through the interconnectivity of the

Internet, must also operate within at least one nation's legal and political boundaries. Those legal and political forces may intentionally or inadvertently foster innovation—or suppress it (Branscomb and Keller, 1998). Society may be more or less well organized to foster economic growth and innovation through, for example, public policies in education, taxation, regulation, and support for basic and applied research (Nelson, 1993). Forces working at these political and legal levels are also critical for the growth of the global Internet economy and of Internet businesses within that economy. We have argued elsewhere for an open communications infrastructure policy framework to foster innovation and growth and take that conclusion as a given for this analysis.[7]

The viability of an Internet business, however, is determined not only by social, political, legal, and cultural factors but also by conventional business factors, such as the quality of the business concept, the strength of the management team, access to labor and capital, and favorable market conditions. In addition, the question of whether the Internet's characteristics are being leveraged in an innovative way to meet a business need is typically the determining factor in separating Internet business winners from losers. One key set of Internet business winners are those firms offering technology and services that enable others to satisfy the above requirements in their Internet business activities. To use the gold rush analogy, the suppliers of the Internet's picks and shovels—the infrastructure to support business on the Internet—will be the big winners in the long run. Whichever service or application or content type turns out to be successful, somehow the bits must be stored and forwarded across the Internet.

We examine these issues in more detail later in this chapter, but first we address a key question: What are the most important "rules" of doing business with the Internet Protocol (IP), or the computer code that is the essence of the Internet?

The technical and architectural features of the Internet are briefly discussed here to illustrate how economic opportunities in the Internet economy derive directly from key features of Internet technologies. First, what exactly is the Internet? The Internet is just a bright idea; there is no "there" there. The Internet is a network of networks. Any network or anything that chooses to speak IP can be part of the Internet. The Internet Protocol, and related standards for interconnecting networks as defined by the Internet Engineering Task Force, is the Internet. Everything else is something else. The unifying power of the IP is analogous to Roman law. Roman law was used, along with the Roman Legions, of course, to demand the submission of opposing (proprietary?) fiefdoms and clans, forcing merchants, kings, and barbarians to bow down to its power. To be on the Internet, you must obey its rules, and the Internet requires that you send and receive messages using the Internet Protocol. Those who refuse banish themselves to a world of darkness, chaos, and incompatible computer systems. Of course, in this case there are no Roman Legions and no law actually requiring one to use IP. There are just legions of users and a host of applications and potential markets. There still is widespread fear of the openness and interconnection resulting from allegiance to the Internet Protocol, because it exposes firms to attack by hackers, thieves, and spies, and subjects users to invasion of privacy and other risks. It must be admitted that such concerns are well founded. Business transactions occur and new business opportunities arise in an inherently vulnerable marketplace.

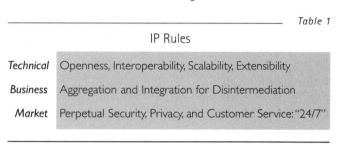

Table 1

IP Rules	
Technical	Openness, Interoperability, Scalability, Extensibility
Business	Aggregation and Integration for Disintermediation
Market	Perpetual Security, Privacy, and Customer Service: "24/7"

The continued growth of Internet businesses therefore depends on balancing the risks and rewards seen by both vendors and consumers. The business requirements to do so stem directly from the Internet's technical characteristics. These business needs have been described by this author as "IP Rules," and are summarized in table 1 above.[8] The most important IP Rules are the technical needs for openness, interoperability, scalability, and extensibility in the Internet. Openness is required at a number of levels, but essentially if one is not open to information transmissions then one cannot participate in the Internet. There are of course some caveats on this point. Most users, especially large organizations, whether in the private, public, or nonprofit sector, must be concerned with the technical integrity of their information systems and therefore must guard against information attacks, whether malicious or benign.[9]

The question of which systems can be trusted in an open network environment is a constant concern of both small and large users (Camp, 2000). "Interoperability" is a variously defined Internet-era term, but essentially it is a corollary to the more general term "open." To be interoperable is to be able to connect disparate systems through a common interface.

On the Internet, of course, that common interface is the Internet Protocol. It may in fact be wise for technical or business reasons to limit the use of the Internet Protocol in certain areas and use other standards and technologies better suited to the task at hand. Still, those technologies must be able to link through some mechanism via the Internet. If not, end users cannot be reached by others on the Internet, whether to try to sell them something or to deliver requested information to them. Interoperability and heterogeneity—diversity —and convergence and divergence—innovation—are all facilitated by the Internet Protocol's properties.

Scalability and extensibility can be discussed together. The Internet is a highly scalable system. Therefore, as demonstrated continually over years of sustained high-growth rates, the Internet is able to support increases in the number of users, volume of traffic, rate of traffic, and variety of uses—all at the same time. Extensibility is a more subtle term and refers to the ability to incrementally improve the hardware and software empowering Internet networks, services, and applications. This is not an accident, as the Internet's engineering designers and systems architects have consciously striven to make continuous improvement possible. At times, a design limit has been reached or been miscalculated. For example, the Internet's address space was not designed with the assumption that there would be billions of users; hence the need to upgrade the protocol occasionally.[10] Nonetheless, the ability of the Internet to scale— that is, to cope with exponential growth in the number of users and in the volume of traffic—is nothing short of astounding.

The Internet permits everyone to make changes in, improve the performance of, or extend the range of features of their own separate technologies, products, and services; and, by maintaining interoperability through the Internet Protocol, they still will be able to "plug in" to the network—and to the Internet marketplace. Figure 1 illustrates this special ability of the Internet to allow one to utilize any network technology, any type of middleware software, and any type of application and service across the same network to reach customers and suppliers worldwide. The National Research Council conceptualized this as an "open data network architecture." As long as one relies on the "bearer service" of the Internet Protocol—which allows it to transport any load—then you can always get there from here across the Internet.[11]

From an economic perspective, the most important element of the Internet stems directly from the technical features we have just reviewed — specifically its ability to cross boundaries, whether of technologies or markets. Taken together, these critical features of the Internet are understood by economists by generalizing the concept of the Internet's bearer service through the idea that the Internet acts as a general purpose technology or platform technology.[12] The reduced transaction costs and positive network externalities often found on the Internet enable new products and services to be brought to market more easily and quickly than in the past. From an incumbent firm's perspective, this heightened risk of competitive entry is unsettling and worrisome but is an inherent aspect of an Internet economy. The lower barriers to entry on the Internet

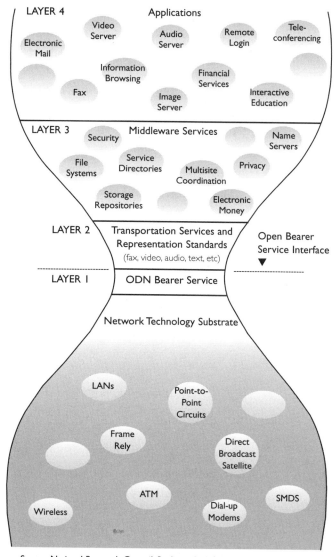

Figure 1

NCR Open Data Network Architecture

LAYER 4 — Applications

Electronic Mail, Video Server, Audio Server, Remote Login, Tele-conferencing, Information Browsing, Financial Services, Fax, Image Server, Interactive Education

LAYER 3 — Middleware Services

Security, Name Servers, File Systems, Service Directories, Multisite Coordination, Privacy, Storage Repositories, Electronic Money

LAYER 2 — Transportation Services and Representation Standards (fax, video, audio, text, etc)

Open Bearer Service Interface ▼

LAYER 1 — ODN Bearer Service

Network Technology Substrate

LANs, Point-to-Point Circuits, Frame Rely, Direct Broadcast Satellite, ATM, Dial-up Modems, SMDS, Wireless

Source: National Research Council, *Realizing the Information Future*, 1994

may be raised intentionally by strategic actions, but the barriers can only be fortified and never wholly solidified, as competitors can always try to find a way to reach one's customer's with their product (Gawer, 2000). There is no way to fully "lock out" anyone. A firm may attempt this, of course, by pursuing both new and classic strategies, as Microsoft has been alleged to do by the U.S. Department of Justice and the courts.

Because of information interoperability across the Internet, it is easier, cheaper, and faster to aggregate information in novel ways and analyze correlations and other relationships within the data sets thereby assembled (Bailey, 1998). In this chapter it is not possible to explore in detail the business implications of this, but it is important to emphasize that for corporate "back-office" functions, and for users searching for information, this may seem to be the most important aspect of the Internet.[13] From a strategic perspective, equally important is the ability to use the Internet as a weapon to disintermediate established firms and industries. Firms and customers on either end of a value chain can more easily reach each other directly, or a new firm may propose to act as a lower-cost, trusted third party or intermediary between the two groups. In the area of business to business transactions, as well as in the business to consumer arena, such new intermediaries may take many forms, such as exchanges, publishers, service providers, storefronts, and so on.

If one is going to do business of any kind on the Internet, then the third set of IP Rules identified in table 1 applies. Because the Internet is "always on," and customers and suppliers somewhere in the world may be trying to reach you, Internet businesses must always be on—must operate "24/7," in the current expression. In practical terms, firms must be perpetually concerned about security, because hackers and viruses also do not sleep. Protection of privacy for customers is a concern, because someone, somewhere could be using the Internet to aggregate information or otherwise violate the privacy of customers. Finally, customer service also must be always on, because users expect to be able to log on at any time from anywhere. If they have a problem and your Internet business cannot fix it quickly and courteously, a competitor just a click away may be only too happy to oblige. We leave it to sociologists and psychologists to assess the social strains of an "always on" life, but only note here that execution of any Internet business model will falter if human and technical requirements are not both satisfied. The Internet may be always on, but we humans need a good night's sleep for peak performance.

It may be helpful here to review a simple conceptual model of the Internet as we delve deeper into Internet business processes. Most Internet businesses operate on the edge of the Internet, which is where the intelligence and processing power resides by design (see figure 2). To reach the Internet, users must contract with some type of Internet Service Provider or ISP. ISPs come in all shapes and sizes, and at present are estimated to number roughly 12,000 in the United States and who knows how many worldwide. Internet Service Providers aggregate the traffic of many customers into larger bundles, which are then handed off to a "backbone provider." The backbone provider can be thought of as a wholesaler of network capacity to ISPs who may act as retailers. In fact, some firms are active in both the backbone and retail ISP markets, but typically

they organize those functions into distinct business units, because the focus in each is so different. Nonetheless, national and local ISPs may compete for end users. It is the backbone providers, however, who truly must be always on, continuously monitoring network performance and traffic patterns. In the open and user-driven Internet, traffic flows, directions, and volumes shift in a chaotic or bursty manner. At one moment users are flocking to a new streaming media release—in the next to an online auction site. Somehow the backbone and ISP engineers must

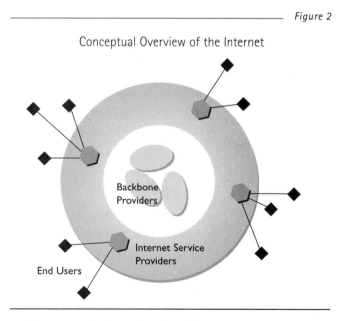

Figure 2

Conceptual Overview of the Internet

Backbone Providers

Internet Service Providers

End Users

accommodate both, in a still largely best-effort network. In performing this task, firms generally are spending twice as much on operations as they receive in revenues. Is there a business model that can justify being in this business?

To answer that question, we offer figure 3, which illustrates the components of an unclouded Internet. The phrase, "the Internet cloud," has long been used to refer to the components of the network of networks that are not visible to the end user. The way in which bits get to their final destination is a variable, automatic process, which Internet users did not need to think about. That is no longer the case, particularly if one is attempting to provide some level of quality assurance beyond the Internet's "best effort" for real-time services such as voice calls, streaming media, or multimedia conferencing.[14] Before those bits get into the Internet cloud, of course, they must traverse some type of local access infrastructure. As figure 3 illustrates, users have many choices for Internet local access technologies, including mobile phones and other portable wireless devices, such as personal digital assistants. These and other devices, such as televisions or traditional personal computers, can access the Internet across analog telephone lines, coaxial cable networks through use of cable modems, Integrated Services Digital Networks (ISDN), Digital Subscriber Lines (DSL), Ethernet data networks prevalent in most corporate and government offices, and higher-capacity digital and fiber optic lines used by businesses. There is no shortage of technology to access the Internet, though many of these alternatives may not be economically viable in particular areas or for particular types of use. The rapidly increasing capabilities of optical networks and falling prices for wireless and satellite packet services used by businesses is in any case encouraging, as it suggests that other businesses should have increased access to the currencies of the Internet, which are packets and bandwidth to carry those packets.[15]

Moving upstream from the edge of the network, Internet traffic typically must pass through an aggregation point (called point of presence, or POP), which also may be variously known as a cable head-end or telephone central office. As figure 3 illustrates, these POPs are sometimes called "telecom hotels," if the traffic aggregation points are owned and operated by neither an incumbent telephone or cable operator, but rather by and for new Internet businesses. National (backbone) ISPs with default-free routing capability and settlements-free interconnection, incur high costs of maintaining default-free routers to operate at the core of the Internet.[16] National backbone ISPs compete for ISP customers and end users.

Through the interconnection of ISPs, users may reach a seemingly infinite array of content, products, and services. New varieties of business operations, such as Application Service Providers, Education Service Providers, and Content Delivery Networks, are relatively easy to invent and deploy because of the Internet's openness and interoperability. User applications, including e-mail, FTP (file transfer), Telnet (terminal sessions), Usenet (news bulletin board service), and of course Web browsing, search, and other services may be combined in service bundles for particular market needs and niches, either by end users or by firms. Additional services are chat groups, message boards, instant messaging, voice services, streaming media, music entertainment, and real-time audio and video conferencing. In addition to the above services, business applications including databases, transaction systems, security systems, and so on can all be accessed across the Internet.

Figure 3

An Unclouded Internet

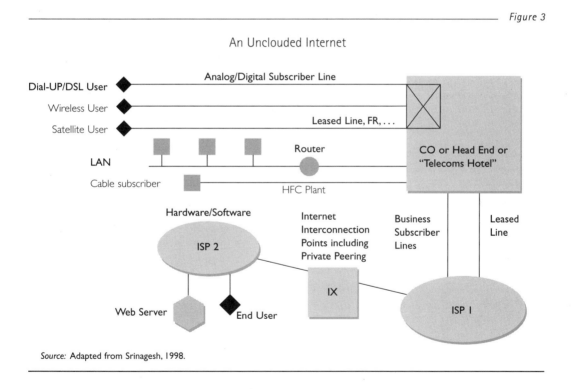

Source: Adapted from Srinagesh, 1998.

Further market segmentation business models can be seen as plugging in at various points in figure 3. Firms may intend to provide services, software, and equipment and conduct e-commerce across the Internet. All they need to get started is a website. Of course, as many first-generation Internet firms quickly discovered, there are other business requirements, such as having an efficient logistics system, strong customer service, and an effective market and branding strategy. And even if all of those requirements are effectively met, it is not sufficient. The business must also have a technology, product, or service that someone, somewhere is willing to spend money to obtain.

Firms may develop business models to offer Internet access, Internet services, Internet applications and application services, Web hosting, caching and/or network storage, as well as ancillary services, such as advertising, marketing, and customer relationship management to support all of the above. Underpinning all of this are the firms that offer the Internet equipment on which all others depend. Engineers at Cisco jokingly describe themselves as the "arms merchants" of the Internet: they will sell their equipment to anybody and really do not care which firm may succeed or fail at disintermediating another through clever use of Internet technologies. It is not their problem.

The three figures together provide a multidimensional picture of the Internet. Figure 1 illustrates conceptually what the Internet Protocol does by acting as a "bearer service"—the general purpose or platform technology linking technologies, software, services, customers, firms, and markets. Figure 2 illustrates the principal actors on the Internet: the backbone providers, the Internet service providers, and the users. Users range from individuals to corporations and governments, all of whom can both consume and produce information for dissemination across the Internet. It is that simple. It also is a bit more complex in practice, as figure 3 illustrates, when one "unclouds" the Internet. There are many different, independent entities that may all be involved to one degree or another in any Internet activity. Because the Internet's intelligence traditionally resides at the edge of the network, the Internet need not be self-aware of all the things for which users may wish to use it. That lack of self-awareness also may be seen as a problem to be overcome or worked around by other businesses, such as content hosting firms and content delivery networks. The viability of any particular business model can be seen as dependent on many other businesses.

New entrants almost always propose an innovative approach that effectively disintermediates other firms upstream and downstream from their intended point of market entry. In the language of William Baumol, author of the preceding chapter, all Internet markets are inherently contestable—that is, open to competitive entry—even if they may be monopolized to a degree at a particular point in time. The framework developed here can be used to categorize and assess the competitive threats and opportunities for various Internet business models. Questions any Internet business must ask include: Which market are we targeting? How can we best use the Internet to serve our customers and develop new markets? Which rival firms and industries can we disintermediate? What types of new technologies could be used to disintermediate us? The following section assesses some Internet business models and whether they have as yet proven their viability.

INTERNET BUSINESS MODELS

Given the preceding analysis, what future business models would not make more sense if they were built around the Internet? It is now evident that the Internet, and Internet business models, are now business as usual.[17] Every firm in every industry, eventually in nearly every country, will use the Internet and incorporate the net into its organizational structure, market research, product development, manufacturing, and distribution strategies. If the Internet innovation engine is irreversibly transforming everything it touches, should not businesses, governments, universities, and individuals seek to harness the net to their advantage? In the terminology of Schumpeterian economic analysis, Internet businesses are founded on and rely on nothing more remarkable than the technological and economic forces of creative destruction—as usual.

If one accepts this point of view, the Internet is no more or no less remarkable than past innovations, such as electric lights, railroads, the telephone and television, which changed our ability to communicate and transport ideas, images, goods, and services. Some may claim that the Internet is more significant than any of those past society-shaping innovations, and hark back to Gutenberg's printing press as the proper comparison of an epoch-shaping technological innovation. In any case, while we may wax rhapsodic about the Internet, it is, after all, only transporting bits from here to there and back again. But that simple function clearly is having broad effects on businesses and societies, for good and ill.

Some claim that Internet marketing is a new form of business-consumer relationship, based on trust. It is certainly true that the networked environment for electronic commerce places a high premium on ensuring that the firm is responsive and trusted by customers and prospective customers. Just because marketers speak of cyber-based virtual communities, however, does not mean there is anything fundamentally new at work from a marketing perspective.[18] There are, however, many new opportunities to track and identify consumers, create "rich media" advertisements, and in other ways personalize the relationship between individuals and organizations hoping to obtain revenue for goods or services offered to that individual. Some may argue that this constitutes only a form of pseudo-personalization, because there is a computer database and not necessarily a person on the other end of the communication exchange. While academics may prefer the term "mass customization" to describe the ability of information technology—now heightened by the Internet—to mass produce customized experiences and interactions, the fact remains that the new tools are being used for the old goals of selling and then maintaining a customer relationship.

The Internet enables aggregation, integration, and analysis of an unprecedented quantity and variety of information at low unit costs. The ability of Internet-centered firms to disintermediate firms operating on different organizational principles and to reintermediate industries in new ways is largely driven by this fact.[19] The easy access to markets for innovative ideas and businesses is driven by the same force—the interoperability and ubiquity of the Internet Protocol. The largely positive network externalities of the Internet stem from the same factor—that is, the value of the Internet to all users increases as others try to do more across the network of networks. All of these benefits are to a degree driven by the statistical sharing of bandwidth, which is the primary technique for ensuring the technical efficiency of the Internet (McKnight and Bailey, 1997, 1998).

Tables 2 and 3 below summarize several Internet commerce and Internet access business models. Table 2 makes clear that few barriers to entry exist in many of the broad categories of Internet commerce that nonetheless have succeeded in attracting significant investment funds. If there are few barriers to entry, and most of the portals, exchanges, and e-commerce stores rely on standardized technology to interface with the greatest number of customers possible, what possible barriers to entry can be erected? Advertising off the net—on radio, in print publications, and on television—has become a potent weapon, one on which venture capitalists are willing to have their money spent. We hope all this advertising is not just a matter of stock promotion, which would be illegal under Securities and Exchange Commission rules, but is instead intended to increase brand awareness, attract traffic to websites, promote sales, and ultimately lead to profitability. But why do we still suspect that many of the advertising campaigns are intended as much to promote the stock as they are the company itself? And why do we feel nervous if the only barrier to entry is a big advertising budget to create a big media campaign? Is this all that many so-called Internet innovations amount to? Isn't anybody really building a better mousetrap?

There are of course many subtleties and nuances in individual firms' e-business models that are not reflected in the generic categories shown in table 2. With regard to technology, all Internet firms by definition rely on the public and open standards that define the Internet in general and the World Wide Web more specifically. Vendors offer proprietary software products for Internet security, transaction processing, auction operations, and content delivery, to name a few specific Internet commerce–related markets. But only a few e-commerce operators have developed unique, proprietary technology that is deeply embedded in their businesses. Perhaps this is not so unusual, because most retailers and wholesalers in the physical world are not also renowned for their technical research divisions and proprietary innovations. Rather, retailers try to distinguish themselves through branding, advertising, and their management of the customer experience—which remains crucially important to e-retailers and wholesalers as well.

We also should note that a few firms already are operating in the black

Table 2

Internet Commerce Business Models

Business Model	B2C Portals	B2C & C2C Auctions & Exchanges	Niche & Vertical Portals	B2B Portals	B2B Auctions & Exchanges
Technology	Standards-based	Standards-based, & proprietary	Standards-based	Standards-based	Standards-based, & proprietary
Profitability	Yes & No	Yes & No	Yes & No	Yes & No	Yes & No

in the Internet marketplace. For example, some niche market portals and e-commerce sites are profitable, and are able to charge a significant premium to advertisers compared to the general-interest portals. Nonetheless, the general lack of profitability combined with the still quite high stock valuations by traditional market metrics has puzzled many analysts. Why should e-business firms be able to make money in the stock market when they can't make money from their business, many wonder. One argument is that just as other firms had to sustain losses while building out their infrastructure and market position (for example, cable television franchise-holders and cellular telephone license holders), so too must investors take the long view with Internet firms and support them while they build their market position over time. While this argument is reassuring to a degree, we may ask, where is the license or franchise in the Internet? With no legal claim to a position in cyberspace, can investors really be confident that the Internet market leader of today will even remain in existence tomorrow, let alone some day become profitable? Perhaps in the Internet access market we may find more promising business strategies.

Table 3 reviews the current status of Internet access businesses in the United States and considers their profitability, or lack thereof. The Internet access market is a battleground for telecoms and Internet firms. For cable modems, the Boston area has one of the largest deployments to date, with more than 10 percent of homes passed by the service subscribing by winter

Table 3

Internet Access Business Models

Internet Access Business Models	"Free email/free ISPs/free computers"	High-speed services (T-1s/ADSL/cable modems/satellite)	Subscription dial-up services (wireless and fixed modems)
Flat-rate or variable prices	Flat rate subscription + advertising support + possible phone charges + possible price of other bundled goods or services	Mainly flat rate, with variable usage—sensitive pricing plans on the horizon	Wireless typically has usage charge, fixed typically does not in US; elsewhere is usage-based
Profitable?	No—in build-out phase	No—in build-out phase (except for very profitable T-1s)	Yes

2001. Other smaller markets have penetration rates up to 25 percent as of this writing. Those fortunate enough to live in areas where such service is available have enjoyed high bandwidth access at a fraction of the price previously charged. This chapter cannot explore in detail the comparative advantages and disadvantages of telephone dial-up, ISDN, DSL, cable modem, fiber optic, cellular, wireless local loop, and satellite technologies, among others, that can offer Internet access. Nor can we explore in detail the important public policy issues raised by debates on "open access," which have occurred at municipal, regional, and national levels.[20] We will, however, briefly touch upon both issues while analyzing Internet access business models, because both the range of technologies and the role of public policy are important factors that affect firms' business strategies in these markets.

In *The Gordian Knot*,[21] we anticipated the efforts to obtain market power through establishment of a controlling position in access markets, and offered four principles for a new information and communication policy architecture: open architecture, open access, universal access, and flexible access. We argued that open access is great, as are equal access and universal access, but we also advocated a flexible policy regime to adapt to rapidly changing technologies, preferences, and needs. For example, if AT&T won't provide open access, then AOL will make deals with satellite, ADSL, and/or other providers. If AOL won't offer open access to its instant messaging users, then others will work around them. If the traditional telecommunications firms, both local and long distance, try to raise phone rates at a time of falling costs, then people will stop using things called phones and work around them with Personal Digital Assistants (PDAs) or other mobile Internet access devices. That's one of the beauties of digital technologies—there's always another way to get from here to there.

The new telecoms division between haves and have-nots is an issue often raised in the global Internet access market. In advanced nations, this issue is debated primarily between those who have access to high-speed Internet services and those who do not. There are a number of reasons that some areas may have access to higher-bandwidth services sooner than others. For example, businesses with a higher willingness to pay will be served first, and higher-income suburbs and city centers may be served before lower-income urban or rural areas. Important public policy questions of social equity must be addressed as we rush forward into an Internet-centric economy. For this and historical reasons, the route to Internet access often still wends its way past federal, state, and municipal regulatory authorities.

The telecoms regulatory process of local loop unbundling requires definition of a seemingly infinite number of specific procedures for network interconnection. In the United States, the functional components of a switched telecoms network are known as UNE, or Unbundled Network Elements. Competitive Local Exchange Carriers (CLECs), the incumbent local exchange carriers, the long distance operators, resellers, and others have all been engaged in discussions of these UNEs, as well as Operating Support Systems (OSS). These arcane debates also are occurring in different forms in other advanced and developing nations where competitive carriers are entering the telecommunications and Internet markets. These discussions are relevant to this chapter on Internet business models, because telecommunications operators are subject to more extensive regulatory oversight than other types of firms, such as cable and satellite operators. In spite of our argument in *The Gordian Knot* that an equitable regulatory environment should be established for all participants in the Internet marketplace, we acknowledge that this vision will remain unrealized for most marketplace participants for some time to come.

There have been numerous mergers and acquisitions involving "next-generation network" and "incumbent telecommunications operator" firms, which affects the Internet access business. Do the deals have a deeper meaning for the evolution of industry structure in telecommunications that will affect investors, users, technology suppliers, and competitors?[22] Or does it merely reflect an inexorable drive toward global scale economies that will leave niche, regional, and even national telecoms players marginalized? Recall again Joseph Schumpeter's characterization of capitalism as a system for creative destruction of technologies, industries, and jobs, as the new obliterates the old. Does it describe the transformation now underway in the telecommunications industry? And is this process creative—or just destructive? The careers of real people with real jobs are at stake.

Current technological, regulatory, organizational, and competitive issues are compelling change in the way telecommunications enterprises and their stakeholders do business in an increasingly global economy. Emerging industry standards are affecting transmission of voice and data, trade in services, and the Internet. There are a wide variety of new trade opportunities—and risks—for telecoms manufacturers, service providers, and software suppliers, which may offer lucrative possibilities in newly opened markets worldwide. The impact of privatization and deregulation on the organizational structure, incentives, and efficiency of telecoms operators and suppliers is also a challenging issue, and may limit the scope and scale of business opportunities for new entrants. The role of international alliances, acquisitions, and divestitures in fostering greater competition and innovation in telecommunications services is also a matter of daily concern in boardrooms worldwide.

Tables 4 and 5 illustrate the relative business success or profitability of key sectors of the global Internet economy—that is, the markets for Internet equipment and software. There are few clear lessons from these tables, except that Microsoft and Cisco are in enviable market positions. We conclude our discussion of Internet business models, with barely a mention of B2B. B2C, B2G, G2C, C2B, or the other market segmentations offered by analysts. (To

Table 4

Internet Equipment Business Models

	Edge (Access) Equipment	Routers and Servers	Carrier-Class
Telco or IP strengths dominant	IP	IP	Telco (at present)
Profitable?	Yes, but highly competitive	Yes—for Cisco	Yes, many new IP-enabled entrants

Table 5

Internet Software Business Models

Internet Software Tools Business Models	Consumer Applications	Business Applications	Common IP Infrastructure— e.g., *domain registries*
Microsoft or Competitive?	Microsoft	Microsoft, Sun, Oracle, Linux	Competitive
Profitable?	Yes	Yes	Not yet

translate, these labels mean business to business, business to consumer, business to government, government to consumer, and consumer to business.) But perhaps the frequent use of all those labels in the business press simply demonstrate that the Internet already is business as usual and will increasingly pervade all areas of the economy. The global Internet economy is not hyperbole, even if the search for successful Internet business models will inevitably be a process of trial and error. And creative destruction—as usual.

CONCLUSION

Business models for Internet commerce, software, access, network infrastructure, and equipment markets must be grounded in the technical realities as well as the business and policy environment of the Internet economy of today and tomorrow. Are they? As academics like to say, it depends. The Internet connects hundreds of millions of people worldwide, and the number of users will grow significantly for years to come. Nonetheless, we should expect that most Internet businesses existing today will fail, as competitive forces and market reality demand that economic value be demonstrated for market acceptance.

More unsettling for business leaders, entrepreneurs, and investors is recognition of the implications of these conclusions. Businesses face creative destruction as usual—disintermediation at a very high data rate, from businesses based anywhere on the planet, including a 15-year-old's bedroom or a 19-year-old's college dorm room. Nonetheless, while many new business opportunities are created by new technologies, most would-be entrepreneurs fail, as do most proposed innovations. Sorting the wheat from the chaff of proposed business models and business plans is done daily by venture capitalists, investment bankers, the media, and markets of many types—not least of which is the stock market. The final arbiter, of course, will be business and residential consumers of goods and services. Some things don't change in an Internet economy.

Businesses, government, and universities face numerous challenges in developing technology policy in an area of incessant innovation, both in technologies and Internet business models. Technology policy in this setting must focus on the research infrastructure, human capital formation, and new tools and techniques needed to support private sector innovation. Which, if any, programs are needed when the private sector is pouring so many resources into new businesses? How should governments harness Internet technologies to better organize their internal operations and more responsively interact with citizens and others? We offer the following suggestions for public policy-makers as they consider how to ensure that their citizenry are prepared to participate in the global Internet economy and to develop their own innovative Internet business models:

- Long-term basic research is needed but is likely to be under-supported by the private sector. For example, the Internet required three decades of subsidies to reach commercial market introduction. Only government can afford to be that patient.

- Support for the education and training needs of "human capital"—that is, people—is a safe and high pay-off bet for societies seeking to ensure future economic growth and innovation.

Thanks to the Internet's innovation engine, there is no way to ignore the implications of an accelerated pace of creative destruction. New technologies and business models will continually spew forth through the Internet. Succeeding in the global Internet economy is difficult, and survival is far from assured. Our final word of "free" advice is to hold on tight—if you think the Internet industry has been on a wild ride, you ain't seen nothing yet. And, because you may need to repeatedly retool your personal skill set throughout your career, don't forget about us in the academy. Say, is that a new e-learning service provider with an innovative business model and proprietary technology I see entering our market niche?[23] Wait a minute . . .

PART3

THE GLOBAL CONTEXT FOR
CREATIVE DESTRUCTION

4 | CREATIVE DESTRUCTION IN LATIN AMERICAN TELECOMMUNICATIONS PRIVATIZATION

Walter T. Molano

Joseph Schumpeter's theory of "creative destruction" presents a dynamic perspective on modern capitalism. By arguing that innovation destroys existing technologies and creates rival products, the theory is a powerful tool to analyze the evolution of current products and markets. The theory is even more powerful, however, when we examine technological development within a political-economic context.

Modern industry has created powerful political and economic forces. Technological innovations have allowed small businesses to consolidate into large corporations, and some sectors have integrated themselves into full monopolies. Public officials broke up many of the cartels, but they could not disassemble all of them. Strategic industries, particularly in infrastructure, required large economies of scale to justify the necessary investment. In response, governments imposed strong regulatory structures on these sectors. In some cases, governments nationalized the industries. The regulatory structures, however, were often obstacles to modernization. Schumpeter's theory of creative destruction suggests that technology is constantly mutating, but governments often lack the flexibility to adapt to radical change.

The interaction between technology and regulation is most evident in the telecommunications industry. The dawn of the telecommunications industry witnessed an explosion of new technologies, and bright prospects for high returns brought a flood of competition. By the beginning of the twentieth century, however, the pace of innovation slowed. At the same time, fierce competition eroded profit margins, and telephone companies were forced to consolidate to survive. Eventually, operating companies consolidated into national monopolies.

Telephone companies around the world used the economies of scale argument to justify their cartels. The large fixed costs associated with telephone networks required monopoly arrangements. The initial response of governments was to impose regulatory structures to prevent abuse. Some governments took a direct role in the sector by nationalizing their telephone companies. The strategy worked well while the pace of technological change was low.[1] Governments used public resources to invest in new equipment and technology. They were ill prepared, however, to confront rapid rates of technological change, and the digital revolution is a good example. Governments were forced to return the telecommunications sector to the private sector when they found themselves unable to make the investment needed to modernize their infrastructure.

The privatization and liberalization of the telecommunications industry in the 1990s led to a competitive explosion. By the end of the decade, the telecommunications market was becoming saturated with a proliferation of technologies and firms. Although competition allowed communications costs to decline, profit margins also fell and companies were forced to consolidate to survive. At the same time, governments began to impose more regulatory control, and it is possible that another wave of re-regulation or nationalization will appear if the pace of technological change decelerates.

This chapter employs Schumpeter's framework to explore the relationship between markets and governments by examining the telecommunications sector of the Southern Cone of Latin America.[2] The main proposition is that the rapid pace of technological change during the 1980s forced governments to relinquish control of the telecommunications sector. Looking forward, we see these governments attempting to exercise more control over the sector once the technology stabilizes and the industry begins to consolidate. The chapter is divided into four sections: First, we review the evolution of the telecommunications sector in the Southern Cone countries. Second, we examine the ability of the countries to confront major technological changes. Third, we look at the impact of privatization on technology innovation. Last, we offer conjectures about the future of the sector.

THE TELECOMMUNICATIONS INDUSTRY IN THE SOUTHERN CONE OF LATIN AMERICA

Brazil was the first Latin American country to acquire telephone service. In 1876 Emperor Pedro II traveled to Philadelphia and witnessed a demonstration by Alexander Graham Bell. He immediately ordered a telephone system for his palace, and the first Brazilian telephone network was installed in 1879.[3] In 1880 the Society du Pantelephone de Loch was established in Buenos Aires, and the Chilean Telephone Company (CTC) was incorporated in Valparaiso. Telephone service arrived in Uruguay in 1886, with the creation of the Compañía Telefónica y de Luz Electrica del Río de la Plata.[4]

Foreign investors took a dominant role in developing the first networks in the region. The first Brazilian network concession was granted to the Telephone Company of Brazil, a company owned by a group of U.S. investors. It provided service between Rio de Janeiro and the suburb of Niterói. In Chile, a group of U.S. investors launched a network in Chile called the West Coast Telephone Company to compete against CTC. In 1881 two U.S.-owned telephone companies, Gower Bell and Continental de Teléfonos Bell, began operations in Buenos Aires. Foreign investors were drawn by the prospects of high growth and wide margins. Unfortunately, the telecommunications market soon became saturated, and fierce competition eventually forced consolidation of the industry.

Chile was the first country to see consolidation of its telephone industry. In 1884, CTC and West Coast Telephone Company merged into a single national network. Argentina soon followed in Chile's footsteps. In 1886, the three major telephone companies in Buenos Aires merged into a single company called Unión Telefónica del Río de la Plata (UTRP). The privately owned company had a monopoly over Argentine telephone service. Within a year after the merger, UTRP increased prices; meanwhile the quality of service deteriorated. Such monopoly abuses quickly led to a public outcry.[5] In 1887 a group of Argentine consumers, upset with UTRP, created the Sociedad Cooperativa Telefónica (SCT) to provide an alternative telephone company. SCT launched operations with 1,000 customers, while UTRP had 7,000. Indirect official assistance, however, allowed SCT to grow at a faster pace than UTRP. SCT eventually became the largest telephone operator in Argentina.

The experience was slightly different in Brazil. The Brazilian government initially granted states and municipalities full control of telephone concessions, and soon there was an explosion of foreign-owned telephone companies. The proliferation of technologies and systems complicated the integration of the telephone systems into a national network. Finally, the Brazilian government took regulatory control of the sector and in 1890 established a national agency to grant all telephone concessions.

The structure of the telephone industry in the Southern Cone of Latin America remained unchanged for the next 30 years. The privately owned companies matured, and government regulation grew at a steady pace. The next major change came during the First World War. Telephone networks expansion stopped during the war because most of the telecommunications equipment was embargoed for military use. The quality of telephone services declined, and the systems decayed further in the early 1920s as the industrialized countries redirected most of their output to postwar rebuilding efforts. The Southern Cone governments retaliated by imposing further regulatory restrictions on the telephone companies. Telephone companies soon faced financial difficulties and desperately needed capital for new equipment and survival. Fortunately, a solution appeared in the mid-1920s.

In 1925, the U.S. government forced AT&T to spin off its international arm, ITT. AT&T was allowed to take a dominant role in the U.S. telecommunications market, while ITT was allowed to focus on the international market. Armed with a strong balance sheet and ample financing, the new company began acquiring Latin American telephone companies. In 1925, ITT bought a stake in the Argentine telephone company, SCT. In 1927, ITT increased its stake in SCT and acquired full control. In 1925, ITT bought the Chilean Telephone Company (CTC), and the Chilean government granted a 50-year operating contract to the new owner. In 1929, ITT acquired UTRP, securing a monopoly over the entire Argentine telecommunications industry. A similar process occurred in Brazil during the 1930s, with German and Canadian multinationals increasing market share.

Uruguay, however, took a different path. In 1903, Uruguay elected Jose Batlle y Ordóñez. The election marked the start of a profound political and economic transformation. President Batlle called for a dominant economic role for the state and advocated the creation of *entes autónomos,* or state enterprises, to enhance the general welfare, increase competition in services, and prevent foreign domination. State-owned companies were granted monopoly rights in the 1917 constitution. Usinas Electricas y Los Teléfonos del Estado (UTE) was given the right to nationalize all telephone services.[6] Unfortunately, the events in Uruguay were a prelude to what would occur in the rest of the region.

Three decades later, Argentina joined the nationalization bandwagon. In 1946, President Juan Peron paid £28 million for ITT's stake in the national telephone company. The name of the company was changed to Empresa Mixta

Telefonica Argentina (EMTA).[7] The pressure to nationalize was also growing in Brazil and Chile.

In the 1930s, Brazilian President Getúlio Vargas advocated a bigger economic role for the state. President Juscelino Kubitschek increased demands for an interventionist state in the postwar period. By the 1950s, the Brazilian government was taking a direct role in setting tariff levels. Unable to pass cost increases onto consumers, telephone operating companies began reducing investment programs. The reduction in private sector investment provided the government with an excuse to take a bigger role. Given the fragmentation of the Brazilian telecommunications sector, long-distance lines were minimal, and the government began calling for the creation of a national long-distance company. In 1965 the government created Embratel, a state-owned long-distance provider. Unfortunately, the creation of Embratel was the first step in the nationalization of the Brazilian telecommunications industry.

In 1966 the government authorized Embratel to acquire a majority stake in Companhia Telefónica Brasileira (CTB). CTB was the largest telephone company in Brazil and the subsidiary of Canadian-owned Brazilian Traction Light & Power. CTB had the concessions of São Paulo, Minas Gerais, and Espírito Santo. In 1972 the government created a federal holding company to integrate all of Brazil's regions under a single technology. The new company, Telebras, was divided into 30 regional subsidiaries.

The path to nationalization was equally fast in Chile. The lack of a national long-distance service was also a troublesome issue for the Chilean government, but CTC had no incentive to build such a network. The need for a national network became painfully evident in 1960, however, when the southern region of Chile was devastated by a powerful earthquake and many towns were completely isolated from the rest of the country. The disaster forced the government to create a state-owned long-distance company, ENTEL, in 1964. The company was placed under the responsibility of the state development agency, Corporación de Fomento de la Producción (CORFO).[8] At the same time, CORFO was authorized to purchase 49 percent of CTC's stock. Relations with ITT deteriorated with the election of Salvador Allende. Consequently, the U.S.-owned company reduced its investment program, leading to further erosion of service. The 50-year concession was coming up for renewal, and the Chilean government informed ITT that it intended to nationalize CTC. CORFO finally acquired the company in 1974 for $125 million.

A look at the history of the telecommunications sector in the Southern Cone of Latin America shows a dynamic relationship between the public and private sectors. At times, the private sector enjoyed full discretion over the telecommunications industry. At other times, the public sector exercised greater control. The variable that determines the ebb and flow of government intervention appears to be technology development.

THE ROLE OF TECHNOLOGY

Technological change is the driving factor in Schumpeter's theory of creative destruction. We believe that the first derivative of technological change is the independent factor in determining the role of the state in the telecommunications industry. Unfortunately, it is difficult to quantify the rate of technological change, but we can take a look at the historical record to see how the rate of technological change affected the role of the state.

Dramatic technological innovation marked the early years of telecommunications. Most of the changes centered on switching equipment technology. In 1876, the first telephone lines were point to point. Operator-assisted switches arrived in the 1880s, allowing users to connect with other phone lines. The first electromechanical switches were installed in the 1890s, increasing the connectivity of the system and reducing operating costs. The pace of technological change decelerated, however, at the turn of the century, although there were improvements in the quality and design of the electromechanical switching equipment. The First World War stymied commercial development of telecommunications technology, because most of the research and development efforts were directed at military applications.

A spurt of technological development followed World War I, when many of the military innovations were reformatted for civilian use. A major technological breakthrough occurred in the 1920s when engineers developed new formats to maximize the signaling rate within a given bandwidth. The pace of technological change slowed again during the Great Depression as companies slashed their R&D budgets. The onset of World War II once more siphoned resources away from the civilian communications market, but many of the telecommunications technologies developed during the war, such as microwave transmission, began to be introduced commercially in the 1950s and

1960s. The telecommunications industry took a quantum leap forward in the 1970s , however, with the development of computer and digital technologies.[9]

A comparison between the rate of technological change and government intervention provides interesting insights. The governments in the Southern Cone of Latin America took no role in the initial development of the telecommunications industry. The first regulatory efforts began in the mid-1890s, however, soon after the pace of technological innovation leveled off. Regulatory efforts steadily increased until the mid-1920s when foreign operators were allowed to purchase monopoly stakes in Brazil, Chile, and Argentina. These purchases coincided with the development of the new signaling technology. Government intervention, this time in the form of nationalization, increased when the foreign companies stopped investing in new equipment during the Second World War. It is interesting to note, however, that government intervention in the telecommunications industry actually increased in the 1970s, just as telecommunications technology was taking another leap forward. The governments expanded their role from the operation of telephone systems to the manufacturing of telecommunications equipment and technology. The framework we developed suggests that the Southern Cone governments should have relinquished their control of the telecommunications sector at this point. Yet, the opposite occurred. Why? A closer look at the region suggests a reason for a break in the trend.

Import substitution was a policy that had existed in development circles since the beginning of the century. The theory gained momentum in the 1950s and 1960s through the work of Raul Prebisch, an Argentine economist. The theory advocated domestic manufacturing of capital goods to foster industrialization and the development of new technology. Unfortunately, the governments lacked the capital to finance import substitution programs. Things changed in the 1970s, however, with the petrodollar boom.[10]

The oil crisis of the 1970s left money center banks with a large amount of capital. Much of this liquidity was channeled into the Southern Cone of Latin America to fund import-substitution programs.[11] In 1974 the Brazilian government established Grupo Ejecutivo Interministerial de Componentes y Materiales (GEICOM) to lead import-substitution programs. In 1976 GEICOM launched CPqD, a telecommunications research and manufacturing center in the city of Campinas. CPqD refined and improved the telecommunications equipment used in Telebras.[12] The government used international syndicated loans to provide incentives and subsidies for foreign telecommunications equipment manufacturers to locate facilities in Brazil. European, Japanese, and North American firms, including Standard Electric-ITT, Ericsson, Nippon Electric, and Siemens, built large equipment plants in Brazil.[13] Most of the facilities were assembly plants, however, providing very little technological development.[14]

A similar pattern occurred in Argentina. In the 1970s the government promoted an import-substitution program in the telecommunications industry. Many of these programs were funded directly or indirectly through international loans. The Argentine state-owned telephone company (ENTEL) was ordered to purchase all equipment from domestic sources. International manufacturers, including Siemens, Equitel, NEC, Allocate, and Telettra, were provided subsidies to locate operations in Argentina. Traditional government suppliers and contractors, such as Perez Companc and Techint, formed joint ventures with international equipment manufacturers. Unfortunately, the strategy had several negative side effects. First, the lack of open competition meant that manufacturers could sell equipment at higher than market prices because the state-owned companies had to use domestic suppliers. Second, the local content rule allowed manufacturers to supply the government with outdated telecommunications technology.[15] The flaws of import substitution became painfully evident in the 1980s when the rest of the world was converging toward digital technology, and the Southern Cone was still mired in an analog straightjacket. It was time to return the reins to the private sector.[16]

Before we examine the privatization wave, it is important to look at the widely different Chilean and Uruguayan experiences with telecommunications technology. Lacking the economies of scale to justify the development of a domestic telecommunications industry, the Chilean state-owned company purchased its equipment abroad. Consequently, the countries had higher levels of telecommunications technology than Argentina and Brazil. In 1986, 36 percent of Chile's telephone lines were digital, compared with 0 percent in Argentina and less than 1 percent in Brazil. The level of digitalization in Uruguay rose in the late 1980s and early 1990s. By 1991, 68 percent of Uruguay's phone lines were digital, compared to 73 percent in Chile.[17] Not surprisingly, the Uruguayan population lacked an urgency to privatize.

THE IMPACT OF PRIVATIZATION

The 1982 Mexican default choked off the flow of capital into Latin America. Unable to fund further investment or subsidies, the telephone systems in the Southern Cone deteriorated. By 1986 Latin America had some of the worst telephone systems in the world. The installation rate of new lines plunged, and consumers had to wait years for a new phone line. The governments in the region tried several gimmicks to generate domestic capital sources. In 1988, for example, the Argentine government announced Megatel. The plan allowed consumers to prepay their phone installation charges, thus providing the state-owned telephone company with the capital to fund the purchase of the equipment. The plan failed miserably. Payment records were lost and consumers lost their money. The public was fed up with the state-owned telephone companies and there were open calls for privatization.

Chile was the first country in the Southern Cone of Latin America to privatize its telephone company. In 1987 the government sold CTC to a group of investors. The sale was driven by ideological reasons. It was clear that the military regime was coming to an end at the end of the 1980s; therefore, the military government wanted to reduce the size of the public sector before turning it back to civilian control.[18] In 1987, the Argentine government also decided to sell its state-owned telephone company; however, political wrangling blocked the transaction until 1989. There were attempts to sell Telebras in the early 1990s, but privatization did not occur until 1998. In Uruguay there was little support for privatization. The government attempted to privatize the national telephone company (ANTEL) in 1990, but a national referendum overturned the measure in 1992.

Privatization brought in a surge of investment and new technology. The level of digitalization in Chile doubled within two years of privatization.[19] Argentina modernized its system, installing a state-of-the-art fiber optic network in Buenos Aires. The privatized Brazilian telephone companies installed the latest wireless technologies. Privatization brought in new data processing and cellular technologies. It also brought in more competition. Personal Communications Services (PCS), cellular, and paging companies appeared across the region. Telebras was split into 12 individual companies. The government also provided mirror licenses to another 12 companies to ensure a competitive environment. Analysts estimated that the Brazilian telecommunications sector would generate $45 billion in investment over the first three years of operation. Yet, within the first year of private ownership, Brazilian firms were already considering consolidation strategies.

Argentina went through a similar pattern. In 1994 foreign direct investment accounted for more than 40 percent of all investment. The government was quite cooperative with the private telephone companies in the initial years of operation, but the relationship soured in the late 1990s, once most of the modernization was completed. In December 1999 the De la Rua government in Argentina unilaterally imposed a series of rate reductions on the phone companies. It seemed that the balance of power was shifting back to the state.

IMPLICATIONS FOR THE FUTURE

Schumpeter's theory of creative destruction is a powerful tool to help understand the dynamic relationship between government and the private sector. The experience in Latin America has shown that governments often lack the resources to finance rapid changes in technology. Therefore, they allow the private sector to lead the investment effort. Once the technology is installed, however, and the pace of change slows, governments attempt to exercise greater control. This observation is consistent with the rent-seeking literature. Theorists have argued that governments are covetous of the rents generated by monopolies. They attempt to capture those rents either through regulatory intervention or nationalization.

We expect that the governments in the Southern Cone of Latin America will increase their intervention in the telecommunications industry once the capital stock has been modernized and the technology stabilizes. It is not clear whether the governments will ever nationalize the telecommunications industry once again; however, the scenario cannot be ruled out. A decline in foreign investment, deterioration of service, consolidation of the sector, and stagnation of the technology base will surely create pressure for nationalization and a destruction of the global telecommunications service providers dominance in Latin American markets. Fortunately, a future spurt in technological innovation will likely force the tide to shift in the opposite direction.

5 | CREATIVE DESTRUCTION IN EUROPEAN INTERNET INDUSTRIES AND POLICIES

Jill Hills and Maria Michalis

Perhaps Schumpeter was only half-right. Decades of technological tumult in Internet-related industries, such as communications, computing, and electronic commerce, support his contention that the capitalist economy "is incessantly being revolutionalized *from within* by new enterprise, i.e., by the intrusion of new commodities or new methods of production or new commercial opportunities into the industrial structure as it exists at any moment" (Schumpeter, 1943: 31). Threats to the existing order—creative destruction—produced by the introduction of new products, markets, methods of production, means of transportation, and new forms of industrial organization are the "fundamental impulse that keeps the capitalist engine in motion" (1943: 83).

We said he may have been only half-right because Schumpeter also thought this process of creative destruction led inevitably to the replacement of entrepreneurial capitalists with socialist economic structures. It was the "likely heir apparent" (1949:418) to capitalism because tendencies toward increased technological complexity, organizational size, and managerial professionalization demanded some degree of economic control and planning. The collapse of most socialist states coupled with the rise of theory and practice celebrating privatization, deregulation, and innovation during the 1980s and 1990s suggest that Schumpeter's prediction about the death of capitalism is at least premature if not out-and-out wrong.

Even given the predictive miscue about the socialism's inevitable triumph, Schumpeter's ideas about the need for some economic control and regulation to rein in the "animal spirits" of capitalism deserves a second look, particularly for Internet-related firms and industries in Europe. At the beginning of the twenty-first century the Internet has spurred a festival of investment in start-up dot.com companies, in companies specializing in Internet infrastructure and software, and in technology that will link licenses for a third generation of mobile phones to the Internet. New markets have been created and, by integrating information and entertainment content with low-cost communications, the Internet has challenged both the old communications network operators and traditional off-air broadcasters. These market actors have responded with adoption of the new technology and with mergers and alliances on a global level. Western governments also have been galvanized. Although states may be increasingly reluctant to engage in explicit "industrial policy" or "targeting," the Internet raises the possibility that some domestic economies can't adapt sufficiently fast to take advantage of new "e-commerce" opportunities. Governments throughout Europe have urged Internet uptake by industry and consumers. At the same time, governments have seen the need for a review and a revision of the traditional system of regulation in Internet-related industries, particularly in communications and the media.

In this chapter we look at the "creative destruction" the Internet is bringing to regulatory policies in the media and communications sector in Europe. Schumpeter understood that heavy-handed rules constrained the dynamics of the capitalist process (1943:85, 101, 154); yet, we might argue that aspects of regulatory policy today, particularly antitrust (antimonopoly) policies, would find favor with him insofar as they encourage competition and innovation. On the other hand, a hiatus in regulatory thinking in Europe might yet be the preferred response from a Schumpeterian perspective.

In either case, the traditional regulatory structure in the communications sector is likely to change dramatically. Traditionally, communications markets were defined by distinct technologies and separated by high entry barriers. Each market segment historically had its own regulatory regime—that is, a set of norms, principles, and rules governing competitive activity in the segment, defining its structures and constraining behavior and performance by incumbents. It is almost axiomatic to say that the Internet has wrought a technological convergence, engendering technologies that overlap previously separate market segments. As it overlaps markets, the Internet also compels a revision of previously separate regulatory regimes. Coming into Europe from the United States, the new regime so far resembles a self-regulatory approach. "Rules" set by an industry elite, or some might say, by an industry cartel might be tolerated for a time in certain European states such as Britain. But self-regulation contrasts with European traditions historically shaped by government ownership and heavy-handed regulation of broadcasting and communications (Maitland, 1985). For Europe, self-regulation—that is, no significant *public* regulation—is not likely, even in Britain. The creative destruction caused by the Internet in Europe requires something more. The state has a hand in guiding this dynamic, even if that hand is light rather than heavy.

To make that point this chapter will first explain the historic basis for current regulation in Britain and continental Europe, and compare previous changes in the regulatory regimes to accommodate new technology with those in the United States. We then focus on the specific problems created by the Internet. In particular, its introduction has produced competition to the existing regulatory system not only from American ideas on self-regulation but from lobbying by industrialists and public interest organizations and from competition between existing regulatory institutions. We conclude that the result has been an adaptation, not destruction, of the regulatory status quo. Rather than the Internet loosening regulation, it seems that it is being integrated into the old European system of content-based regulation, which in turn is likely to lead to clashes with the United States and create further problems in establishing a coherent international regulatory regime for the Internet.

HISTORIC REGULATORY CONCEPTS

Regulation forms part of a political process in which states control markets and distribute economic goods. Within Europe only in Britain is regulation part of the tradition of the British system of common law. It has had no place within the continental tradition of civil law. The American system grew from the British, but in Britain the nineteenth-century attempts at regulation of communications were gradually replaced by what was considered a more public-interest-oriented system of state ownership aligned with continental European tradition. In the United States, however, the concept of regulation by government agencies flourished. New Deal legislation created new agencies of social regulation, with increasing demands on business, so that by the 1970s a backlash had begun to occur. Stigler (1971) concluded that regulation was ineffective on behalf of the "public interest" and served the interests of the regulated. Others challenged it on the grounds of politicization (Quirk, 1981). The ensuing movement toward deregulation under Presidents Carter and Reagan was less effective than might have been expected, leading to an acknowledgment that reregulation, rather than deregulation, had occurred. As Harris and Milkis (1991) suggest, the reason for this failure to roll back the state could be explained by the institutionalization of regulation and the effectiveness of public-interest lobby groups.

In Britain under the 1980s government of Mrs. Thatcher, the free-market ideology went hand in hand with a desire for a strong centralized state. Initial manifesto commitments to roll back the number of quasi-independent regulatory agencies gave way to an increase in their number. Those public-sector institutions that found themselves privatized, such as the network operator British Telecom (BT), became subject to more rigorous regulation than was previously their case under public ownership (Hills, 1986). Reflecting this emphasis on the role of regulatory agencies as the mediators between government and industry, and between competitors within the industry, rather than on their role as champions of the consumer, much of the academic literature on the subject of regulation from both sides of the Atlantic during the 1980s and 1990s was primarily concerned with the mechanisms of economic regulation.[1]

With the entry of competition into telecommunications markets, regulation of such matters as interconnection and costing is in the interests of new competitors. The introduction of a regulatory annex into the WTO agreement of 1997 bore witness to this industrial interest and has led to an assumption that regulators are simply the enforcers of rules to shape markets and that there is one model of regulation to suit all countries (for a critique, see Hills, 1998). If regulation is to be subject to the political goals of a government, however, then the achievement of those goals may involve several alternative, but equally legitimate, models of implementation. This linkage between political goals and regulation has been reinforced recently. A swing toward concern with consumer access has produced a reoccurrence of direct political intervention in regulatory agencies in both the United States and Britain.[2] More than ever the introduction of the Internet has demonstrated that regulation is part of a political process in which there are trade-offs between the various stakeholders in the markets affected.

The Internet is the latest in a long line of technologies that have been identified as "convergent" and therefore requiring new regulatory demarcations of markets. Communications markets can be conceptualized in a number of ways: They can be seen as local, national, and international; divided by technology; divided by types of content; divided according to infrastructure; divided according to services; and divided according to the value chain of information creation, packaging, distribution, and customer equipment. Regulation along one or more of these fault lines (or the lack of such regulation) can then be used to delineate and insulate one market from another, thereby promoting the interests of one set of actors against another. In addition, where specific markets or sectors have their own designated regulatory institution, the fault lines between markets can be defended by those institutions, just as such institutions can also aim to expand their regulatory scope across them.

In the next section we review the way in which such previous convergent technologies have been incorporated into existing regulatory regimes. To draw out differences between European and U.S. traditions, we compare the alternative regulatory treatments of these technologies.

STRUCTURATION OF MARKETS THROUGH REGULATION

Traditional Terrestrial (Public Service) Broadcasting and Telecommunications

When broadcasting was introduced in the U.K., it was done through the telephone, and legislation was already in existence that regulated through licenses the use of the radio spectrum and the telephone. The limitation of broadcasting channels in each country to a monopoly was originally based on spectrum scarcity, particularly with regard to the overlapping of the medium wave in Europe. Those monopolies then became state controlled, either formally, as on the European continent, or informally, as in Britain.[3] Censorship of content arose because of political sensitivity to anything marginally controversial, and from a desire by politicians to placate the powerful newspaper lobby, but was justified in the name of spectrum scarcity.

To control quality and diversity and to protect minors, the regulation of both state-owned and advertising-financed public-service broadcasting in Europe has taken place primarily through licensing of the distribution network (often with an obligation to provide universal access). In addition a traditional policy objective in Europe has been to protect a plurality of information sources through regulation of cross-ownership of newspapers, television, and radio. At the same time, domestic program creation has been supported by quotas on imports and subsidies for local production. French antagonism to the "cultural imperialism" of American products and attachment to the French language has fueled European Union policy. But gradually, in both the EU and its member states, partly as a reflection of the internationalization of mass media conglomerates, there has been less emphasis on the protection of plurality in broadcasting through cross-ownership restrictions. In Britain, for instance, a £8bn ($12.8bn) merger between United News & Media and Carlton Communications proposed at the end of 1999 created a company with annual turnover of £3.6bn ($5.8bn), 65 percent of the British advertising based off-air television market (around 36 million people or 14.9 percent of audience share), and at least 36 percent of the British market for television advertising (Harding and Larsen, 1999).[4]

Under the American Communications Act of 1934, local broadcasters were subject to an obligation to hold their licenses in trust for the public, but the growth of satellite transmission and deregulation has subsequently reduced the emphasis on local programming in favor of national distribution. Title III of the Act also directed the FCC to promote diversity, an objective carried out through regulation of cross-ownership. Again, deregulatory moves have allowed greater concentration of ownership since the 1980s. Broadcasting in the United States, both in terms of content and in terms of ownership, has gone through a steeper deregulatory curve than has occurred in Britain or other EU countries. Whereas public-service broadcasters in Europe, such as the British BBC and ITV,[5] still control the majority share of audiences, and are therefore important players, public-service broadcasting in the United States is a minority-interest channel (Tracey, 1998). Since the 1980s commercial broadcasters and right-wing politicians in Europe have targeted public-service broadcasting for attack, challenging the extent to which the EU's Amsterdam Treaty of 1997 actually defends the right of states to finance their broadcasters through license fees.

In contrast, telecommunications in Europe traditionally was regulated as a textbook case of natural monopoly, with the emphasis primarily on tariffs and standards. While the 1934 Communications Act was interpreted in the United States to include a provision obliging AT&T to provide universal service at affordable prices, until the 1980s there was little concern in Europe for universal access. In common with the U.S. regulatory provisions, however, European state ownership protected producers as against business users.

In neither the United States nor Europe was content over the telephone regarded as requiring regulation. Hence the regulatory regimes applied to broadcasting and telecommunications displayed entirely different characteristics, and the separate markets remained relatively undisturbed until the 1980s. Then, once liberalization had enabled new services in Britain to arise, content over the telephone, such as pornographic and other chat lines were regulated first by Oftel, the telecommunications regulator, and then by industry self-regulation.

Although economic and industrial policy arguments have been dominant in both sectors, at the EU level telecommunications and broadcasting policies have also developed separately. Because of an inherent weakness, however, in its enabling treaties that gives the EU power over economics but leaves culture to member states, the European Commission's entry into broadcasting regulation has always been weak and has failed to take account of the sector's cultural importance. As the logical consequence of the diverse interests they represent, there have been infighting and rivalries between different Directorates General (DGs)[6]—for example between DG IV, competition; DG III, industry; DG X, culture and audiovisual; DG XIII, information society and telecommunications; and DG XV, internal market. Of these, DG X has been the weakest. To date, the commission has failed to address directly the issues of pluralism, media ownership, and the role of broadcasting in citizens' rights. Recently, with the growing political clout of commercial broadcasters reflected in policy, national production of programs for cultural diversity has been regarded as a cause of European economic weakness in the audiovisual sector. The fragmentation of audiences by language and culture has been seen as reason for regulators to prefer a "pan-European" approach, with the development of market niches serving market segments across Europe (European Commission, 1994). In general, at EU level there has been little interest in or support for national, geographically based public-service broadcasters. It has been telecommunications that has held center stage.

Convergence between Telecommunications and Data Processing

Introduction of the microchip and the microprocessor in the 1970s challenged the traditional separate market structure of telecommunications and data processing and introduced the concept of digital convergence, first used in the 1970s to refer to the digitalization of telecommunications switching and transmission. The Computer I and II inquiries of 1971 and 1980 in the United States were attempts to protect AT&T's monopoly of telecommunications while at the same time allowing the expansion of data processing transmission between large corporations. Because of the ubiquity of digitalization and the difficulty of determining whether a byte comprised voice or data carriage, it was almost impossible to keep the markets apart. IBM pushed to enter the telecommunications monopoly and AT&T pushed to enter data transmission. Within a short time the U.S. regulatory framework, distinguishing between "basic" and "value-added" services, was followed in Britain and then in the EU. In effect, data processing, which turned out to be a relatively small market compared to voice transmission, was swallowed into that of telecommunications.

In the United States, divestiture of AT&T in 1984 also redefined the market so that long-distance and local markets were overlaid on the existing definitions of "value added" and "basic," with AT&T facing competition in "long-distance basic" and value-added services and the Regional Bell Operating Companies controlling "local basic." The U.S. telecommunications sector was therefore only partially liberalized. In Britain under Mrs. Thatcher's government, and in response to pressure from London's large users, full liberalization of the market took place. A duopoly in long distance was created and regulation developed in terms of licensing, interconnection, price control, universal access, and quality of service. This regulatory regime was then adopted at EU level.

Convergence between Telecommunications, Broadcasting, and Cable TV

The resurrection of the term "convergence" came about during the early 1980s, when information technology was to become the growth engine to lift Europe out of the oil-induced recession. In particular the drop in price of fiber optics and its high-bandwidth potential led to governments seeing cable television as the infrastructure of the future. The concept of the information society was built on this potential. To quote a report of the time:

> ... the main role of cable systems eventually will be the delivery of many information, financial and other services to the home and the joining of businesses and homes by high capacity data links (ITAP, 1982:7).

With the promise of longer licenses, the British government even went so far as to induce cable TV operators to use optic fiber. The high up-front costs, however, of laying fiber-optic networks, low demand, and over-optimism regarding optical switching led to retrenchment on the part of cable operators. Those that could afford to invest in cable TV were once again the existing telecoms operators and the state. Hence Deutche Telekom came to own the cable network in West Germany, local authorities owned cable operations in France and the Netherlands, and BT was the primary investor in cable TV in Britain.

In the United States, where cable TV was introduced in the 1950s, operators ignored the new fiber-optic technology and continued to install coaxial cable in a tree and branch configuration and did not install the two-way amplifiers required for two-way interactivity. There was therefore no possibility for most cable TV systems to carry point-to-point communications. Given its rapid spread, the established broadcasters feared cable's encroachment onto their territory. From the 1960s until 1996, cable TV companies were prevented from entering the telecommunications market and telecommunications companies were prevented from entering the cable TV market.

U.S. cable TV service, which did not fit into the prevalent broadcasting or telecommunications regulatory models, evaded regulation until it began to pose a threat to broadcast television. From the 1970s until 1980, when it virtually eliminated all federal cable TV regulation, the FCC regulated cable TV as an "ancillary" to broadcasting. In 1984 Congress acted on behalf of the industry to lift virtually all regulation (Hills, 1991:94–99). The resulting hikes in cable TV subscriptions led six years later to the Cable TV Act, once more reimposing regulation. However, with public-service broadcasting of minority interest, content regulation at a minimum, and one regulatory authority for broadcasting, cable TV, and telecommunications, the issue of telecommunications as against broadcast regulation for cable TV has had little of the political saliency it had in Europe. To quote one legal authority, writing of the U.S. 1980s regime:

. . . subscription services have combined characteristics of broadcasting with elements of point-to-point communications. When delivered over the air, they are regulated either like a broadcast service (STV) or like a common carrier (MDS or microwave distribution service). If delivered by a cable system they are considered a cable television service (and are called pay-cable). When delivered directly to subscribers they may be considered either a common carrier service (if the satellite operator allows third parties to provide programming) or broadcasting (if the satellite operator selects its own programming) (Bruce, 1986:162).

After giving the new technology time to establish itself without regulation, the existing regulatory regime was simply adapted to accommodate it.

Traditionally in the U.K., each new technology has invoked a new regulatory regime. Bowing to the interests of the cable television lobby, in 1990 a new regime treated cable TV as neither telecommunications nor broadcasting. Instead, in terms of transmission, it was to be regulated as telecommunications by the telecommunications regulator, Oftel, but in terms of content to be less regulated than public-service broadcasting. In an argument that was to be expanded later, restricted regulation of content was justified on the grounds that viewers had a level of choice denied them in public-service broadcasting. Hence cable and satellite subscription TV required less content regulation than that over which the viewer had no choice. A new regulatory institution was created mirroring the hybrid nature of the cable technology. The Cable Authority held a peculiar status as both the promoter of investment in cable TV (and therefore the lobbyist within central government on behalf of potential investors) and its regulator of content.

As a direct result of the market divisions instituted by regulation in the United States and the desire of U.S. telecommunications companies to gain experience in cable delivery, in 1992 cable TV companies were allowed to provide telecommunications in the U.K. market. In a symbolic acceptance of cable TV's primarily telecommunications role, the Cable Authority was abolished and a loose regime of content regulation was placed under the Independent Television Commission (ITC), a new regulator of all commercial television (satellite, cable, and off-air public-service broadcasting). With the policy objective of creating competition in local voice delivery, North American telecommunications companies dominated cable TV in Britain. In that BT and Mercury were prevented from exploiting technological convergence to provide both telecommunications and cable television, however, the market was asymmetrically regulated.[7] Hence the market was partially restructured through regulation to take account of the new transmission medium and to promote competition in the local loop. In 2001 the two markets will be enabled to become convergent when BT is allowed to provide video signals over telephone wires. In the meantime, cable companies are now concentrated into three groups (CWC, NTL, and Telewest).[8]

At the EU level, because entertainment services were seen as potential cross-subsidizers of telecommunications, broadband delivery was perceived as a means in the short term by which the telecommunications operators could modernize their local networks (Hills, 1991: 191–201). The 1995 Commission Directive that, following the U.K. example, abolished the restrictions on use of cable television networks for the infrastructural provision of telecommunications also abolished the distinction between cable TV and telecommunications but said nothing of content regulation, which was left to member states (Commission Directive 95/51/EC).

Convergence and Digital TV: Broadcasting, Software, and Telecommunications

In Europe the technological overlap between telecommunications and broadcasting in the digital broadcasting market was originally seen as primarily a matter of the set-top box that pay-TV customers would have to buy (but now get free) to access digital television. The set-top box is also important to the development of e-commerce in that it will give access to online banking and retailing, again with the potential for restriction of competition. "Conditional access" refers to the mechanisms used within pay-TV systems to ensure that service to nonpayers is denied through encryption of the signal. The term is also used to cover the subscriber management services through which customers are billed. Using control of these services by proprietary standards, one operator can lock out service suppliers from the delivery network. The issues are similar to those of "bottlenecks" restricting interconnection with the network infrastructure for service suppliers in the telecommunications market which have been the subject of open network provision regulations in the EU and open network architecture measures in the United States (Hills and Michalis, 1997a and 1997b).

The issues have been salient in Europe because public-service broadcasters feared they would be excluded from the digital market by the major media conglomerates of pay-TV—BSkyB, CanalPlus/Nethold, and FilmNet. In particular, these broadcasters saw the possibility in Britain of domination of the digital market by an unregulated BskyB, as had happened in the analog satellite television market. At that point, BSkyB controlled the whole value chain of analog pay-TV from satellite through encryption to distribution and reception, with very little regulation of content or transmission (Goodwin, 1998). A number of regulatory issues were associated with this virtual vertical monopoly.[9] The BBC fought hard but unsuccessfully at the EU level to get open standards for the set-top box. Instead the EU failed to specify standards (Directive 95/47/EC), thereby leaving the question of conditional access to national regulation and setting the scene for competition between telecommunications and broadcasting regulatory agencies, both of which claimed competence.

The regulatory implications of the convergence of telecommunications and broadcasting through digital TV were placed on the political agenda of both the U.K. government and the EU because of the 1994 initiative of the U.K. telecommunications regulator, Don Cruickshank (*Telecommunications Markets,* 1994). A year later, in response to the U.S. initiative on the information superhighway, the EU's Bangemann report, and the British government's "Information Society Initiative," Oftel produced the groundbreaking document, "Beyond the Telephone, the Television and the PC," which laid out a proposed regulatory framework for digital television (Oftel, 1995).[10] As Oftel itself admitted, much of the report's content was necessarily conjectural, but given that "economic characteristics of the emerging markets" would resemble those of the old and that there might be "a tendency for a few large companies to dominate at least the network elements of the new markets," it wished to set out a regulatory framework to encourage competition (p. 6). This framework divided the market into four components that created the value chain: content creation, service provision, distribution networks, and consumer equipment. This approach to potential bottlenecks in the value chain was to underlie its further interventions in relation to digital broadcasting.

The report's publication coincided with discussions engendered by the

Conservative government's White Paper on broadcasting, which proposed that the licenses for the ITV broadcasting franchises should go to the highest bidder without reference to quality of programming. This proposed regulatory regime would have undermined the existence of the Independent Television Commission, responsible for content regulation. Oftel's document can therefore be viewed as an indirect attempt to take over the rump of the ITC's duties. In fact the attempt at regulatory restructuring was foiled by public resistance to the government's proposals, and the ITC was not only saved but given the time to regroup.

The second attempt by Oftel to compete with the ITC revolved around the issue of conditional access and set-top boxes within the digital television market. In effect Oftel saw itself as the economics regulator of all transmission networks, with the ITC responsible only for content regulation. Oftel seemed to have won the argument at the end of 1996 but then was reduced to publicly criticizing the ITC one year later. (Hills and Michalis, 1997A:91). Such was the level of acrimony between the two regulators that the government stepped in to establish two committees to discuss cross-cutting issues and ensure cooperation: G3, chaired by the Office of Fair Trading, and G6, which included representatives of the Departments of Culture, Media and Sport and the Department of Trade and Industry (DTI, 1999: 7).

The Internet emerged to challenge this system of regulation, which still is based on a separation at EU and national level between broadcasting and telecommunications. Thrown into question are the very principles on which the EU regulatory regime is based.

CREATIVE DESTRUCTION: THE INTERNET CHALLENGES REGULATORY REGIMES

The Internet and Telecommunications Regulation

The technology of the Internet, based on distributed packet-data processing, is a potential substitute for voice telephony and the fax. In particular, because a user makes only a local call to an Internet service provider (ISP), the penetration of the Internet is dependent on local call tariffs. And local call tariff levels are dependent on the particular form of costing of the network. European regulation is based on the concepts introduced in the AT&T antitrust case in the

United States. To reduce the costs to distributed business in the United States, the network was construed as divided between local and long distance. The capital costs of the local network were then construed as being "caused" by the end user, leaving long-distance tariffs to reflect only the lower capital costs of the trunk network, thereby allowing their reduction. But Congressional opposition led to only partial implementation of these costings.

In contrast, the British implemented full rebalancing and cost-based tariffs, followed by the EU's adoption of the less rigorous concept of cost-oriented tariffs. The intention was to cheapen long-distance communications for business at a time of European recession. Because high-priced, timed, local call tariffs resulted from these costings, however, the fear now is that European companies may be hampered in their development of e-commerce. As a result, political pressure has been brought to bear on the British regulator to ensure that local call tariffs for the Internet by BT are decreased. The whole regulatory basis of costing is thrown into confusion.

In addition, the Internet and associated e-commerce applications have raised the strategic importance of access to the local loop. In an attempt to expand the broadband communication market to residential and small business customers, the European Commission and a growing number of national governments currently are pushing for unbundling of the local loop.[11] (On the issue of unbundling in the United States and the EU, see Michalis, 1999.) In response to this proposed competition, incumbent operators have speeded up the roll-out of ADSL.[12] Faced with strong objections, however, particularly from Britain, the European Commission was only able to make December 2000 an aspirational rather than a legal deadline (European Commission, 2000). In Britain it took criticism from Oftel (Oftel, 1999a) for BT to commit itself to implement ADSL throughout the country by mid-2001 (see Oftel, 1999b). There are strong pressures, however, to bring the deadline forward. In addition to the European Commission, the Office of the United States Trade Representative is considering lodging a complaint against Britain with the World Trade Organization concerning the current prohibition of access to BT's local loop for potential DSL service providers (Dudman, 2000).

Cable modems and interconnection between ISPs are more evident as regulatory problems in the United States than in Europe. Although it is noticeable in the U.K. that cable TV companies have just begun interactive service, in the

United States cable modems are now one of the fastest growing technologies. Some of those investing in cable infrastructure to provide fast interactive access to the Internet may have assumed that such investment was not covered by common carrier legislation and that they would not be subject to the same requirements as telecommunications companies to open access to those networks. But such cable infrastructure is now subject to access-opening legislation by the States, anxious to get broadband access opened to competition (Public Network Europe, November 1999, 5). Hence the Internet is bringing cable companies under telecommunications-type regulation, and creating concern about the disincentive for network investment.

The question of bottlenecks in interconnection creates a clash between the traditional self-regulated computer industry and that of heavily regulated telecommunications. For instance, some of the backbone Internet service providers in the United States that own their own infrastructure have prevented access on equal terms to small ISPs—a telecommunications issue of interconnection. They are not, however, regulated as common carriers under the 1996 Telecommunications Act and therefore are not subject to the same regulation as say AT&T; nor do Internet service providers contribute to universal service funds as do telecommunications operators. Hence, while the FCC is prepared to allow a new service to develop without regulation, some state regulators see the Internet as providing "unfair" competition to telecommunications operators, and local legislative activities on broadband are creating problems for the FCC. In contrast, ISPs in Britain buy bulk leased lines from the telecommunications operators and use the arbitrage available to absorb the costs of "free" access to the customer. Responding to pressure from telecommunications operators worried about additional competition, the European Commission examined the status of voice communications over the Internet (Commission Notice, 1998). It ruled that voice over the Internet does not come under the legal definition of voice telephony services. This ruling means that ISPs do not have to contribute to the provision of universal service.

If, as in the United States, the Internet is seen as a technology competitive to traditional telecommunications, then questions of cross-ownership arise. As a result, when WorldCom bought MCI, the latter company was forced to sell its Internet service on the grounds that together the two companies would have too great a market concentration. Although, the measurement of Internet traffic and market concentration is extremely complicated and difficult (see OECD, 1998a and 1998b), in this case Internet provision was treated as telecommunications operation. The ruling, made jointly by the European Commission and the FCC, indicates that different Directorates General within the EU currently are perceiving Internet provision differently. One (DG XIII) sees it as telecommunications, another does not (DG IV).

The Internet and Broadcasting Regulation

The Internet also arouses issues of content regulation, particularly in regard to pornography and terrorism. There have been attempts—by Germany, for instance—to censor pornographic sites, but given the international nature of the distribution such national actions have proved difficult to implement. In the U.K., self-regulation to prevent the distribution of illegal material is used via the Internet Watch Foundation in a manner similar to the self-regulation used among premium-rate telephone service providers. Although some coordination is effected in the U.K. by having one Independent Television Commission member on the policy board of the Internet Watch Foundation, content is self-regulated by the industry, not by the broadcasting regulator. As we shall see below, this model based on current telecommunications regulation appeals to the EU's DG XIII (information society). This model of industry self-regulation of content has recently been strengthened by the courts. In 1999 following a case brought for defamatory Internet postings, which despite complaints were not removed by the ISP, a high court judge in Britain ruled against the ISP. An ISP has thereby been judged to be equivalent to a publisher in its responsibility for defamation and libel. Following this case, ISPs in Britain are prepared to control controversial content that they host rather than risk being drawn into legal battles (see Akdeniz, 2000).

In direct contrast, the American courts have taken the opposite view. In a recent case a number of courts have ruled that the ISP was not liable for either objectionable e-mail or bulletin board messages. The New York Court of Appeals ruled that

> Prodigy's role in transmitting e-mail is akin to that of a telephone company, which one neither wants nor expects to superintend the content of

its subscribers' conversations. In this respect, an ISP, like a telephone company, is merely a conduit. Thus, we conclude that [...] Prodigy was not a publisher of the e-mail transmitted through its system by a third party.[13]

The entry of broadcasters and telecommunications operators into e-commerce channels is also posing new problems for British regulators. In this regard, *Open* (a new service launched in October 1999 by a joint venture between BT, BSkyB, Matsushita, and HSBC's Bank) is an initial case. The service gives limited access via subscribers' television sets to those Internet sites and suppliers (initially 25) linked to the new service—a form of a proprietary Internet.[14] Such new interactive services are seen as only the tip of potential applications.

But this expansion into interactive services by broadcasters is raising the prospect of intervention by the Independent Television Commission under its broadcast regulation remit. The ITC argues that its authority covers all connected services as well as consumer protection. Concerned that programs should not be driven by advertising content, that viewers may not be aware that they are "in a buying zone rather than an entertainment or an information zone," and that consumers should not be "ripped off," the ITC states that "we can't just step back and let it develop by itself." The prospect of regulatory intervention is raising opposition from the broadcasters, however, on the basis that any restrictions would raise the cost of running interactive services and limit their profitability (*Broadcast*, 6 August 1999, 5).

In addition, the public-service broadcasters' expansion into the Internet has caused a rethinking of their regulation and of their role in the converging communications market. In Britain, the BBC's Internet involvement has raised a number of complaints. Other Internet content providers are concerned by use of the BBC's brand name to attract users to its commercial sites and by the hypertext link from the BBC's noncommercial to commercial sites.[15] The British Internet Publishers' Alliance has also questioned whether the BBC's online activities and the provision of numerous types of content (such as sports and pop music) are a necessary extension of the corporation's public-service obligations, and how far such activities may distort "the commercial basis of the wider market for Internet services" (BIPA, 1999:6). The expansion of public-service broadcasters into the Internet is leading to challenges to the whole concept of public-service broadcasting.

THE INTERNET'S INFLUENCE ON THE EU REGULATORY DEBATE

The regulatory implications of the potential technological convergence of telecommunications, broadcasting, and the Internet were not brought to the forefront of the European regulatory agenda until the late 1990s. Behind this increase in importance lay U.S. initiatives on information superhighways, the Bangemann report on a future information society, and the advent of digital television. The objective of the 1997 Green Paper reiterates the European Commission's 1994 rhetoric:

> The European Union should give priority to the early creation of a European information area, thanks to the development of technologically advanced information infrastructures, liberalization of the services that will be using these infrastructures, standardization, and the creation of an open environment in terms of conditional access systems. (European Commission, 1994, Section 5.1.1(i))

Initial drafts of the Green Paper on convergence were prepared by DG XIII (information society and telecommunications) and drew heavily on a 1996 consultancy report that advocated deregulation to create a single market. In brief, the Green Paper puts forward two opposing views of regulation in the era of convergence (European Commission, 1997). The starting point of the minimalist approach is that convergence will be a limited phenomenon. In this model, media policy is construed as promoting social, cultural, and ethical values and these values would remain unchanged regardless of the underlying technology used. The approach makes a distinction between those matters requiring economic regulation (e.g., competition issues, interconnection, access), which would be handled by one regulator, and those of content and specific public policy goals, which involve non-economic regulation to be handled by a separate regulator. The approach replicates that underlying the turf war between Oftel and the ITC, in which Oftel sought to become the "economic" regulator of all transmission and services.

According to the alternative maximalist view, current sector-specific regulatory regimes would result in regulatory uncertainty and would seriously impede convergence. A new approach would be technology- and medium-neutral, based on a reconsideration of fundamental principles, and more focused on the international rather than national level of regulation. Despite the intervention of DG X (culture and audiovisual) and the subsequent turf war in latter stages of the drafting process, the model implicitly favored by the authors suggests that regulation of content should be based on self-regulation, albeit with some European-level coordination (European Commission, 1997: 22). In other words, content regulation would be the same as that currently applied to the Internet. Besides enhancing the role of DG XIII at the expense of DG X, the maximalist approach also would have had the effect of expanding the current regulatory powers of the EU in relation to those of the member states.

The Green Paper concluded with three options for a future regulatory regime. The first option would leave "current vertical regulatory models . . . in place." The second would "develop a separate regulatory model for new activities, to coexist with telecommunications and broadcasting regulation." This model flags a return to the concept of new regimes for new services and implies the FCC model of little or no regulation for new services. The third option would introduce a regulatory model to cover the whole range of existing and new services. In essence, the third option is a reiteration of the maximalist model, but again without any detail on the basis for regulatory mechanisms.

It later became evident that a European-wide horizontal framework that negated the regulation of content for all content providers across all markets, as favored by the Green Paper, would not be politically possible. In particular, separate regulatory structures based on a division between person-to-person and "public," i.e., broadcast, communications is part of the constitutional division of responsibilities within the German federal state structure. Telecommunications and the Internet are federal responsibilities, whereas authority over broadcasting rests with the Länder (states). Without constitutional alterations, it would not be possible for the German federal government to sign on to a EU regulatory framework that negated content regulation on broadcast communications. The situation in German broadcasting would be the same as in the telecommunications sector, where only after Deutsche Bundespost and the German government altered its attitude to liberalization was the EU able to initiate changes in the regulatory regime.

The reaction of public-service broadcasters, made known in consultation meetings in Brussels, in a European audiovisual conference, and in written comments, was most unfavorable. Using the European Commission's own value system, the BBC pointed out its contribution to exports and industrial policy potential. Overall, the broadcasters supported the first option—the maintenance of the status quo with vertical regulatory structures—but have become proponents of a new regulatory regime for content regulation. Under this regime, the Internet as an interactive technology over which the viewer has complete command would feature at one end of a spectrum of content regulation, subject to few rules, while, at the other end of the spectrum free-to-air broadcasting, over which the viewer has no choice, would continue to be heavily regulated. In this model, the Internet would be assumed into a broadcasting style of regulation.

In March 1999 the European Commission, in its communication on the results of public consultation on the Green Paper, indicated that the regulatory model to be adopted at some time in the future is actually different from any mentioned in the Green Paper (European Commission, 1999a). Instead of a completely horizontal split of the markets between infrastructure and almost nonregulated information services, there will be a horizontal split in terms of infrastructure, but a sector-specific differentiation in terms of content. This approach, as was acknowledged in the Working Paper, accepts a separate regulatory framework for content. This regulatory framework has been confirmed again in the European Commission's 1999 Communications Review (European Commission, 1999b).

A comprehensive review of the framework for electronic communications services, resulting in legislation in July 2000, was announced by EU Commissioner for the Information Society Erkki Liikanen in late 1999. The proposals acknowledge the need for a separate regulatory framework for content, and by implication the continuation of existing institutional divisions, but will bring fixed line, cellular mobile telecommunications, and cable TV transmission under one regime and attempt to enforce similar regulatory principles across Europe (European Commission, 1999b). Institutionally, the split between telecommunications and broadcasting (with the Internet in terms of transmission classified as telecommunications and the Internet in terms of content classified as a less regulated form of pay-TV) has been confirmed at EU level.

Yet the debate continues. In May 2000 the British government announced it was conducting a review of communications regulation that might involve the closure of both the telecommunications regulatory agency (Oftel) and that for commercial broadcasting (ITC), with the creation of one regulator on the lines of the FCC in their stead, or else a reliance on competition law as against sector-specific regulation. Ministries are split on the issue (Groom and Larsen, 2000), and further contradictions are evident. This seeming concern for liberalization had been preceded by disclosure that, under new legislation, all ISPs in Britain will be obliged to be hard-wired to a government center empowered to monitor access to e-mail and the Web, and that all consumers will be obliged to divulge passwords and encryption codes. Such potential policy returns Britain to the traditions of the 1920s and contrasts with policy in the Republic of Ireland, where the government has taken a directly opposite stance on state control of Internet technology (Rufford, 2000). The Internet continues not only to force rethinking of communication regulation in Europe but to produce divergence and potential conflict within and between states.

CONCLUSION

Regulation is about the distribution of resources and is part of the political process. Companies may compete through that regulatory process for the market structure and rules that suit their interests. Simply by its existence the EU's single market places pressure on those markets that are delineated in terms of geographical space, national versus EU, rather than delineated by market segment across the whole EU. This pressure is compounded by the competition between EU regulatory institutions and those of member states. It has been inevitable that public-service broadcasting, based as it is on language and geographical area, should come under attack from those using the growth of the Internet to argue for one regulatory regime with minimum content regulation throughout the single market. Similarly, nationally based telecommunications regimes, dominated by the old operators, have been the focus of market-opening pressure.

A redrawing of regulatory boundaries has been attempted at both the EU and national level, and has involved not only commercial interests but also those of regulatory institutions. The resulting debate, however, has not yet produced one super-model of regulation for all modes of transmission and content. Rather, as demonstrated here, the debate has been messy. The Internet may spawn a whole new regulatory structure as the European Commission would prefer; or it may simply be bolted on to the old, as value-added services were in the 1970s; or it may be assumed under the current regulatory regimes of telecommunications and broadcasting.

We have described here a process of adaptation of regulatory regimes to a series of technologies that have affected market structure and regulatory rules and institutions. The Internet is the latest in this series and the process of rethinking regulation is ongoing. Even though that process has been spread over a number of years, Schumpeter probably would argue that the waves of creation and destruction from new technology could take a far longer period than that covered here. Given that the Internet has a lower penetration in Europe than in the United States and that the competitive opportunities created by unbundling of the local loop have only recently occurred, we might well agree. Yet broadcasting regulatory traditions in the United States are different from those in Europe, where freedom of speech is more circumscribed and libel law is more utilized. Between Britain and the rest of Europe, there is division about the acceptability of pornography and differing political priorities regarding state control of the Internet. At this stage of the debate, with so many conflicting interests and institutions involved, it seems unlikely that one worldwide regulatory regime for the Internet is likely to emerge in the near future. In Europe, it is more likely that political priorities coupled with economic interests will determine the outcome of the "creative destruction" that has been instigated by the Internet.

6 | SOCIAL COMMUNICATIONS INNOVATION AND DESTRUCTION IN JAPAN

Leslie Helm

Exodus in the Hopeful Country, a novel serialized in one of Japan's leading intellectual journals,[1] portrays a newly politicized Japanese youth using Internet technology to rebel against a decaying society. Students boycott schools and join forces over the Internet to build a prosperous network of online businesses that is unfathomable to the elders of the old economy. The story builds on the utopian notion of the World Wide Web as a powerful force for social and economic change.[2] The notion, popular among Internet pundits, is that new digital networks cut across old socioeconomic boundaries (including national borders), undermining them and recreating society in the open, democratic image of the Internet itself. By offering the masses direct access to millions of other people and to previously unavailable information, Internet activists argue, the Internet eliminates middlemen, empowers consumers, encourages political participation, decentralizes power, and fosters a flowering of creativity and individualism.[3]

For Japan, such change would indeed be nothing short of a revolution. The nation's Byzantine multilayered distribution systems, centralized bureaucracies, and moribund schools would all fall prey to quicker, smarter solutions delivered over the World Wide Web. The reality, of course, is far more complex. While the Net is triggering seismic shifts in the United States economy, Japan has been slow to change. The "creative gales of destruction" Joseph Schumpeter argues are critical to innovation have been held at bay. Novelist Murakami finds the notion of Japan transforming itself today so improbable that in *Exodus* his rebel youngsters buy land in Japan's northern island of Hokkaido to build society anew.

When considering the impact of the Internet tsunami on Japan's social and economic landscape, therefore, it is critical to examine the substantial institutional breakwaters that act to block change. Japanese government institutions and corporate systems were developed over the past century with the goal of maintaining social stability while "catching up" with the West.[4] Japanese industrial policies concentrated scarce resources in strategic sectors. Its peculiar brand of Japanese-style management mobilized workers from the chief executive down to the janitor to accomplish corporate and national goals. Those efforts helped drive Japan's dominance of industries ranging from steel to semiconductors. This chapter suggests that as Japan transitions from a manufacturing-based economy to a mature knowledge- and service-based economy, these same institutions have now become barriers to growth.

These barriers are particularly evident in Japan's slow adoption of Internet-based technologies. Management practices such as lifetime employment and seniority wages have generated a steady flow of incremental innovations in the automobile industry, for example, but have proved to be obstacles in new Internet-enabled technologies such as electronic commerce where successful companies must be capable of making radical changes quickly to keep up with constant changes in the business environment.

Japan's powerful bureaucrats were effective strategists for industrial development as long as they could predict the direction in which industry was moving and chart a clear course.[5] They protected domestic markets while helping companies import, match, and then improve on Western technology. These policies are problematic, however, in new Internet sectors where the direction of technology is unclear and new technology makes the protection of markets more difficult. Time windows are also short. Entire new industries can blossom then consolidate before government officials have the chance to put their policies in place.

Japan is not unusual in its efforts to shelter and direct its economy. France, for example, has had a similar *dirigiste* economy, and it has also been slow to exploit the Internet. Indeed, the United States may be the outlier in its willingness to give such free rein to market forces. But Japan's past success in a variety of high-tech sectors, such as consumer electronics and semiconductors, makes it a case worth examining.

Japan's particular variant of capitalism also sheds light on what Schumpeter has argued is capitalism's most enduring characteristic: its ability to obliterate the old while spawning the new. "The problem that is usually being visualized is how capitalism administers existing structures, whereas the relevant problem is how it creates and destroys them," explains Schumpeter.[6]

Scholars have long pointed to Japan's inability to destroy inefficient old structures without significant external pressure. In the late nineteenth century, the cannons of Commodore Perry's black ships forced Japan to open itself up to trade after two and a half centuries of isolation. Japan's new leaders recognized they had little choice but to demolish the nation's feudal structures and start anew if the country was to protect itself from Western imperialism. Later, the U.S. Occupation, established following Japan's defeat in World War II, broke up Japan's family-based *zaibatsu* and set the stage for the nation's postwar economic miracle. At each stage, external political forces initiated major changes in key economic institutions. Japan's inability to pull itself out of the decade-long economic slump that followed the collapse of its late 1980s bubble economy, many argue, is yet another example of its powerlessness in the face of severe systemic problems.

The Internet case adds to a growing body of recent scholarship that seeks to explain Japan's fall in the technology world from world leader to struggling follower. Robert Cole argues that Japanese high-tech companies have failed because they are characterized by "organizational continuity" at a time when success in many high-tech sectors favors small companies with the ability to deal with discontinuity. Labor policies such as lifetime employment and the widespread practice among Japanese companies of channeling business to a network of companies with which they have close ties, offers Japanese companies an advantage only when technological change is slow and its direction predictable.[7] Marie Anchordoguy suggests that the industrial policies that were so successful in Japan in such sectors as mainframe computers have been ineffective in the software sector because the pace of change and the first-mover advantages in software make it difficult for government officials to effectively select and pursue software targets.[8] Carlile and Tilton argue that the Japanese regulatory framework, designed to protect small companies by eliminating "excessive competition" in areas like retail and distribution, is unlikely to change in spite of recent efforts at deregulation because of strong vested interests.[9] Given the swift, unpredictable nature of change in the Internet technology world and the fact that its applications are overwhelmingly in the service sector, this critical "new economy" sector provides a substantial challenge to Japan's catch-up system.

The slow pace at which Japan has adopted Internet technologies is well documented. At the end of 1999, only about 12 percent of the Japanese population had access to the Internet compared to more than 30 percent in the United States.[10] Many analysts believe the Japanese numbers actually overstate Internet use in Japan because millions of office workers with access to the Internet seldom use it. The amount of commerce taking place over the Web in Japan is a small fraction of the U.S. level, and only 19 percent of Japanese schools had at least one connection to the Internet at the end of 1999 compared to more than 90 percent of American schools.[11]

The low penetration rate of personal computers in Japanese homes and offices, a function of the difficulty of inputting the thousands of characters used in the Japanese language into a computer keyboard, is one reason for the low level of Internet access. The high cost of converting Internet software into Japanese is another significant obstacle. But these obstacles are also present in other newly industrialized countries in Asia. They don't explain why Japan, as late as 1998, lagged significantly behind such less-developed neighbors as Taiwan, Singapore, and Hong Kong in its level of Internet access.[12]

There is some evidence Japan began to more aggressively embrace the Internet at the end of 1999. The use of cell phones to access the Internet has shown strong growth, for example. But it is too early to predict whether the moves will be sufficient to help Japan regain its position as a technology leader. The outcome is critical. The rate at which Japan adopts the Net is important because it has a potential impact on everything from the nation's cost of doing business to the effectiveness of its educational institutions. The Internet is widely regarded by Japan's leaders as a significant tool for increasing the efficiency of Japanese businesses and revitalizing the economy. Japan's ultimate effectiveness in using the Net may be a proxy for its broader effectiveness in making the transition from manufacturing to a knowledge-based service economy.

In the following section, Japan's state policies toward the Internet are first reviewed. The impact of Japanese management practices on the use of Internet technologies is then assessed. The final section looks at the potential for more significant changes in these state and corporate practices and the broader potential for the Internet to act as an agent of change in Japan.

JAPAN INC. TARGETS THE INTERNET

In the turmoil and recession following the oil crisis of 1973, Japanese bureaucrats recognized that the days of high-speed growth in the nation's industrial sector were over and that the country needed to begin the transformation into an "information society." In the ensuing years, the Ministry of International Trade and Industry (MITI) established numerous collaborative research projects designed to reverse engineer and then improve upon U.S. semiconductor and computer technology. Those efforts were so successful that by the mid-1980s U.S. technology leaders such as Intel and IBM identified Japanese electronics companies such as Fujitsu and NEC as their primary competitors. Japan set ambitious targets for creating a national optical fiber network and had one of the most advanced telecommunications networks in the world by the early 1990s.

But Japan's vision was clouded by its experiences in the industrial world. Its leaders failed to recognize that success in the emerging information sector was less and less a function of being able to build low-priced, high-quality components and to put in place sophisticated infrastructure and increasingly a function of understanding how information could be shared and manipulated to solve problems. Japan was blindsided, therefore, by emergence in the United States during the 1980s of a computer network that was technically clumsy yet showed explosive growth because users, impressed by its ability to connect diverse computer systems, spent long hours developing new applications to take advantage of the network and improve upon it.

Japan's first computer networks were designed to share computer capacity, not information. The first academic network, the Science Information Network, was built in the late 1970s to connect the regional computing centers at Japan's three top universities with the nation's three mainframe computer companies and its telephone monopoly.[13] The system used a standard[14] that Japanese engineers still believe today to be technically superior to Internet standards but which was never widely adopted. E-mail was not even offered as a feature of the system until 1989.[15]

In 1984, Jun Murai, a maverick associate professor at Keio, led a volunteer effort to build a new Internet-based computer network called JUNET. The goal was to offer Japanese scientists e-mail and allow them to tap into the increasingly active academic discourse taking place over the Internet. Japanese regulators tolerated JUNET as an academic network but fought broader use of the Net. Some officials saw the Net, with its English-language content and U.S.-based standards, as American technological imperialism, and such terms as "Pax Digital Americana" entered the lexicon. Bureaucrats also saw the Internet as a challenge to the regulatory framework they had constructed. In 1992, when Murai and a few of his students sought permission from the Ministry of Post and Telecommunications (MPT) to begin offering a commercial Internet service, the request was turned down.[16]

Not until President Clinton began promoting his National Information Infrastructure (NII) initiative did Japan take notice of this powerful new phenomenon. Izumi Aizu of Glocom, a think tank that was an early advocate in Japan for the Internet, recalls the wintry day in early 1993 when the president of NTT (Nippon Telegraph and Telephone Co.), Japan's telephone monopoly, called him and asked: "What is all this about the Internet?"[17] Japanese bureaucrats, eager to enhance their prestige, soon were offering blueprints for Japan's own information highway. In the spring of 1994, MITI published a plan that proposed digitizing government documents, creating electronic libraries and helping the elderly access medical services. The Ministry of Post and Telecommunications spoke of building a "High-Performance Info-Communications Infrastructure that would generate an intellectually creative society."[18]

Japanese officials talked the talk, but they found it difficult to walk the walk. MPT misinterpreted (some say deliberately) the Clinton initiative to mean that the U.S. government would subsidize the cost of building an elaborate communications network, just as it had built the national highway system. MPT proposed a massive project to extend fiber-optic cable to every home at a cost to the government of as much as $450 billion. MITI attributed the success of the Internet to the early role of the Pentagon and set out to boost the capabilities of Japanese companies by establishing its own government-subsidized projects. Both ministries, raised in the tradition of *kanson mimpi* (revere the bureaucrats, despise the people), failed to understand the user-driven nature of the Internet.

NTT, which accounted for the bulk of Japan's telecommunications R&D, had evolved as Japan's only *national champion* in an increasingly competitive global telecommunications business. The Japanese government was also the largest owner of NTT shares and it had a stake in keeping NTT a profitable company. Few objected when NTT insisted it be put in charge of building the fiber-optic network and asked permission to increase local phone rates to help pay for the investments. The government even offered NTT subsidized loans to help pay for the construction. Within a month, NTT's stock price surged.[19]

MPT's first step toward building the information highway turned out to be a major step backward. Already, high local telephone charges had proved a major obstacle to consumer use of the Internet. Consumers forced to pay NTT ten cents for every three minutes they were connected to the Web, not including the charges levied by Internet service providers, often ended up with bills totaling hundreds of dollars a month and canceled their services. Now NTT was raising connection rates for many consumers.[20] In 1999, when NTT finally began offering fixed rates for Internet connections but only after 11 P.M., usage in that time period soared. People began arriving at work bleary-eyed after spending the night surfing the Web.

MITI also made a major error. It led the nation down the wrong information highway. MITI, working with other ministries, was instrumental in budgeting billions of dollars for a range of multimedia projects, including satellites for distance learning projects, multimedia software development projects, interactive medical systems, and video-on-demand pilot projects.[21] The projects used broadband technology that proved commercially unfeasible.

To be sure, U.S. phone and cable companies also marched down the same blind alley by announcing multibillion dollar projects to build out broadband interactive systems. But U.S. companies quickly abandoned the projects when it became clear the networks would be too costly to build and that the future was with Internet access systems that exploited existing narrow and mid-band copper and coaxial cables. When the technology winds shifted in the mid-1990s, companies like Cisco that had continued to bet on the Internet were there to respond to the surge in new demand for Internet standards-based equipment.

Japan, by contrast, found itself adrift. With all its telecommunications companies working with NTT on proprietary technology, Japan had no major companies with Internet experience. Rather than chart a new course, Japanese companies continued to promote outdated technologies. NTT, which had invested tens of billions of dollars in research to develop expensive ATM (asynchronous transfer mode) switches capable of handling massive amounts of multimedia traffic, was not about to admit that less reliable, Internet-based systems from a bunch of small Silicon Valley companies might be more appropriate for data networks. While the minor disruptions in data transfer common on Internet-based networks will lower the quality of voice connections, they are seldom noticeable when transferring data. Yet, as recently as 1999, the Japanese government was still paying NTT to build an experimental ATM-based data network to connect leading research institutions that at half a billion dollars was many times more costly than an Internet-based system would have been.

While NTT remains a reluctant convert to the Internet-based technologies, MITI has recognized the problems with its earlier policies and has established new projects aimed at developing Internet technologies and applications. Since 1998, MITI has budgeted several hundred million dollars to pay for 158 projects in the area of electronic commerce, and dozens of projects to help Japanese companies catch up in the area of Internet infrastructure.

In 1998, MITI launched the Real Internet Project, which subsidized research by a who's who of telecom companies and research institutes including Hitachi, NEC Corp. Furukawa Electric, Sumitomo Electric Industries, the Tokyo Institute of Technology, Kyoto University, and Kyushu University. The goal was to build high-speed routers, critical devices that act as traffic cops for the Internet.[22] Hitachi would use its supercomputer technology, also developed with government aid, to develop a high-end machine. NEC would build a low-end model. Both companies hope to exploit the change in technology that will come with the shift to Internet V6, a new-generation network that can better deal with security problems and the huge demand for new Internet addresses.[23]

Fujitsu has received money to work with the Japan Biological Informatics Consortium, a group of research institutions, to build an Internet-based system for handling purchases of materials and equipment used in research. *Pia,* Japan's leading entertainment review, has received money to develop a digital ticket management system.[24] There are 17 supply-chain management projects, including ones to help Toshiba and Matsushita acquire components online. There are also projects to create online securities trading systems, automated materials purchasing systems, systems for accessing the Net from home televisions, and automated sales systems for dental offices, fish paste companies, and clothing designers.

MITI is also promoting additional standards to speed adoption of the Internet. In March 2000 delegates of the "Forum for Agreeable Living with Intelligence"[25] were scheduled to announce a program to encourage builders to install a uniform receptacle in all new residential buildings that would allow residents to quickly hook up to various high-speed Internet access offerings. The Japan Internet Payment Promotion Association, made up of MPT and 278 companies in the financial and Internet services sector, are planning to test new ways of making payments on the Net that will be less costly to merchants and more secure than using credit cards online.

This approach is reminiscent of Japanese efforts to reverse engineer and then improve upon American products in the 1960s and 1970s. Because the projects appear aimed at reproducing technology that already exists in the United States, they may have a better chance of success than such failed MITI software projects as the effort to develop fifth-generation computers with artificial intelligence capability. If successful, the projects could also prove controversial because they represent a return to using government subsidies to support domestic industry, which MITI rejected a decade ago following heavy criticism from the United States.

J-STYLE MANAGEMENT IN A DOT COM WORLD

What many scholars have come to describe as the "J-style" company has greatly influenced Japan's approach to the Internet. In the 1970s and 1980s, when Japanese companies were outselling their U.S. counterparts in industries from autos to machine tools, American managers looked to Japan for lessons. Popular books like William Ouchi's *Theory Z*[26] suggested that Japanese practices such as consensus management and lifetime employment were key to Japan's success and urged American managers to learn from Japan. Later, scholars attributed other characteristics of Japanese companies—including their participation in *keiretsu*, horizontal industrial organizations tied together with interlocking shareholdings—to the ability of Japanese companies to make risky, long-term investments. But practices that helped Japan in manufacturing sectors, where major competitive advantage can come from incremental advantages in design and production processes, suddenly appeared as weaknesses when new technologies caused a major discontinuity in the way business was conducted.

Cole argues that Japanese companies are less able to contend with the discontinuity because of their propensity to maintain stable relationships with their employees and with suppliers and other business partners.[27] These relationships, which Hitotsubashi University professor Hiroyuki Itami has called "human-capitalism,"[28] have long been a major bulwark of the Japanese company. In this model, the employee is the biggest stakeholder in the company. The firm's goal is "value added that can provide the basis for long-term job stability."[29] Firms also maintain close relationships with business partners, owning shares in their businesses and exchanging information and personnel. Personal relationships develop that reinforce these ties.[30]

John Barlow, the former Grateful Dead lyricist and co-founder of the Electronic Frontier Foundation, is reported to have once suggested that Japan did not need a new digital network because it already had an effectively debugged personal network. The problem is that personal networks, while effective among a group of homogeneous, geographically close companies, are far less effective in an increasingly global economy, where suppliers may be scattered about the world and market trends can change overnight. Companies that own shares in suppliers will be less willing, for example, to engage in the kind of online search for lower-cost suppliers that is helping U.S. companies cut costs. They are also less likely to move to dramatically new business models that will cut out those partners. Japanese personal computer companies, for example, have been slow to adopt Dell Computers' practice of selling directly to customers for fear of alienating their dealers and resellers.

The Japanese company's system of governance, with boards dominated by management insiders and interlocking shareholdings, was established to insulate companies from shareholders and from hostile acquisitions. Scholars such as W. Carl Kester have argued that this approach has allowed Japanese managers to have "acute long-term vision" with respect to investments.[31] But these investments tend to focus corporate investment in areas that will help maintain the competitiveness of legacy businesses that provide the bulk of existing jobs and profits. This kind of management structure is less willing to shift resources to Internet-type businesses that produce few new jobs, while simultaneously threatening to undercut existing businesses that support large numbers of employees in the company or its broader *keiretsu*.

Labor practices such as lifetime employment also limit a firm's strategic choices. The Internet has helped drive American companies increasingly to outsource manufacturing so they can focus on high-value activities like software and hardware design and marketing. Companies such as Cisco and IBM often turn to specialist manufacturers such as Solectron to manufacture their products, which relieves them of worry about keeping plants fully utilized and upgraded and allows them to focus on high-value parts of the business. Because the companies are connected to their suppliers over the Internet, they can closely monitor product quality. At the same time, because they are subcontractors, Cisco can move its production if other manufacturers offer lower costs. At a time when businesses are going global, companies like Cisco are proving that computer networks can be far more efficient than personal networks.

Japanese companies, also aware of the trend, have begun selling many of their American factories.[32] But commitments to lifetime employment have made it difficult to sell plants located in Japan. The inability to unload those factories, in turn, forces Japan to pursue strategies that result in promoting manufactured goods rather than the kind of higher-valued services and software that drives Internet usage.

Consensus-making, another typical characteristic of the Japanese firms, is said to improve implementation of decisions by mobilizing employees behind management objectives. Young Japanese executives, however, complain that consensus decision making only serves to slow decisions. Many of the first e-commerce sites came from large Japanese companies that were so cautious they did not even offer products for sale.[33] Caution, while important in the manufacturing arena where a single defect will be multiplied a million times on the production line, can be an obstacle on the Web where first-mover advantages are significant and products can be improved on an ongoing basis in response to customer feedback.

Japan's seniority system also can be a significant obstacle. Most strategic decisions are made by men in their 40s and 50s who do not feel comfortable with technology and do not understand its benefits. In a survey of 6,000 people conducted in November 1999 by *Nikkei Business,* only about 45 percent of those in their 40s and 50s felt productivity had climbed as a result of e-mail, while less than 25 percent felt they had better access to information. Less than 15 percent of those in that age group felt the Net helped in sales. Reflecting such anxieties, a recent television program depicted a group of young computer programmers who were assigned to debug a company's computer system, but instead used their privileged access to the computer network and management ignorance about technology to steal company secrets.

In interviews with young employees of leading electronics firms, *Nikkei Business* reporters found that automated accounting systems, e-mail systems, and other Internet-based technologies put in place were often left unused. Some managers, embarrassed to admit they did not even know how to read their e-mail, did not respond to important mail. Other young employees cited instances of managers demanding to be faxed copies of every e-mail message sent by subordinates.[34]

Such attitudes, combined with a continued focus on production, have contributed to Japan's low investment in information technology. While American companies put 33.9 percent of their capital investments in computer systems in 1997, Japan allocated only 12.5 percent. Information technology investments accounted for 4 percent of Gross Domestic Product in the United States that year, while it accounted for only 2.3 percent of GNP in Japan.[35] The problem of low spending on information technology is accentuated by the fact that Japanese companies maintain highly centralized management information systems departments that resist efforts by individual business divisions to develop and implement their own Internet strategies. Seniority employment also makes it difficult to promote more competent, Internet-savvy executives to senior positions of responsibility.

Japan's market structures, typically dominated by a few large companies, also make it less likely that entirely new Internet-based strategies will emerge. Government-approved cartels are common throughout the economy, as are "price stabilization" regulations that forbid discounting. This environment makes it difficult for new companies to challenge incumbents, and raises the overall cost of products and services to consumers and businesses.

Consider the publishing business in Japan. Books from hundreds of publishers are channeled through two large book distributors. Those two distributors, in turn, decide what books should go to which of 30,000 bookstores. Because booksellers have the right to return books that aren't sold (they typically send back about 40 percent of the books placed with them after just a few weeks on the shelves), the system is hugely inefficient. Such inefficiencies would suggest a perfect opportunity for online bookstores. Yet, under Japan's retail price-maintenance system, book prices are fixed. Without discounts, customers are reluctant to purchase online because the cost of freight makes online purchases more costly. A similar regulation prevents discounts of music CDs.[36]

Currently, the largest online bookstore, Kinokuniya, is also one of the largest brick and mortar bookstore chains. One would expect a company that continues to make the bulk of its profits through its stores to be less aggressive in the online space. And indeed, Kinokuniya's site is poorly designed and rarely updated. It requires users to register before conducting book searches, a move that seems designed to scare away users. Company executives admit they do not expect online sales to exceed 10 percent of total sales anytime in the next few years.[37] By comparison, Amazon's creation as an exclusively online book retailer forced it to be responsive to customer demands, and the company developed proprietary technology to make it easy to search for and purchase books, CDs, and other products. Amazon's early success in selling books and its soaring stock valuation forced Barnes & Noble to respond with aggressive online plans of its own. Competition among online retailers has continued to drive down book prices while boosting services.

Japanese companies are making some adjustments to exploit the capabilities of the Internet. NEC, Hitachi, Toshiba, Matsushita, and Fujitsu, Japan's leading electronics companies, have all announced major plans for restructuring their companies to better exploit the Net. The plans typically involve buying supplies over the Internet, introducing merit pay increases, cutting unproductive divisions, and seeking acquisitions in key technology sectors.

So far the measures have been relatively moderate. Consider Fujitsu, Japan's premier computer company. It also is one of Japan's largest Internet service providers and plans to be a major provider of Internet solutions for business customers. In 1988, Fujitsu installed a system for purchasing office

products over the Net that enables employees to place an order for office supplies. The system required a substantial investment by Fujitsu, using up 100
man-months of programming time, but Fujitsu employees can now put out
specifications for the product they want to purchase and electronically forward
the request to a purchasing manager. The purchasing manager approves the
request and gives it an order number. The request is put on the web site, and
interested companies offer a bid. The purchasing manager decides which supplier to use and electronically orders the product.

Fujitsu says the system has shortened the order process and eliminated
7,000 order forms that used to circulate around the company for various seals
of approval. The process enabled the company to move 87 employees to more
productive positions. The company also estimates its purchase costs dropped
by about 5 percent . Fujitsu's savings, while substantial, were limited by its decision to automate existing procedures rather than change the way purchases are
handled to eliminate the approval process for small purchases as many American companies have done. In addition, all but 11 of the 289 companies that use
the system are the same suppliers that worked with Fujitsu before. This suggests Fujitsu may not have organized the system to find the lowest-cost suppliers available. Fujitsu says that logistics dictated those decisions.

CREATIVE DESTRUCTION: JAPANESE STYLE

Richard Samuels argues in *Rich Nation, Strong Army* that Japan, in its effort to
catch up with the West, has developed an ideology of techno-nationalism that
"precedes and informs" Japanese institutions.[38] As Japan's industrial sector
matures and the country is forced to move toward a knowledge-based service
economy, many of these institutions are no longer appropriate. Government
intervention and corporate practices reduce the speed and flexibility with
which Japan can respond to new technologies and new markets. Yet past experience suggests Japan has difficulty changing without significant external pressure. In the short term there may be justification for policies that help
companies make the transition to the "new economy" to avoid widespread lay-
offs. Schumpeter argues, for example, "Situations emerge in the process of creative destruction in which many firms may have to perish that nevertheless

would be able to live on vigorously and usefully if they could weather a particular storm."[39] Schumpeter goes so far as to suggest that "in the process of creative destruction, restrictive practices may do much to steady the ship and to alleviate temporary difficulties."[40]

But many of the practices designed to help Japan cross over may actually be serving to block the transition. By avoiding "destruction," Japan may be leaving less room for "creation." Consider MITI's policies. On the one hand the Ministry is returning to its early experience in promoting industrial policies targeted at clearly defined niches. Its efforts to develop e-commerce software and next-generation routers are examples of this approach. The strength of the approach is that the funds often are given to a consortium that encourages member companies to establish standards and to pool their resources in joint research that will help raise the technological level of all members. The programs also assure a smoother transition to new technologies. Because incumbent companies, often organized into industry association, receive subsidies to develop the technology they need to increase efficiency, there is less danger of companies going bankrupt and being forced to lay off employees. On the other hand, by supporting incumbent companies, MITI makes it less likely that a completely new organization, perhaps better suited to exploiting the Internet, will emerge triumphant. These policies, therefore, contradict other efforts by MITI to use changes in tax laws and subsidies to encourage new start-ups.

Another problem with MITI's projects is that technology changes so rapidly that by the time the projects are completed they are likely to be outdated. Even if they are not outdated and the technology is good, they may be rendered ineffective because of the huge first-mover advantage in software. The companies that originally designed the software will tend to move quickly to global distribution, establishing worldwide standards and earning money to help finance continued improvements. Video game software is the one area in which Japan has led the way. Japanese companies such as Nintendo and Sony have played pioneering roles, and Japan's large base of sophisticated consumers and talented cartoonists gives it a strong advantage. But this model assumes monopolistic control over a standard so that license fees can be charged to software companies. This model may be increasingly difficult to pursue as the more "open" Internet model gains momentum.

MPT's policies also remain problematic. In private conversations, MPT officials admit that their prestige is tied to the success of Japan's telecommunications sector. They fear the loss of face experienced by the Ministry of Finance when Japanese banks began to fail in the late 1990s. The Ministry of Finance realized too late that protecting banks in the short term would not assure the long-term health of the banks without structural changes. MPT has recently increased pressure on NTT to lower prices for Internet access. NTT announced in February 2000 it would offer unlimited use of telephone lines for Internet access for $40 by the end of the year, 50 percent below what it had previously announced. But NTT is only offering the service to a limited group of customers on a test basis, and this pressure does not solve the structural problem. The inability of competitors to access NTT's network at competitive rates puts NTT in a position to squash its competitors virtually at will. The lack of competition, in turn, assures a slower rate of decline in prices and a much slower pace in the adoption of new technologies for high-speed access. The prices charged for leased lines used by e-commerce sites, while declining, remain several times higher in Japan than in the United States.

There may be some areas in which Japan does well in spite of the heavy role of government and national monopolies. Consider the wireless market. While the American cellular phone market remains fragmented as many firms struggle to promote different standards, the Japanese mobile phone market is dominated by the same telephone that sets most standards. With more than 50 million cellular phones in use, Japan has one of the highest rates of cell phone usage in the world. MPT expects that nearly 80 million people, 60 percent of the population, will have cell phones by 2010.[41] Because NTT Docomo has a dominant 57 percent share of the Japanese cell phone market with 26 million subscribers, the company had a large enough base to promote I-mode, its own technology for using cell phones to access the Internet. The system allows consumers to access e-mail and certain specially formatted websites from their cell phones. After just two years, the service already had 12 million subscribers by October 2000. Accessing short e-mail messages using cell phones fits the Japanese lifestyle, in which millions of people spend hours each day on commuter trains and access to the Net from home computers is still relatively low. Japanese teenagers, who have little privacy at home and seldom have access to a second home phone line, use their mobile phones to exchange e-mail. These phones will be combined with "smart cards" to handle a variety of online transactions, acting as identification cards, electronic money, and train passes. A growing number of companies are using I-mode phones as corporate intranets. While small, the phones are sufficient for handling such basic functions as updating inventory information, coordinating schedules, and providing cost estimates. Insurance salesman, for example, can input basic information and have corporate servers calculate premiums.[42]

While NTT Docomo has done well, Japanese telecommunications suppliers have done poorly on world markets because NTT chose its own proprietary standard to build its wireless networks. Learning from its past mistakes, Docomo, with MPT's support, is moving aggressively to be the first to introduce broadband CDMA, a technology widely expected to be one of two global standards. The system, to be put in place by the spring of 2001 following a massive investment in a new infrastructure, will allow cell phone users to send images to each other. If Japanese manufacturers are among the first to build the equipment, they could once again become competitive players in the global market.

Japan's strong investments in wideband CDMA, however, run the risk of moving too far ahead of market forces and building capabilities for which there is no consumer demand. The wireless market also has benefited from unusual circumstances. Aggressive pressure by the U.S. government on behalf of Motorola resulted in substantial deregulation of the wireless market in 1994. The $1,000 deposit previously required to get a cell phone was eliminated and it became possible for consumers to buy their own cell phones, for example. Because NTT still demands a $700 deposit on landlines, cell phones are now cheaper to acquire than regular phones.[43] While cell phone use continues to soar, the use of landline telephones is actually declining.

Japanese companies also face a dilemma in trying to maintain traditional business practices while at the same time adjusting to the new economy. To paraphrase Napoleon, they want to make omelets without breaking any eggs. Practices like lifetime employment and seniority wages create a nurturing environment that allows for innovation in the factory. But they do not help produce the kind of entrepreneurship required to exploit Web technologies. Japanese executives admit as much. Junichi Miyazu, president of NTT, suggested that his employees "should all quit and start companies like in the

United States and that would help nurture the information communications industry." But he went on to dismiss the capacity of his employees, arguing that, "our people just aren't that resourceful."[44]

But if Japanese companies find it difficult to change internally, what will finally spur innovation? The decade-long slump in Japan's manufacturing sector may prove a necessary but insufficient condition of change. Two other important catalysts are directly related to the emergence of the Internet. One is the pressure from American companies threatening to exploit the Internet to break into the Japanese market. Another source of change may be the Japanese companies that win important competitive advantages by being first to exploit the Web and are rewarded by the stock market for their boldness.

Although Japan remains a difficult country for foreign businesses to penetrate, many U.S. start-ups are moving into the market in joint ventures with traditional Japanese partners. Rival Japanese trading companies have paired up with U.S. venture companies to launch websites for trading steel, for example. Itochu Corp. and Marubeni Corp have established a joint venture with MetalSite to sell steel online. They expect to cut brokerage commissions to 1 percent of sales from the current 3 percent to 5 percent. Included in the exchange will be 1,000 companies tied to the two trading companies, including steel makers, wholesalers, and users. Later, other companies will be invited to participate in the exchange.[45] The very decision of those companies to invest in a business that will substantially undercut their traditional trading businesses suggests an admission that change is inevitable.

Many argue that Japanese companies, while slow to reach a consensus, move fast once that consensus has been reached. When Matsushita, Japan's consumer electronics giant, said the 11 main companies in its industrial group would purchase virtually all their supplies online by March 2001, they put their 3,000 domestic suppliers on a forced march. If the suppliers want to bid for the $20 billion in purchases Matsushita makes annually, many will have to take crash courses in e-commerce. Less than 40 percent of small companies in Japan today own personal computers and only 20 percent of companies have Internet access, according to Goldman Sachs. In the United States, 80 percent of small businesses have PCs and about 60 percent are online.

Initially, many of these electronic networks may do little more than squeeze inefficiencies from existing relationships. But the Internet, like the first railroads, creates new conditions that could set the stage for more fundamental change. Those changes will come first in areas where the companies face the most competition. A major catalyst of that competition in many sectors will be innovative companies like Sony and Softbank. Sony, which does not have the extensive retail chains of companies like Matsushita, Toshiba, and Hitachi, has been the most aggressive in selling its products online. Sony is also positioning its Playstation II as a device that will double as a DVD player, and in the future, as an appliance for accessing the Internet. Sony has also announced plans to exploit the power of the Web to get into the banking business and to expand its nascent insurance franchise.

Another catalyst for change will be Softbank, a company founded by Masayoshi Son, an ethnic Korean who was born in Japan and went to high school and university in the United States, in part to escape discrimination.[46] Son's net worth at one point exceeded $70 billion, largely as a result of Softbank's early investments in successful American venture companies like Yahoo. Those investments have provided the money and technology for Son's attack on the Japanese establishment. He has joint ventured with E*Trade and E-Loan, two of his early investments, to offer similar services in Japan. He prodded Tokyo Electric Power Company, Japan's largest electrical utility, into forming a joint venture with Softbank and Microsoft to use TEPCO's extensive fiber-optic network to bypass NTT's network to offer Internet Access Services.[47] In 1999, Softbank teamed up with Japan's four leading toy makers to establish an online toy store. In February 2000 Softbank received permission to acquire Nippon Credit Bank. The same month Son established a $1.4 billion fund to invest in Japanese Internet start-ups.

Son's efforts already have had some impact. In late 1999, soon after he announced plans to establish jointly with NASDAQ a new stock exchange in Japan that would be more friendly to start-up companies, the Tokyo Stock Exchange responded with plans to launch MOTHERS (market of high-growth and emerging stocks.) Although MOTHERS, racked by huge volatility and charges of insider trading, has had a rough beginning, over time the two exchanges should make it easier for Japanese start-ups to finance their companies and for venture capitalists to cash in on their investments.

A few of Japan's innovators from an earlier generation are also getting aggressive. Ito Yokado, a discount retail chain, has announced it will use its

9,300 retail outlets, including the convenience stores of its subsidiary Seven-Eleven Japan Co., to offer banking services over ATM machines.[48] The move is part of a broader plan to transform its network of stores into a critical arm of Japan's e-commerce system. Online customers of many websites now have the option of picking up their purchases and paying for them at the closest convenience store. For example, Seven-Eleven created a joint venture with NEC, Sony, and others called 7dream.com to pursue this strategy.[49] These ventures have hit some potholes, however. Seven-Eleven discovered that it could not make its banking service profitable within three years, a requirement for getting a banking license from the Ministry of Finance. Still, companies like Seven-Eleven will likely provide the distribution infrastructure to support a new constellation of Internet-based retail companies.

While efforts to accelerate Internet and e-commerce growth represent a challenge to old Japan, they are neither a convergence toward a U.S.-style market economy nor do they represent a broader transformation of the Japanese economy. With so little labor mobility and the nation's technical and capital resources focused in a few large companies, Japan can change only if the large companies that employ most of its workers also change. NEC's chief executive argues, for example: "Venture companies will help drag in the cutting-edge technology and for that they are critical. But ultimately, I expect it will be the established company converting to the new structure that brings change."[50]

That conversion will take a long time. Despite a great deal of talk about increasing merit pay, most workers are still paid by seniority. Stock options are rare. Even at venture companies and successful wireless companies such as Docomo, executives responsible for important innovations complain of receiving just $100 to $300 in incentive pay. Even Softbank, the most venture-like of the new breed, does not make heavy use of stock options. And while it looks to America for its technology, it looks to old Japan for its business model. Softbank's Son says his goal is to build an information *zaibatsu* that will control the key chokepoints of the information economy, just as Japan's early *zaibatsu* dominated such key sectors as shipping and finance.[51]

The potential of the Internet will continue to be constrained by the old establishment in other ways. Recognizing the importance of training youngsters to exploit the Internet, the Ministry of Education has promoted an aggressive plan aimed at connecting all Japanese schools to the Internet by

2003. But half or more of those connections are going to staff rooms or a head-master's office where they are often left unused. In a system where central bureaucrats have tight control over the content of education and where teachers already complain that they are required to teach too much content to students, it is unclear how much opportunity teachers will have to use the computers in class.

Once in place, however, the Internet can have unintended consequences. The Ministry of Education has begun discussing changes in its curriculum to include a subject called "information" that would require computer use. In the summer of 1999, a Wakayama man used his Internet home page to criticize the principal of his son's school for not taking appropriate action after some boys at the school cut up his son's shirt, forcing him to spend the day at school in an undershirt. The 56-year-old principal resigned one month later after the father's Web account of his son's bullying incident generated a flood of telephone calls criticizing the principal's handling of the affair.[52] A consumer received an apology from Toshiba's chief executive after the recording of a telephone conversation with a rude Toshiba customer service representative that he put on the Web received wide press coverage.

CONCLUSION

This chapter has argued that the institutions Japan created to catch up with the West in the industrial era have now become anchors that prevent the Japanese economy from moving forward. Government policies, management practices, and market structures that helped protect and nurture industrial-age companies have had the effect of holding back growth in information-based sectors that are at the heart of the new Internet economy. The emergence of a few powerful new companies, however, seems to signal changes.

But the Internet won't drive a convergence toward the same kinds of social values as Internet advocates have predicted for the United States. Internet usage is not going to lower consumer costs if regulations forbid it. Without broad and heavy use by consumers, new ways of exploiting the Web are less likely to evolve. As long as Japan's "old economy" companies are driving the Net rather than a new generation of more efficiently organized companies, Internet adoption is likely to be slow. "Old economy" managers will not have incentive to alter labor rules and governance structures that limit change unless they are faced with strong competition from new organizations more capable of exploiting the technology. Key information will not be available if bureaucrats do not share it. Japan's government-directed growth, so successful in the industrial age, is inappropriate for an era when new technology requires fast-paced change to adapt to unpredictable trends.

Management structures and government policies may slow adoption of the Internet, but they will not block it, and once in place, the Internet will lay the foundation for potentially sweeping changes. Once transactions are electronic and use established rules, business relationships may become less personal and more formal. Companies with such electronic systems may find it easier to cut off inefficient suppliers or to pit suppliers against each other in online auctions. Just as the U.S. Occupation built the framework of Japan's democracy in its own image only to see the institutions operated by the Japanese in their own inimitable fashion, the Internet will take root in a way that reflects Japanese values. Novelist Murakami no doubt hopes the values will reflect those of a revitalized, public-spirited youth rather than those of their dispirited elders.

PART4

BUSINESS DESTRUCTION
STRATEGIES IN THE GLOBAL
INTERNET ECONOMY

7 ALLIANCE ENTERPRISE STRATEGIES DESTROYING FIRM BOUNDARIES

Peter Pekar, Jr.

Strategic alliances are sweeping through nearly every industry. Interorganizational links seem particularly popular and important in industries experiencing creatively destructive technological, organizational, and institutional innovations. Telecommunications, airlines, and media are but three industries whose firms have been forced by changes in rates of new product development, deregulation, and privatization to shake up management practices, competitive positioning, and product and business portfolios, in large part by drawing on interorganizational relationships. As these and other industries destruct and reconstruct under new arrangements, such relationships become an essential driver of superior corporate growth and profitability.

Interfirm alliances figure substantially in individual firm valuation. Based on research summarized in *Smart Alliances* (Harbison and Pekar, 1998), we estimate that over the next five years alliance relationships will add between $30 and $50 trillion to the market value of allied firms. In another chapter of this volume, Paul Vaaler reports additional evidence of the link between the establishment of interfirm alliances and increased share value (see Chapter 9).

The rise of strategic alliances may be explained initially by the quest for value among leading firms. The current craze, however, may also owe something to the feedback effects these leading firms have on others in the industry. The surge in alliances engenders nothing less than a worldwide restructuring in organizational relationships, management practices, and investment priorities. Making alliances becomes an increasingly attractive investment approach compared to outright mergers and acquisitions.

A series of longitudinal research studies conducted at Booz·Allen & Hamilton, covering 1987–2000,[1] revealed that

- more than 20 percent of the revenue generated from the top 2,000 U.S. and European firms now derives from alliance-based business ventures rather than from individual firm-managed ventures, with more predicted in the near future;

- these same firms earn higher returns on their alliance-based business than from their individual firm–managed businesses;

- successful firms create a "concentration" of alliances with multiple links to certain partners, with the intent of using these key partnerships to rapidly overpower rivals; and

- traditional "command-and-control" organizational approaches are inadequate to manage these complex sets of relationships forming outside the direct control of the corporation.

This study and others suggest that industry restructuring follows from alliance forming and reforming processes. Instead of striking a two- or three-firm joint venture agreement to serve a discrete, limited purpose, leading firms increasingly consider the creation of looser "cooperatives" and "constellations" with multiple peers and broader terms of interorganizational commitment. In this way, these firms create options to leverage a vast array of capabilities, some of which they may not even be aware of or interested in exploiting at the time the relationships are initially established. Firms insisting on a "go-it-alone" competitive strategy often lose out on these options and gradually lose ground to rivals with apt alliance relationships.

As alliances have become an essential element of successful businesses, it is not surprising that alliance announcements are often linked to surges in the stock prices of partnered firms. My own work indicates that alliance-intensive firms earn approximately a 70 percent higher return on equity and are more likely to see higher market valuations for their stock. Firms such as Hewlett-Packard and Oracle see the ability to form successful alliances as a core competency to be developed and nurtured.

Something is missing, however. Firms are building up portfolios of alliances, but too often they are managed as discrete linkages of secondary importance. This rather limited view of alliance management is probably inadequate to take full advantage of options provided by this new type of inter-organizational structure. New models are necessary to unleash the power of a truly "allianced enterprise" with a portfolio of interorganizational relationships and embedded options.

What is the allianced enterprise? How will it work, particularly in the volatile industry settings where Schumpeter's process of creative destruction is busily at work? This chapter provides answers to these questions, builds alternative models for structuring the allianced enterprise, and discusses implications for managers and public policy makers.

BACKGROUND

Two or three decades ago, competition among firms may have been simpler. Firms did not need to excel in all capabilities or participate across the globe—one capability serving one major market region often was sufficient. The pace of change in technologies and markets was modest compared with today's activity, and industry boundaries were well defined and generally not global. If a firm lacked a capability, it either took the time to develop it or bought it through an acquisition.

Shareholders then may have been more patient and less demanding about profitability and returns. "Hot" ideas of the day for strategic thinkers and planners were market segmentation, application of portfolio models to categorize the firms' different businesses to determine resource allocation, and competitive strategies. A command-and-control model emphasizing the internalization of competence within the formal boundaries of the firm was dominant and, apparently, working successfully.

Some writers, however, suggested that a new pattern was emerging. Gary Hamel (Doz and Hamel, 1998) at the London Business School, and Barry Nalebuff of Yale and Adam Brandenburger of Harvard (Brandenburger and Nalebuff, 1997) developed new and interesting models of interorganizational cooperation. Their models suggest a new type of business entity—a less discrete enterprise that featured clusters of common activities in the midst of a network of relationships, the aim being to share knowledge and core capabilities to rapidly increase value to customers.

Their work complemented research on alliances by Michael Hammer (Hammer, 1998) of MIT, Sumantra Ghoshal of the London Business School and Christopher Bartlett of the Harvard Business School (Ghoshal and Bartlett, 1999), and Michael Yoshino (Yoshino and Rangan, 1995) of Harvard, who predicted that the traditional concept of management and control was at the end its life cycle. Ben Gomes-Casseres (Gomes-Casseres, 1996) at Brandeis used the term "constellations" to describe this new era. Recently, a task force at Booz·Allen & Hamilton, headed by Bruce Pasternack and Albert Viscio (Pasternack and Viscio, 1998), studied this emerging trend. They concluded that we are moving toward what John Dunning (Dunning, 1997) of Rutgers first described as a "centerless corporation"—an organization in which competitive strength will be based on harnessing capabilities, knowledge, and the power of people in ways previously unknown. Meanwhile, in another forum, James F. Moore (Moore, 1997) of the Harvard Business School is predicting the emergence of "business ecosystems." These commentators and others[2] agree that we are in the early phases of a new era that will see cooperative business models become a dominant force in the world economy.

THE ALLIANCED ENTERPRISE AS AN ALTERNATIVE GROWTH ENGINE

When firms team with other firms, the relationships range from transactional conventional sourcing and servicing arrangements at one extreme to acquisitions and mergers at the other. In the middle of the spectrum are what we call strategic alliances.

Strategic alliances are not transactional (arm's length) in nature—they are arrangements in which the partners are willing to act in unison and share core capabilities. A survey of more than 2,000 U.S. and European firms reveals that more than 20,000 alliances have been formed worldwide in the past two years, more than half of them between competitors. All participants said that alliances are increasing within their industry, and more than 75 percent noted that the alliances are effective. Acquisitions and mergers over the same period also remained strong, with more than 15,000 completed. Their success rate, however, is less than 50 percent.

The percentage of revenue earned by the top 1,000 United States firms from strategic alliances is now 18 percent. (The figure for Europe is almost 30 percent). By 2004, these same firms expect more than 30 percent (U.S.) and nearly 40 percent (Europe) of their revenue to come from alliances.

The top two reasons stated for forming alliances were (1) to accelerate the growth trajectory (75 percent), and (2) to gain access to external core capabilities (67 percent).

Strategic alliances have consistently produced a return on investment of nearly 17 percent among the top 2,000 firms in the world for more than ten years. This is 50 percent more than the average return on investment that firms produced overall. The 25 Fortune 500 firms most active in alliances earn 17.2 percent return on equity, compared to 10.1 percent for the 25 firms least active in alliances.

Executives strongly stated (two-thirds of respondents) that the current command-and-control model is inappropriate in the allianced-enterprises era. (See figure 1.)

Figure 1

Today's Organization Model Is Flawed

Americans and Europeans Rate Organizational Structure Appropriateness

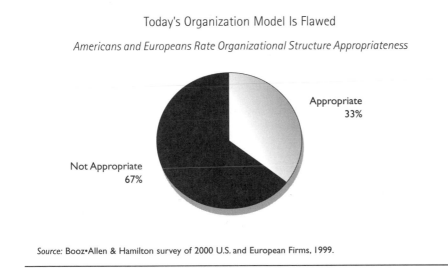

Appropriate
33%

Not Appropriate
67%

Source: Booz•Allen & Hamilton survey of 2000 U.S. and European Firms, 1999.

If these battle-tested alliance executives believe their current business model is not appropriate, then what will work? To begin to answer these questions, let's examine the forces behind the explosion in alliances.

DYNAMIC FORCES DRIVING STRATEGIC ALLIANCES

Certain environmental conditions favor the formation of alliances and explain the increasing cooperation in the last decade:

- Competitive boundaries have blurred as technology advances have created crossover opportunities to merge formerly distinct industries.

- Advances in communications (voice-mail, e-mail, and e-business) and the trend toward global markets link formerly disparate products, markets, and geographical regions and facilitate the open communication essential between partners.

- Intensifying competition and increasingly demanding customers require advantaged capabilities across the board, and no firm has the time or resources to develop these capabilities themselves.

- The drive for technology standards and compatibility in a globally linked world is insatiable.

- Alliances create an additional degree of strategic freedom, providing access to a largely unexplored set of opportunities.

- A growing number of firms have successfully scaled the alliance learning curve, and there now exists a global body of expertise to ensure successful alliance formulation and execution.

Defending the Ramparts: Retrenchment into Core—Our studies reveal that in 1985 only 26 percent of the revenue of top U.S. firms was coming from their core businesses. Diversification was still the standard of the day. By 1998, this had changed. Today we find the core generating more than 60 percent (U.S.) and 67 percent (Europe) of these firms' revenue. Effectively identifying, protecting, and enhancing the core business without giving up the key elements of the value chain where the core is not positioned is a key test now. As competition intensifies, alliances fill in capability gaps to protect the core business.

Global Reach—Fifteen years ago U.S. firms produced only 14 percent of their revenue overseas. Most U.S. firms saw competition confined to U.S. borders. Not so today. The numbers show that 35 percent of U.S. revenue (and 45 percent of European revenue) comes from international sales—making all firms vulnerable to threats from global players, especially from experienced cooperative international partners.

Holding the High Ground: Turbocharging the Development Engine— Research and development took a back seat in the early 1980s, with only about 2 percent of revenue being spent on R&D. By 1995 a dramatic change had occurred, with nearly 6 percent of revenue being allocated to R&D in the United States and Europe. We believe this change was directly related to the increasing importance of new product development to a firm's competitive position. Our surveys clearly show that since 1990 new products have accounted for a steady stream of more than 20 percent of the revenue every two years. Accommodating such rapid innovation has put pressure on management to act faster and smarter with fewer resources—hence the move toward alliances.

Wall Street's Watchful Eye: Rewards for the Best—Recent studies at Booz• Allen & Hamilton reveal the link between growth and market capitalization. Table 1 illustrates the achievements of high performers. Clearly they generate growth, but that growth also translates into high shareholder returns and earnings. It is not surprising that these firms have much higher price earnings and market caps than their competitors or the market in general.

Table 1

Growth Drives Performance

Financial Performance 1985–1994

	Annual Rates of Growth			Ten-Year Cumulative Growth		
	Shareholder Returns*	Earnings	Revenue	Shareholder Returns*	Earnings	Revenue
90th Percentile	23.7%	25.9%	21.1%	841%	997%	678%
80th Percentile	19.1%	17.8%	13.3%	573%	516%	347%
50th Percentile	12.7%	9.6%	8.5%	331%	251%	226%

*Shareholder returns reflect stock price appreciation plus dividend reinvestment, adjusting for stock split

Source: B•A&H Analysis, 10X Growth Study

Where do alliances fit in? The majority of these top performers are leading alliance firms, and they experience significantly higher return on investments than on their core businesses, gain a higher percentage of revenue from alliances, and earn 70 percent more return on shareholders' equity than their less-allianced competitors.

The Business Life Cycle—In 1956, Booz•Allen introduced the concept of the product life cycle in a landmark *Harvard Business Review* article. Business life cycle phase is a key driver of alliance imperatives and suggests at least five growth engine trigger points. The chart below illustrates alliance imperatives at each life cycle phase.

Figure 2

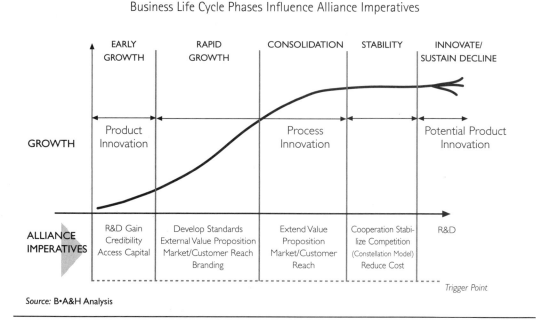

Business Life Cycle Phases Influence Alliance Imperatives

Source: B•A&H Analysis

In the early growth stage, product innovation and credibility are the main drivers of alliance initiatives. In the rapid growth phase, the development of standards and market reach are of key importance. The drivers change again in the stability phase when reduced cost, product extension, and value-chain strengthening are important. Organizations increasingly recognize alliance-enabled opportunities to close these strategic gaps.

Microsoft is a firm that recognized alliance opportunities. From its market capitalization of $0.6 billion at its 1986 IPO, the firm has grown to almost $500 billion in market cap. Few people understand, however, the critical role that alliances have played in this evolution. Microsoft's first breakthrough was an alliance with IBM to develop DOS. Its second breakthrough was dominance of operating systems through Windows and its "Wintel" alliances with Intel. The pace has never slackened. In the past two years, the firm announced on average *two alliances per day.* Microsoft's investments in these partnerships have paid huge dividends—for example, their equity investment in Apple has risen more than 900 percent in just two years.

Business life cycle phase is the key driver of alliance strategy imperatives (see figure 2). Once the linkage between these imperatives and the corporate and business strategies and objectives are clear, the next step is determining where alliances can be effective in meeting the objectives. Processes for identifying alliance opportunities encompass traditional industry analysis, brainstorming, and a new breed of tools we call "forcing techniques." Figure 3 illustrates a forcing technique designed to identify alliance opportunities for a retail fund manager seeking to expand distribution.

Figure 3

Forcing Techniques to Surface Alliance Options

	Acquire Funds to Invest	Identify Investment Needs	Investigate Available Products	Effect Transaction	Monitor Investment Performance	Manage Tax	Sell Investment
Potential Partners and Investment Houses ▶	• Financial institutions without investment offering (e.g., credit unions, small banks) • Employers • Professional associations/affinity groups • Real estate agents • HR consultants	• Accountants • Independent financial advisers • Investment magazines • Investment clubs • Financial planning software • Financial planning Internet sites	• Independent financial advisers • Investment magazines • Investment clubs • Investment Internet sites	• Stockbrokers • Credit unions/small banks • Financial management software (e.g., Quicken, MS Money) • Utilities • Credit card companies	• Investment magazines/ finance papers • Financial management software (e.g., Quicken, MS Money) • Investment tracking Internet sites	• Accountants • Tax return preparation agents	• Independent financial advisers • Stockbrokers

Source: B•A&H Analysis

It is important to understand and anticipate alliance activities of competitors and those firms that could become competitors. Figure 4 is an analysis of the consumer products area that illustrates how firms have been developing extensive alliance portfolios. Some of these firms were in the early stages of forming breakout alliances. By using this analysis, one firm positioned itself against the new wave of competition very early in the game.

Figure 4

Analysis of Alliances in the Consumer Products Area

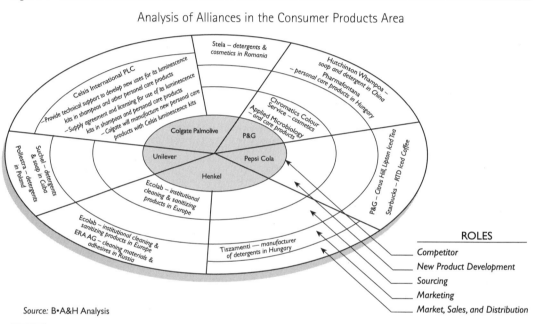

Source: B•A&H Analysis

ALLIANCE MODES: THE SEARCH FOR ADVANTAGED CAPABILITIES

Many firms see alliances as only filling a hole here or there—primarily where the firm cannot purchase a capability or develop it. These firms miss the real power of this new tool to become a superior growth engine. Real alliance power comes not from discrete alliances but from using a group of alliances in a concentrated manner to create a string or class of interconnected alliances to rapidly overpower the competition.

In today's dynamic environment, successful firms need to select, build, and deploy the critical capabilities that will enable them to gain competitive advantage, enhance customer value, and drive their markets. The emphasis should be on future differentiators, not historical ones. The competitive focus must switch from how to compete better with current capabilities to how to select and build better future capabilities—especially those emerging capabilities that will drive the market (figure 5).

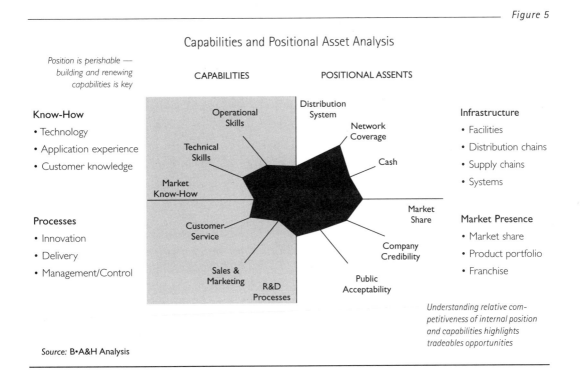

Figure 5

Capabilities and Positional Asset Analysis

Position is perishable — building and renewing capabilities is key

Understanding relative competitiveness of internal position and capabilities highlights tradeables opportunities

Source: B•A&H Analysis

Competition is no longer for position itself, but for change in position. Positional assets such as facilities, market share, and brand franchise are transitory, while capabilities are continuing assets. The goal is to focus on capabilities that the firm can use to constantly renew and extend its position. In this section, we describe how alliances are being used. Later we will discuss how these modes can be grouped into classes of interconnected alliances, thus leveraging a vast array of capabilities to increase value to the consumer and to overwhelm the competition.

Filling Single- and Multiple-Gap Deficiencies: Capabilities are know-how leveraged by cost-effective, responsive business processes and systems for innovation and delivery of enhanced customer value. Capabilities are intrinsically cross-functional—based on horizontally organized teams working according to well-designed, pre-engineered processes, and empowered by policy to make decisions within an established framework of rules.

Competitive advantage in capabilities comes from precision tailoring and sharp focus—no firm can afford to build advantaged capabilities against all aspects of value-added stream. Consider the Internet service provider world where firms are teaming together to capture segments of the value-added chain.

Alliances are an excellent solution for filling critical gaps when a firm lacks the resources or the time to build its own capability to world-class levels. Alliances should not be viewed as static. The strategy linkage is particularly important when thinking about the changing know-how needs and emerging critical processes that will affect the firm in the future. At a minimum, alliances should be seen as a way to fill key single or multiple gaps in a firm's value-added chain.

Creating Integrated Products and Services: In using the alliance approach to build integrated products or services, a team of partners can significantly raise the competitive bar to outflank a single competitor or force them to respond—thus placing a severe strain on their internal resources.

Global airline alliances are perhaps the most obvious example of initiatives to provide an integrated product or service offering (figure 6). Member airlines coordinate schedules for rapid, more hassle-free connections; frequent travelers are provided recognition and special services even when far from home; and customers can earn and redeem miles almost anywhere they travel. Alliance members have been especially successful in stimulating markets that neither carrier could serve effectively on their own, by providing more competitive offerings between medium-sized cities that were not aggressively marketed and the more traditional interline relationships. Member airlines also are rewarded with richer yields, attracting a higher proportion of the frequent travelers.

Significant opportunities remain untapped, however, in the largest (new) alliances. The lack of effective cross-firm compensation schemes, lack of antitrust immunity in some instances, and a natural reluctance to violate corporate sovereignty may be inhibiting further integration. We expect that the winning alliance(s) will find ways to act more effectively as one, potentially leveraging regional JVs and other mechanisms to fully combine revenue management, while integrating operations more effectively over time. The group that is most successful with these initiatives will not only further stimulate travel, but will gain share of high-yield traffic over time at the expense of other groups.

Figure 6

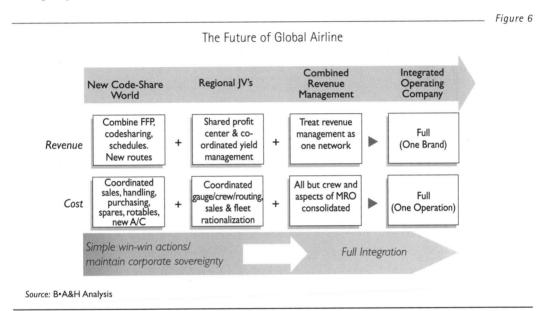

The Future of Global Airline

Source: B•A&H Analysis

Airlines also are developing additional alliances and relationships in related businesses such as maintenance, and are beginning to explore potential breakout strategies by leveraging their key capabilities and market positions in the e-commerce and loyalty management businesses.

Forming a Breakout Strategy: Some firms are using alliances to develop a breakout strategy to leap over competition and grab the high ground before competition can react. Consider figure 7, which shows how a constellation has developed in the Excite@Home cable broadband Internet delivery market.

Since its founding in 1995, Excite@Home has reached affiliate agreements with 23 leading cable firms worldwide. Their goal is to create a broadband alternative to AOL (America Online) by marrying a graphics-intensive portal/search engine (Excite) to @Home's exclusive distribution arrangement with the cable TV firms. The service offering to customers is integrated (for example, Cox@home, Comcast@home, etcetera), and the customer probably is not even aware that there are multiple firms behind the service offering.

Figure 7

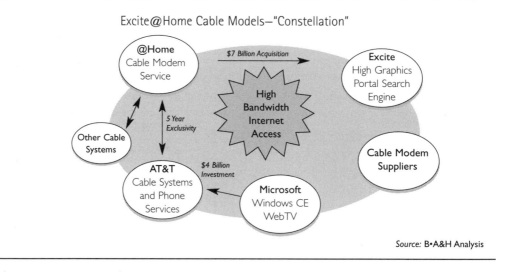

Excite@Home Cable Models—"Constellation"

Source: B•A&H Analysis

In the breakout environment, successful partners select, build, and deploy the critical capabilities that will enable them to gain competitive advantage, enhance customer value, and drive their markets, thus putting their competitors on the defensive.

CONTROLLING THE BATTLEFIELD: EMERGENCE OF ALLIANCE CLASSES

The exploding number and scope of alliances is creating challenges for executives who are trying to manage complex activity that increasingly is outside the direct control of the corporation. Firms are forming vast arrays of alliances that on the surface seem a collection of unconnected arrangements. These alliances increasingly are becoming an interrelated tapestry of activities, however, linked in ways to gain competitive advantage and control the battlefield. The need to adapt the organizational model is compelling.

Leading-edge firms are beginning to use alliance architecture models that are defined in terms of the role strategic alliances can play. The key issue is how should these alliances be governed, controlled, and managed? Many of these alliances could dwarf the size of any one partner. Yet, many of these highly dynamic and competitively strong entities have no definable business models.

Alliances cannot use the command-and-control business model to span multiple partners. They require a model more flexible and dynamic to reflect the market environment and the partnership structure. Four models are emerging for firms with multiple alliances: franchise, portfolio, cooperative, and constellation, and each of these "pure tones" will have a different set of implications in terms of the appropriate governance model.

These pure tone models are shown in figure 8:

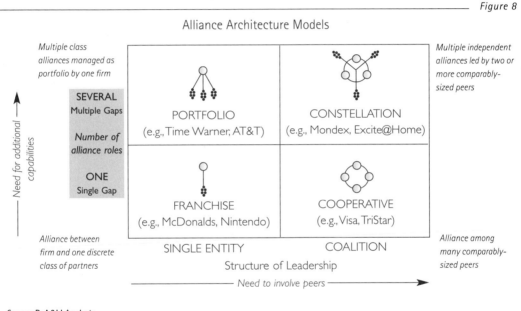

Figure 8

Alliance Architecture Models

Source: B•A&H Analysis

FRANCHISE MODEL: *Deep Bench Strength*—This model is used by firms to fill a single critical gap in their value chain. The needs in that gap area, however, are greater than any one partner can fill, so the firm develops a replicable alliance model for a class of partnerships.

For example, Nintendo is using this franchise model to fill in a key capability need—the development of games for its consoles. Nintendo is positioned in the center, closely controlling the activities of its alliance partners (figure 9). The franchise model develops a single alliance role that can be refined and quickly replicated to create scale, producing an alliance growth corridor for the alliance initiator. This alliance architecture is a significant part of the business model of e-business firms that use the franchise architecture to develop and manage referral affiliates (e.g., Next Card), content partners (AOL), or distribution partners (First USA).

Franchise alliance partners are, in a sense, extended employees of the firm. The partnership is analogous to what we see emerging between a firm and its employees—the partner is responsible for his or her own destiny, while the dominant partner provides an opportunity for the other partners to grow and develop.

Figure 9

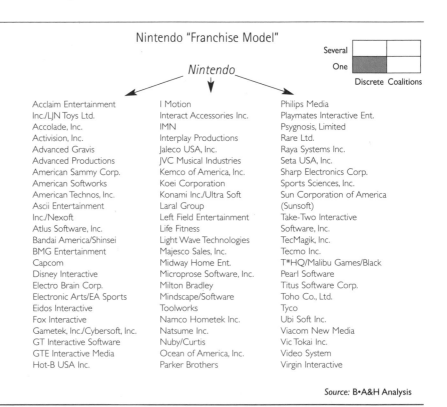

Nintendo "Franchise Model"

Nintendo

| | Acclaim Entertainment Inc./LJN Toys Ltd. | I Motion | Philips Media |

Acclaim Entertainment Inc./LJN Toys Ltd.
Accolade, Inc.
Activision, Inc.
Advanced Gravis
Advanced Productions
American Sammy Corp.
American Softworks
American Technos, Inc.
Ascii Entertainment Inc./Nexoft
Atlus Software, Inc.
Bandai America/Shinsei
BMG Entertainment
Capcom
Disney Interactive
Electro Brain Corp.
Electronic Arts/EA Sports
Eidos Interactive
Fox Interactive
Gametek, Inc./Cybersoft, Inc.
GT Interactive Software
GTE Interactive Media
Hot-B USA Inc.

I Motion
Interact Accessories Inc.
IMN
Interplay Productions
Jaleco USA, Inc.
JVC Musical Industries
Kemco of America, Inc.
Koei Corporation
Konami Inc./Ultra Soft
Laral Group
Left Field Entertainment
Life Fitness
Light Wave Technologies
Majesco Sales, Inc.
Midway Home Ent.
Microprose Software, Inc.
Milton Bradley
Mindscape/Software Toolworks
Namco Hometek Inc.
Natsume Inc.
Nuby/Curtis
Ocean of America, Inc.
Parker Brothers

Philips Media
Playmates Interactive Ent.
Psygnosis, Limited
Rare Ltd.
Raya Systems Inc.
Seta USA, Inc.
Sharp Electronics Corp.
Sports Sciences, Inc.
Sun Corporation of America (Sunsoft)
Take-Two Interactive Software, Inc.
TecMagik, Inc.
Tecmo Inc.
T*HQ/Malibu Games/Black Pearl Software
Titus Software Corp.
Toho Co., Ltd.
Tyco
Ubi Soft Inc.
Viacom New Media
Vic Tokai Inc.
Video System
Virgin Interactive

Source: B•A&H Analysis

PORTFOLIO MODEL: *Hub and Spoke*—The portfolio model is a major step up from the franchise approach. Firms that adopt this approach are finding that the value-added chain contains far too many elements for it to command all of the capabilities necessary to compete. Instead of forming a number of single discrete arrangements to fill each gap, however, thus making itself vulnerable if a partner experiences difficulty or the market changes rapidly, the firm decides to create multiple class alliances managed as a portfolio. These firms are still in the center, but they are weaving together a portfolio of distinct and often unrelated partnerships. The external partners are connected directly to the firm, but they have little relationship to each other—only to the (distant) firm at the center.

For example, Time Warner is trying to cover multiple gaps in the key elements of the value chain—including content, applications, distribution, software, and service (figure 10). In each of these areas, it has formed alliances with a variety of partners, though a similar class of firms. It manages these classes as a portfolio, thus directing the arrangements to meet its strategic needs. Although Time Warner acts in consort with its portfolio partners, it never loses its sense of direction or control of its future. By adopting the portfolio approach, it can move quickly within a class adjusting its position or partners.

The biggest advantage of the franchise and portfolio models is that the forming firm sits in the control position directing and managing the intercon-

Figure 10

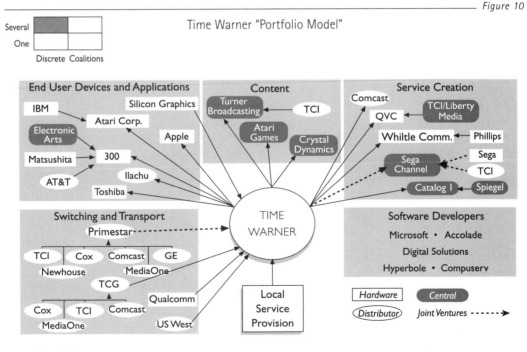

Time Warner "Portfolio Model"

Source: B•A&H Analysis

nectedness of the arrangements. In the portfolio model, the forming firm acts as the "corporate core." Through its actions it formulates strategic leadership and capability building. It manages this process through forming and dissolving its alliances as its primary control mechanism. The more dominant the position of the forming partner, the easier it is to implement this model.

COOPERATIVE MODEL: *Mutual Benefit*—In the cooperative model, a partner moves from a center position to a more cooperative role. The alliance is at the center, and the customer relationship often shifts from the firm to the alliance. Typically, we find that firms adopt the cooperative model to outflank the competition. The distinguishing feature of the cooperative model is that no one firm is in control—all work together to raise the competitive bar.

TriStar, the cooperative effort of CBS, Columbia Pictures, and HBO, for example, formed a film firm and motion picture studio with an initial investment of $300 million in the 1980s. Through TriStar, HBO was guaranteed an additional source of feature films. CBS obtained a toehold in cable TV services and gained a source of feature films for commercial broadcasting (figure 11). Columbia Pictures gained access to new distribution channels and extra studio capacity when space was scarce.

Figure 11

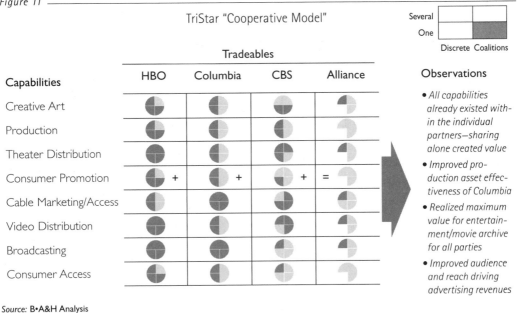

TriStar "Cooperative Model"

Several / One — Discrete Coalitions

Tradeables

Capabilities	HBO	Columbia	CBS	Alliance
Creative Art				
Production				
Theater Distribution				
Consumer Promotion	+	+	+	=
Cable Marketing/Access				
Video Distribution				
Broadcasting				
Consumer Access				

Observations

- *All capabilities already existed within the individual partners—sharing alone created value*
- *Improved production asset effectiveness of Columbia*
- *Realized maximum value for entertainment/movie archive for all parties*
- *Improved audience and reach driving advertising revenues*

Source: B•A&H Analysis

Although TriStar operated separately from its parent firms, it did not have its own distribution system. The parent firms distributed TriStar's films through their respective distribution systems, thus raising the effectiveness and productivity of the partners. TriStar is notable because its movies were made, sold, and distributed through TV, cable, and theaters in a more seamless manner. It helped establish cable and made HBO the dominant force in the paid cable area.

The cooperative model requires a different business model. While the relative size of the partners may differ, they are equals at the point of intersection (the specific product or service provided to the marketplace). All firms are working toward the same goal in that specific dimension. These arrangements are analogous to outsourcing agreements and should be governed by a prescribed set of standards. The day-to-day operation is not under direct control of any partner.

CONSTELLATION MODEL: *Integrated Service Offering*—Firms that use constellations develop a breakout strategy that leapfrogs the competition and

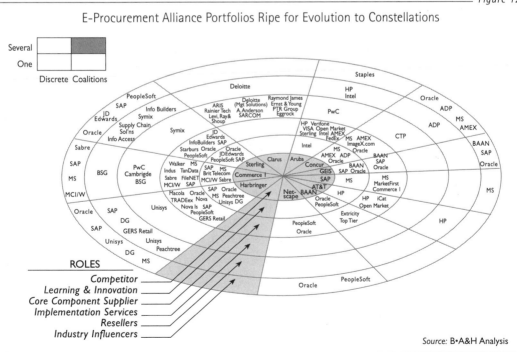

Figure 12

E-Procurement Alliance Portfolios Ripe for Evolution to Constellations

Source: B·A&H Analysis

puts industry competitors on the defensive, while moving the market into a high-growth phase.

E-procurement is a good example of an industry with emerging alliance constellations. Entering this industry requires a very substantial set of partners playing multiple alliance roles (portfolio architecture). Requirements for global scale, standardization, and substantial capital injections, however, are forcing early players to share leadership and equity with selected partners through migration to a constellation model (figure 12). These constellations will mature as constellation partners discover new ways to work together to change the rules of the game.

Constellations initially are composed of a set of equity joint ventures that should naturally evolve into independent firms. They will have all the "organization" required and be self-contained. They will be governed through board processes and create their own identity in the marketplace.

A recent survey of more than 2000 alliances clearly shows that gap-filling dominates the alliance landscape for major U.S. and European firms. More than 30 percent of alliances, however, fall into the cooperative and constellation mode.

Table 2

Each "Pure Tone" Alliance Class Has a Unique Set of Characteristics

	Governance	Integrated Offerings	Industry Focus
Franchise	Easiest — Operationally managed	Little (fill single gap)	Single Concentrate on current customer/market segments
Portfolio	Easier — Internal oversight committee crosses various areas	Possible (multiple gap focus)	Single Concentrate on current customer/ market segments
Cooperative	Intricate — External shared leadership and governance	High (create new value proposition within industry	Multiple Focus on creating new value position to extend reach into customer/market segments
Constellation	Difficult — External broad structure, shared governance crosses industry boundaries	High (breakout industry boundaries leapfrog current competitive structure)	Multiple Rapid expansion into new high-growth and high-value market areas unobtainable previously

MANAGING ALLIANCE MODELS: THE ART OF VIRTUAL COHERENCE

Each alliance model has a different set of characteristics, governance issues, and strategic focus (table 2). Trying to manage these models under the old command-and-control structure inhibits the formation and management of these models. It has been our experience that firms that form and manage alliance models successfully do not want to team up with firms that have not learned this lesson.

There is little doubt that successful firms in the next decade will harness the full potential of the alliance models and tailor their organizational structures to take full advantage of the "pure tone" alliance style that best fits their strategic needs. The business world will be difficult to navigate as firms are shaken loose from traditional ways (figure 13).

Firms must develop coherence among the many seemingly disparate pieces of the business, establishing a potent binding force and sense of direction where all the pieces mutually reinforce each other and provide a platform for growth. Coherence is what allows the firm to de-emphasize a rigid organiza-

Figure 13

Emerging New Business Model Contains Elements of Control and Cooperation

Source: B•A&H Analysis

tional structure. A staggering failure of the old business model is that it chokes the potential of the firm.

How is coherence established in an alliance? How should these alliances interact with the partners? The answers must be tailored for each kind of alliance.

The *franchise* model is operational in nature. Franchise alliances are an extension of a specific part of a firm, and that's where the alliance should be managed.

The *portfolio* model is de facto a new business model. Because it usually involves one primary part of the dominant partner, it is managed not by an operations group but by a business center. That center acts as the "corporate center" for the alliances. It must treat its partners as a business unit within a centerless corporation—adding value only where the businesses cannot (figure 14). The business center must focus on knowledge and people and work to build coherence internally and externally.

Figure 14

The Centerless Corporation

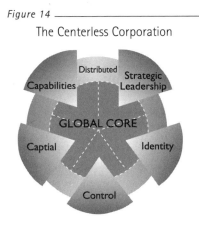

The *cooperative* model is a shared business model that needs its own leadership, but with few "owners," it must develop a cooperative governance structure. The challenge with these models is to establish a set of operating and performance parameters. This model is very much what firms do when they establish a shared services organization within the corporation or use an outsourcing agreement.

The *constellation* must be thought of as a new firm, with its partners the businesses. The constellation requires its own corporate center, which is focused on creating value for the extended entity. Our view is that the only areas in which a corporate center adds value are in strategic leadership, capability brokering, identity, control, and capital. This holds true for a corporation and for a constellation.

The more an alliance must mirror a single business model, the more it must focus on knowledge creation and dissemination, people strategies, and creating coherence throughout the entity. Without this focus, the venture is doomed from the start. This business model will have strong analogies to a

Figure 15

New Business Model for Alliances

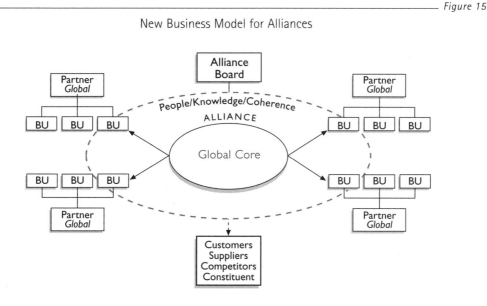

Source: B•A&H Analysis

single business, but as figure 15 illustrates, it must cross corporate borders. While the basic principles hold, their application will differ. These new models will be the growth engines of the future, and will provide great value to early adopters.

To a large extent we are entering new territory. As the word spreads and more firms seek alliances as a growth vehicle, the differentiator will shift from being able to form an alliance to being able to manage one. Obviously, those in the game the longest have the most experience, but the game is so new that standards have yet to be set.

ALLIANCES AS A CORE COMPETENCY

Regardless of which of the four alliance models is appropriate, firms no doubt will be compelled to form multiple kinds of alliances and will need a disciplined process to decide which type of alliance is optimal in a particular situation. Pragmatic executives are often suspicious of simple formulas. Some executives even maintain that seat-of-the-pants management and pure luck play an important role in any alliance. Luck always helps a business alliance succeed, but studies show that the chances of alliance success without experience, learning, and best-practice adoption are at best only one in five.

Alliances come in different flavors and each flavor has different characteristics. As figure 16 illustrates, each alliance needs to be treated differently for such issues as best practices, governance, success measurements, and implementation.

Figure 16

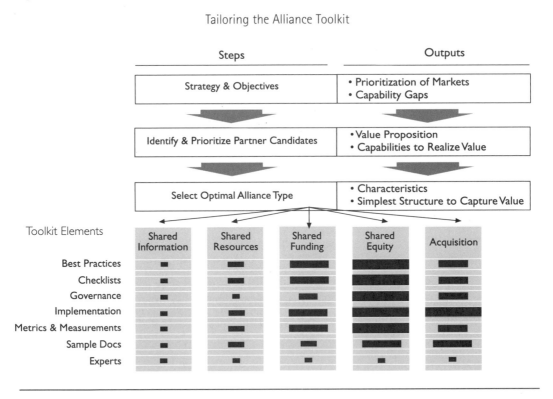

Tailoring the Alliance Toolkit

The alliance tool-kit approach supports learning and institutionalization and thus avoids an ad hoc approach in developing an alliance process as a core competency. As figure 17 illustrates, successful alliance firms are using alliance tool-kits to generate an alliance transaction stream while increasing and reinforcing their alliance proficiency.

Figure 17

The Alliance Toolkit

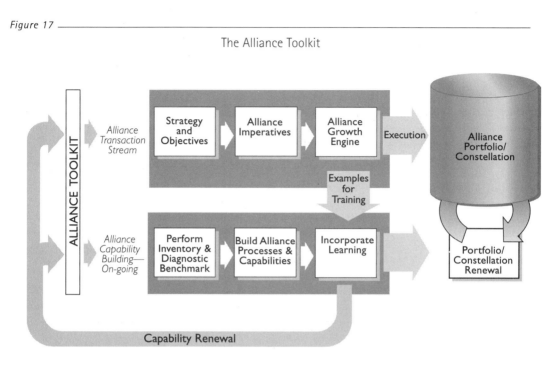

CONCLUSION

Global industry has entered an unprecedented era of structural change. Per-haps not since the industrial revolution have new technology development and adoption, rapid market expansion, and revolutionary business processes invaded managerial space so forcefully. The old command-and-control model that worked successfully for nearly two centuries is now challenged by the allianced enterprise. This new organizational ecosystem places a high premium on growth, market leadership, and capability absorption—and it delivers.

Leading-edge firms are transforming their organizations and are reaping the benefits of this new business model, but only if they have carefully tailored the model to their own circumstances. One allianced enterprise does not fit all firms, but perhaps one of the different schemes discussed in this chapter offers enough tailoring to fit firms that have not yet gotten on the alliance bandwagon, or have gotten on but feel uncomfortable in their present seat. This chapter outlined technological, organizational, legal, regulatory, and competitive forces that undermine the strategy and performance of firms that persist in going it alone. In the gradual destruction of this old approach to doing business, however, firms still have an opportunity to shape their destiny through the interorganizational relationships they make and rely on in competition. The new age of allianced enterprises is upon us. The sooner managers realize that, think carefully through the implications for their firms, and then implement the appropriate interorganizational strategies, the greater will be their prospects for survival and profitability in this new age.

8 | CREATING AND DESTROYING SHAREHOLDER VALUE ACROSS BORDERS

Paul M. Vaaler

This chapter continues our survey of strategies to deal with the forces of creative destruction currently engulfing industries in the Internet economy. The effects of creative destruction on shareholders is the principal concern of this chapter. How shareholder value can be created—and can be destroyed—across national borders in the Internet economy will be illustrated by this analysis.[1] We will focus on the telecommunications industry, for which it has become almost axiomatic to note profound change motivated notably by enterprise privatization. Accelerating technological, organizational, and institutional change have undermined an "Old Regime" of state-owned telecommunications enterprises (telecoms) offering integrated services with simple and predictable pricing schemes for consumers, predictable returns for suppliers, and predictable state-sanctioned protection from competition by would-be rival firms. At the dawn of the new millennium, a "New Regime" of privatized telecoms is emerging. They enjoy wider latitude to rise or fall based on their own choices of which markets to serve, which technologies to adopt, how to price services to different consumer groups, and how to react to entry by competitors. As more countries embrace this transformative process—call it an institutional form of creative destruction—the remaining hold-outs come under increasing pressure from peers, international organizations, and international capital markets to abandon the Old Regime and get on the telecoms privatization bandwagon.

As this unprecedented transformation continues, however, at least in the near term we will be living with telecoms exhibiting characteristics of both the old and emerging new regimes. Lingering equity stakes held by the state in these privatizing firms provides part of the reason. At the end of 1999, privatizing telecoms such as Deutsche Telekom, France Telecom, and Japan's Nippon Telephone & Telegraph (NTT) still kept a majority of their respective firms' equity under government ownership or control, which may create a split personality among top managers and directors. Instead of being guided by sound business principles, government-owned or government-controlled telecoms are vulnerable to "misuse" for political ends. Even privatizing telecoms with minimal or no formal government equity ownership may face residual political pressure from former government masters.

This near-term situation raises interesting issues for international business strategy research and practice. By almost any measure, privatizing telecommunications firms have been busily engaged in major international transactions such as mergers and acquisitions, capital investments, alliances, joint ventures, and licensing agreements. Deutsche Telekom's July 2000 proposal to spend $46 billion to acquire U.S. mobile telephone service provider VoiceStream, Inc. (*Financial Times,* 2000) is just one example of a foreign investment binge apparently affecting many privatized telecommunications firms. Between 1997 and 1999, privatizing telecoms announced hundreds of foreign investment transactions worth billions of dollars.

Does the privatizing status of these telecommunications enterprises make a difference in foreign investment deals? How does the mix of state- and private-ownership relate to the quality of foreign investment decisions taken by these telecommunications firms? Second, how does increased experience with private-sector owners and institutions relate to the investment decisions of these telecommunications firms? These questions imply a link between lingering state-ownership and the quality of foreign investment decisions, as well as a link between time in the private sector, no matter the lingering ownership role of the state, and the quality of foreign investment decisions. Both issues compel closer examination of a multitude of foreign investment decisions.

This chapter provides some preliminary answers, first by examining in greater depth the conceptual basis for linking these privatization-related factors to the quality of foreign investment decisions taken by privatizing telecoms. Next, we report results from empirical investigation of more than 400 foreign investment decisions announced by 11 privatizing telecoms during the 1997–1999 period. The telecoms we examine include privatizing stalwarts from developed countries: British Telecom, Deutsche Telekom, France Telecom, NTT, Tele-Danmark, Telecom Italia, Spain's Telefonica, and Australia's Telstra. We also include in this investigation less well-known privatizing telecoms from emerging-market countries: SK Telecom, Telmex, and Telecom Argentina. Using an event-study methodology explained in greater detail below, we find that abnormal share-price returns associated with foreign investment announcements by these firms, are positively related both to the extent of a telecom's private (versus lingering state) share ownership, and to the number of years of experience a telecom has in the private sector. These results have important implications for privatizing telecoms and their stakeholders. We conclude by discussing some of these implications and by suggesting practical strategies for managers, investors, and other stakeholders dealing with such trends.

PRIVATIZATION AND FOREIGN INVESTMENT: CONCEPTUAL LINKS

The Concept and Practice of Enterprise Privatization

Both as policy and research subject matters, privatization is a recent phenomenon. Some scholars consider West German Chancellor Konrad Adenauer's "denationalization" program in the early 1960s to be the first large-scale attempt to move state-owned or -controlled assets to the private sector (Megginson and Netter, 1999). More commentators, however, look to British Prime Minister Margaret Thatcher and her privatization program of the 1980s as the first wholesale shift in assets and managerial mind-set from state- to market-oriented control principles. Prominent among the sell-offs in Britain was the 1984 offering of British Telecom, then the largest worldwide initial public offering of shares in history. Thatcher and other leading ideologists in the British Conservative Party, such as Enoch Powell, are credited with first coining and then popularizing the term "privatization," rather than denationalization, to describe their policies (Yergin and Stanislaw, 1998).

The application of privatization policies during the last two decades has enjoyed global scope. Several researchers have chronicled the progress of these policies on a country-by-country basis, including Guislain (1997) and Megginson (1998). In the developed world, French governments in the mid-1980s and again in the mid-1990s privatized more than 30 companies, including such state-controlled icons as automaker Renault and France Telecom. The Japanese experience with privatization since the 1980s saw the largest enterprise sell-off in the world to date when NTT was sold to shareholders in 1987 and 1988. The subsequent spin-off of NTT's cellular division, NTT Do-Co-Mo, in late 1998 instantly created the third largest company in terms of market capitalization on the Nikkei; NTT without Do-Co-Mo remained the largest (Fox et al., 2000). The U.S. experience with privatization in the 1980s also saw a substantial transfer of assets to private hands, although many of these transfers involved assets that were state and local government-owned or -controlled rather than federal government-owned or -controlled (Vernon, 1988). While not a formal privatization, the 1984 break-up of the regulated private telephone giant, AT&T, represented a fundamental change in U.S. telecommunications industry structure, and spurred a wave of new entries in local and long-distance voice, data, and video segments previously thought to be better served by a single dominant supplier. Research on the privatization experience in smaller developed countries such as Belgium (Vincent, 1995), Sweden (Prokopenko, 1995), and New Zealand (Duncan and Bollard, 1992) suggests that the movement from state- to market-oriented principles was no less dramatic.

The privatization phenomenon found its way to emerging-market countries starting in the late 1980s and has been widespread in the last decade. Chile, Argentina, and Mexico embarked on privatization programs earliest in Latin America, and perhaps most ambitiously in terms of the number of enterprises and dollar-value sold (Guislain, 1997; LaPorta and Lopez-de-Silanes, 1997). In Central and Eastern Europe, privatization efforts in the Czech Republic, Hungary, Poland (Borish and Noël, 1996), and Russia (Boycko et al., 1995) have received substantial attention, while policies undertaken in Bulgaria (Due and Schmidt, 1995), Romania (Lhomel, 1993), and countries of the former Soviet Union (Rozenfelds, 1993; Joskow et al., 1994; OECD, 1995) have received less coverage. Megginson (1999) holds that the privatization phenomenon in Sub-Saharan Africa is particularly under-reported, even though research by Kerf and Smith (1996) and others note substantial progress and future potential. Here again we see that early privatization of state-owned telecoms in developing countries has at least two important effects. It deepens local capital markets by providing additional share or voucher market liquidity, and also signals a commitment by the state to carry through future privatizations in other infrastructure industries, such as electricity, transportation, and water (Guislain, 1997).

Stanbury (1994) suggests that emerging-market countries should have led rather than followed industrialized countries in implementing privatization programs in the 1980s and 1990s. Fiscal concerns were more acute in emerging-market countries compared to industrialized countries, and made the burden of maintaining state-owned or -controlled enterprises more onerous. Ramamurti (1992) echoes this point by showing that countries running higher budget deficits, accruing more foreign debt, and experiencing greater productive inefficiency in the administration of state-owned enterprises—a description of many emerging-market countries in the 1980s and 1990s—are more likely to implement privatization policies. Despite their predisposition to embrace privatization policies, emerging-market countries may be stifled in the implementation of such policies because of the absence of key factors, including professional management expertise, capital, or a stable legal and regulatory framework. Research by Galal et al. (1994) highlights the small absolute size of national economies and slower economic growth rates of many developing countries as potentially limiting factors in the successful implementation of state privatization programs. At a minimum, such country-level, industry- (regulatory-) and enterprise-specific contingencies explain varying degrees of success in privatization programs across emerging-market countries in Latin America, Central and Eastern Europe, and elsewhere.

Privatization–Related Organizational Transformation and Performance

Almost as soon as policies were implemented, researchers began to study the performance of privatized enterprises. Early research by Caves and Christenson (1980) in Canada and Yarrow (1986) and Vickers and Yarrow (1988) in the U.K. suggested that privatized enterprises were no more productively efficient than their nationalized counterparts. Later, however, a steady flow of empirical research led by Megginson and his collaborators (Megginson et al., 1994; Megginson, 1998; D'Souza and Megginson, 1999; Megginson and Netter, 1999) established that, for a range of countries and industries, enterprise privatization was associated with superior operating returns, increased employee productivity, and turnover in top-management teams and directorial boards.

Many of these observed changes in enterprise behavior and performance are justified in terms of the realignment of enterprise stakeholder incentives, particularly the incentives of enterprise owners (principals) and enterprise managers (agents) (Jensen and Meckling, 1976; Holmström, 1979). As Hart, Shleifer, and Vishny (1997) point out, private ownership provides strong incentives for managers to innovate new products and markets, but it also entails costs. When managers and directors fail in this regard, wealth-maximizing shareholders can replace them. When shareholders fail to guide these agents toward a wealth-maximizing business strategy, the market for corporate control will lead to a transfer of shares to more vigilant holders willing to pay more. Post-privatization turnover in management and directors, as well as enhanced employee productivity and firm performance are consistent with this principal-agent perspective on enterprise privatization.

Foreign investment by privatizing enterprises reinforces the process of transforming it from state- to private-shareholder orientation. Kogut (1996) suggests that the positive contribution of foreign investment by privatizing enterprises is the result of greater access to more sophisticated individuals and capabilities. Because foreign investment frequently involves a transfer of equity to foreign individuals and institutions, there is an added beneficial effect in the form of better monitoring of enterprise managers. These different factors raise the probability that the enterprise will be able to draw on a broader international menu of organizational practices associated with higher performance.

Foreign investment may undermine the domestic state's role in guiding privatized enterprises, but it gives the new firm a broader portfolio of competencies *outside* the control of the state. Indeed, foreign investment policies undertaken by newly privatized enterprises may even have the principal purpose of simply raising the costs of state interference in enterprise affairs. States may become more hesitant to impose their political agendas on newly privatized enterprises if they anticipate a backlash from the foreign investment community (Guislain, 1997).

This brief review of the privatization literature suggests that performance is likely to improve after a telecom first confronts private shareholders and subsequently is forced to reorient its policies and personnel to serve their interests. Similarly, this process also may be affected by the extent to which the state lingers as an equity holder and thereby induces conflicts with the interests of the telecom's private shareholders. Can we assess the evidence to understand how, if at all, these factors affect the quality of foreign investments undertaken by newly privatized telecoms? The event study methods detailed below facilitate a response to this question.

PRIVATIZATION AND FOREIGN INVESTMENT: EMPIRICAL LINKS

Event Study Methods

Most empirical research on privatization and performance rests on methods that compare the operating returns of private sector and state-owned firms in the same country and industries, or that track the operating performance of firms whose ownership is transferred from state to private ownership (Megginson and Netter, 1999). This approach, however, does not isolate the performance implications of specific actions taken by a privatizing enterprise. Instead, it aggregates across a range of managerial decisions over time to provide a general sense of the privatization impact on organizational performance.

An alternative event study methodology facilitates a different, more fine-grained analysis of specific managerial actions in the newly privatized firm. This methodology is used primarily in the finance field, but increasingly it has been applied to business strategy, accounting, law, organizational behavior, and marketing research questions. The event study method uses share price or asset price changes to assess the performance implications of organizational decision making and to measure investor reactions to various events. These prices are supposed to reflect the true value of firms, because they reflect the discounted value of all future cash flows and incorporate all relevant information (McWilliams and Siegel, 1997).

The viability of event study methodology rests on the efficient market hypothesis, under which the price of a security reflects all available information about the firm's current and future potential cash flows. Any new information or event that affects the firm's potential cash flows results in an instant change in the firm's stock price as soon as the market learns of the event. The degree of change in the stock price reflects the value of the specific information or event to the company. Accounting-based measures of profit, which can be easily manipulated by managers, are not used, making the event study method a popular way to evaluate firm performance (McWilliams and Siegel 1997).

This informational assumption requires some adjustment in the context of newly privatized enterprises, particularly those from developing countries. In developing countries, less well-developed rules related to informational disclosure and diffusion to certain investors suggests a less robust relationship between an event and its impact on firm share and asset prices (Aggarwal and Harper, 2000). Practically speaking, researchers take this into consideration by experimenting with broader "windows" of time associated with an event and its associated share or asset returns.

With this adjustment in mind, the event study method for addressing the questions posed above is relatively straightforward and may be summarized in the five steps listed in table 1.

Table 1.

Steps for Implementing the Event Study

Step 1	Define an event that will have a financial impact, is unanticipated, and provides new information to the share price market.
Step 2	Identify event dates and the firms that experience the event.
Step 3	Outline a theory that justifies a financial response to the new information.
Step 4	Choose an appropriate event window and justify its length.
Step 5	Compute "abnormal" returns during the event window and assess their significance.

Following Steps 1 and 2, we chose to examine foreign investment announcement events during the 1997–1999 period, and assess their impact on the share price returns of 11 telecoms privatized between 1984 and 1997. As we noted earlier, the 11 telecoms came from developed and developing economies located in the Americas, Europe, and Asia. The foreign investment announcements made during the 1997–1999 period ranged from divestitures and cross-border merger and acquisition deals, to international joint venture, alliance, and technology licensing agreements. In all, more than 400 such foreign investment announcements were recorded as events for investigation.

Following Step 3, we drew primarily on principal-agent theory to justify the financial response to new information tied to each foreign investment event. As firms acquired experience in the private sector, we reasoned that managers would improve their ability to choose foreign investment opportunities consistent with the interests of their private shareholders, who, in turn, would reward the telecom managers with share price increases. Similarly, as state equity stakes decreased, we thought that the likelihood of state interference in the decision making of telecom managers would also decrease. Again, this would benefit the private shareholders and bid up the telecom's share price. Table 2 provides information on the privatization experience and extent of state ownership associated with each privatizing telecom included in our study.

The information in table 2 requires two further comments. Telefonica was never entirely government owned, but until late 1989 it was heavily regulated to the point of simulating government ownership. Thus, the date used to represent privatization for Telefonica was October 1989, when changes in Spanish telecommunications regulation substantially broadened managerial and investor discretion. Second, several telecoms in our study had, by the end of 1999, eliminated formal state ownership of enterprise equity. On the other hand, in certain cases the state retained "golden-share" rights, which most often permitted the state to veto a limited number of extraordinary transactions proposed by enterprise management. These rights might be exercised in

Table 2.

Telecom Privatization History

Telecom	Date Telecom Equity First Offered to Private Investors	Percentage of Government-Owned Equity at End of 1997	Percentage of Government-Owned Equity at End of 1998	Percentage of Government-Owned Equity in June 1999
British Telecom	11/26/84	0	0	0
Deutsche Telekom	11/1/96	74	74	74
France Telecom	10/20/97	75	63.6	63.6
NTT	10/1/86	65.48	65.48	59.2
SK Telecom	11/7/89	18.35	18.28	17.86
Tele-Danmark	4/27/94	51	0	0
Telecom Argentina	11/8/90	0	0	0
Telecom Italia	8/1/94	5.17	3.95	3.46
Telefonica	10/2/89	0	0	0
Telmex	12/20/90	0	0	0
Telstra	11/17/97	67.7	67.7	50.1

the event of a merger or sale of substantially all of the enterprise's assets deemed inimical to state interests. For the telecoms in our event study, the golden share rights were limited in scope and never actually exercised. Accordingly, we treated privatizing telecoms with global share provisions alone as having no state equity ownership or control.

Step 4 in the event study methodology requires that we define an event window over which the share price returns associated with a foreign investment event may be measured. Traditionally, researchers in finance would start with rather narrow windows that might include the date of the event itself, as well as the day before and after a foreign investment announcement. We expanded the window from this traditional three-day period to a five-day period—share price returns on the event date itself and over the two days before and after the event date—to take into the consideration the possibility of slower informational diffusion in certain share markets.

Step 5 requires computation and assessment of "abnormal" returns associated with an event. In event studies, abnormal returns are often computed as the difference between the percentage share price change observed for the firm over the event-window period less the percentage change observed over the same period measured by some local share market index. The indices relevant to our 11 privatizing telecoms are listed in table 3.

While popular, this approach is not the only one available to researchers. In using share price indices, we are assuming that the local markets have similar types of listed firms, local currency price fluctuations, and other institutional trading arrangements. This could be problematic, particularly given the inclusion of telecoms from several smaller and less-diversified share market indices from developing economies. Accordingly, we also took an alternative

Table 3.

Local Share Price Indices

Telecom	Country	Local Share Price Index Name
British Telecom	Great Britain	FTSE
Deutsche Telekom	Germany	DAX
France Telecom	France	CAC
NTT	Japan	NIKKEI
SK Telecom	South Korea	KOSPI
Tele-Danmark	Denmark	DS
Telecom Argentina	Argentina	MERVAL
Telecom Italia	Italy	COMIT
Telefonica	Spain	IBEX
Telmex	Mexico	BOLSA
Telstra	Australia	TOTMKAZ

approach to computing abnormal returns. In addition to using local share price changes, we used price changes of so-called American Depositary Receipts (ADRs) issued in U.S. share markets for each of the 11 privatizing telecoms. ADRs allow foreign-based telecoms to access U.S.-based equity investors more easily. For a relevant share market index to go with these ADRs, we created a synthetic index based on changes in the pricing of a market basket of U.S.-based firms in communications and equipment production, broadcast and media, and telephone services industries. This alternative market index was tailored to each of the 11 privatizing telecoms we studied. By using ADRs we controlled for many sources of distortion in share price changes that could be tied to the local share markets where the telecoms were based. By using the synthetic index, we created a measure of "normal" returns, perhaps more closely resembling those of the average telecommunications enterprise rather than the share market in general. Electronic databases provided by Datastream and Bloomberg, as well as information from 1997–1999 annual reports for the telecoms, allowed us to collect the data necessary to compute abnormal returns using both the traditional (local share market prices) and alternative (ADR prices) approaches discussed above.

Assessing the Abnormal Returns of Privatizing Telecoms

We identified 401 foreign investment events to investigate for abnormal returns during the 1997–1999 period. The propositions for investigation were that abnormal share-price returns associated with foreign investment announcements by the 11 privatizing telecoms would be positively related both to the extent of their private share ownership and to the number of years of experience they had as private-sector firms. To assess the evidence related to these propositions, we examined the abnormal returns associated with these foreign investment events in two ways. First, we simply plotted the data and examined it descriptively. Next, we performed several statistical tests using analysis of variance (ANOVA) models.

Descriptive Data Analyses and Results

Charting the share/ADR price data and associated abnormal returns reveals several interesting trends relevant to the two propositions under investigation.

To illustrate this point, we have charted and descriptively analyzed the data for three privatizing telecoms from developed economies—British Telecom, France Telecom, and Tele-Danmark—and one privatizing telecom from a developing economy—Telmex.

British Telecom. The share price (£) and ADR price ($) data for 1996–1999 is charted in figure 1. Not surprisingly, the two measures of equity value in the privatizing telecom move together nearly perfectly. The historically close correlation of U.K. and U.S. equity market prices engender this close correspondence. The steady rise in value over the 1997–1999 period follows a general increase in the value of U.K. and U.S. equity markets.

British Telecom's abnormal returns based on local share price and ADR price changes over five-day event windows for the first quarter of 1997 are charted in figure 2. The chart gives a sense of the types of events that engender marked reactions from shareholders. Foreign investments in Latin America

Figure 1

British Telecom Stock Price and ADR Price 12/31/96 to 6/30/99

Figure 2

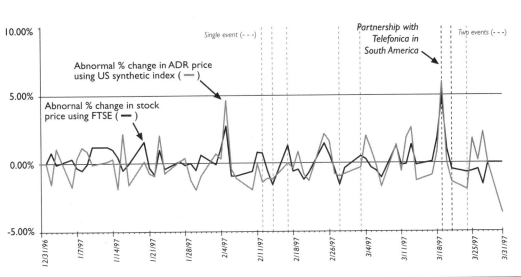

British Telecom Abnormal Returns 12/31/96 to 3/31/97

apparently create significant abnormal returns for British Telecom. For example, the March 19, 1997, announcement of an investment partnership with Spain's Telefonica in Latin America brought returns during the event window in excess of 5 percent higher than the changes in both the local share market (FTSE) and U.S. ADR (synthetic) indices for the same time period.

Another jump in abnormal returns occurs around the July 14, 1997, announcement of a joint venture with a Brazilian telecommunications equipment producer.

France Telecom. Figure 3 illustrates local share and ADR prices for France Telecom equity from the beginning of 1997, when it was privatized, to the end of our study period in 1999. An initial evaluation of France Telecom immediately after shares were first sold to the public on October 21, 1997, shows that the stock price increased at a steady pace for the first 18 months, then leveled off by the end of our study period in mid-1999. Again, as in the case of British Telecom, the local share and ADR price movements exhibit close correlation.

Unlike British Telecom, however, the geographic focus of foreign investment approved by shareholders is Western Europe rather than South America.

Figure 3

France Telecom Stock Price and ADR Price 12/31/96 to 6/30/99

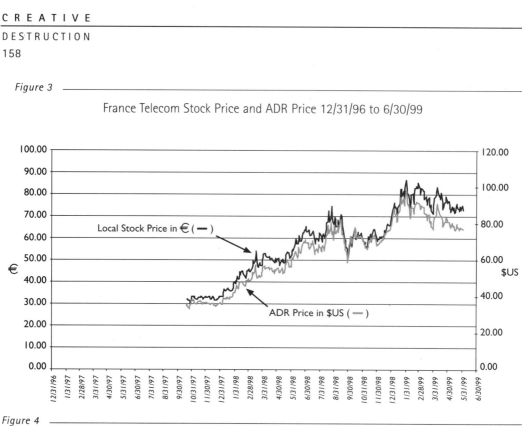

Figure 4

France Telecom Abnormal Returns 4/1/98 to 6/30/98

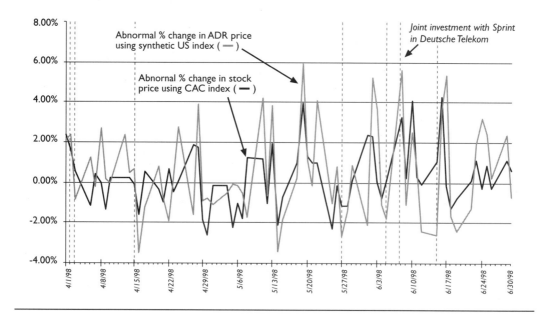

As figure 4 indicates, investments in the Netherlands and Belgium appear to yield positive abnormal returns for France Telecom. The announcement of joint investment projects with Deutsche Telekom also appears to yield positive abnormal returns. Announcement of a strategic alliance with Deutsche Telekom in late October 1997 yields local share and ADR returns 4 percent above their respective index returns. Likewise, the announcement of a joint investment with Deutsche Telekom in U.S.-based Sprint in early June 1998 produces abnormal local share returns of approximately 3 percent and ADR returns of approximately 5 percent. The variance in abnormal returns associated with this event highlights the value of using alternative measures. The greater precision in measurement achieved by using the ADR-based approach suggests that true abnormal returns associated with the Sprint investment probably are closer to 5 percent than 3 percent.

Tele-Danmark. The local share (DK) and ADR ($) prices for Tele-Danmark are given in figure 5. Once again, the two prices correlate closely in movement. They are relatively flat until November 1997, after which they steadily increase until early 1999. Interestingly, the increase in 1998 corresponds to the period when the Danish government sold its remaining 51 percent stake.

Figure 5

Tele-Danmark Stock Price and ADR Price 12/31/96 to 6/30/99

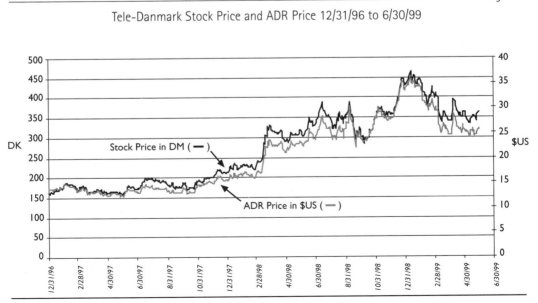

Figure 6 tracks abnormal returns for a portion of 1997 and yields insight on the types of foreign investment decisions attractive to Tele-Danmark investors. The figure shows a dramatic increase in both local share and ADR abnormal returns in the run-up to October 28, 1997, when it was publicly announced that U.S.-based telecom Ameritech would be purchasing 34 percent of Tele-Danmark's equity for $3.2 billion. Again, the ADR-based measure of abnormal returns is higher (13 percent) than the local share-based measure (9 percent), and probably better reflects the actual abnormal returns generated around this event.

Figure 6

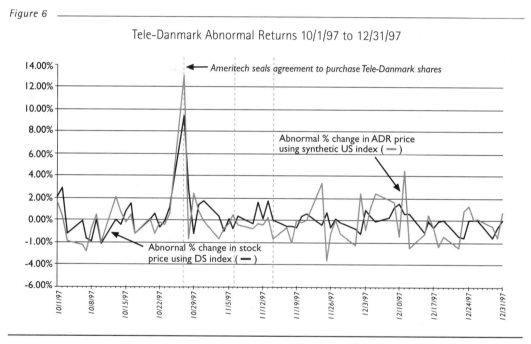

Tele-Danmark Abnormal Returns 10/1/97 to 12/31/97

No other events appear to produce substantial abnormal returns, however they are measured. With the exception of the Ameritech investment, Tele-Danmark foreign investment events appear to produce little response from Tele-Danmark shareholders during this period. Again, this also coincides with a lingering state equity stake of 51 percent.

Telmex. Local share (MP) and ADR ($) prices are given in figure 7. Prices were relatively flat until late 1998 when they began increasing steadily as the company became more active in forging joint ventures and alliances.

Abnormal returns charted in figure 8 give us a sense of shareholder responses to Telmex's more aggressive foreign investment strategy in the first half of 1999. Announcements of joint ventures with U.S.-based local telecommunications service provider SBC yield positive overall abnormal returns during late April 1999. Similar positive abnormal returns follow the announce-

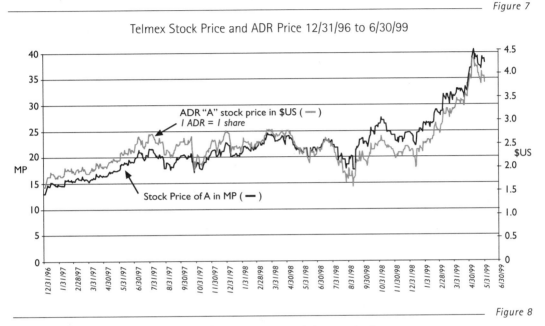

Figure 7

Telmex Stock Price and ADR Price 12/31/96 to 6/30/99

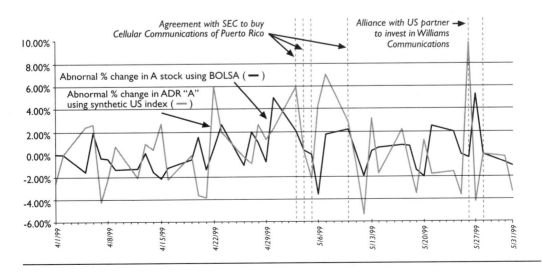

Figure 8

Telmex Abnormal Returns 4/1/99 to 5/31/99

ment of investment agreements with U.S.-based Williams Communications.

These descriptive analyses yield two interesting insights regarding the overall quality of foreign investments undertaken by privatizing telecoms. First, and perhaps foremost, the analyses suggest that cooperative joint venture- or alliance-based foreign investments may be associated with higher positive abnormal returns than foreign investments undertaken by the privatizing telecom on its own. This observation is consistent with Kogut's (1996) point that foreign investment provides access to a broader range of managerial and shareholding competence, especially when the investments involve sophisticated foreign counterparties.

Our descriptive analyses also highlight important differences among the privatizing telecoms and their respective foreign investment patterns. The differences we observed have a geographic dimension. The privatizing telecoms we examined successfully chose foreign investment projects and partners from different regions: British Telecom found favorable shareholder responses to their South American investment decisions; France Telecom found favor in its Western European investments and investors; Telmex garnered positive abnormal returns from investments involving U.S.-based locations and counterparties. We should exercise caution before making final conclusions, but these results suggest the importance of geographic focus and consistency to shareholders in these privatizing telecoms.

Statistical Analyses and Results

While helpful, the descriptive analyses provide no formal tests related to the central propositions linking favorably received foreign investment decisions to a telecom's time in the private sector and the extent of private ownership. To fill this gap, we conducted two such tests using the ADR-based abnormal returns measure and ANOVA models designed to indicate whether differences in average abnormal returns are statistically significant. To perform our first test, we divided the 11 privatizing telecoms into two groups. The first group comprised six telecoms privatized before 1991: British Telecom, NTT, Telefonica, SK Telecom, Telecom Argentina, and Telmex. The second group comprised the remaining five telecoms, all of which were first privatized after 1991: Tele-

Table 4

Private Sector Experience ANOVA Test Results

TELECOM	Date telecom equity first offered to private investors	Average percent abnormal returns (ADR), 1997–1999	Statistically significant difference between groups?
First Group: *Telecoms Privatizing by 1990*			
British Telecom	11/26/84	1.68	Yes, statistically significant at 90 percent (p<.10) level
NTT	10/1/86		
Telefonica	10/2/89		
SK Telecom	11/7/89		
Telecom Argentina	11/8/90		
Telmex	12/20/90		
Second Group: *Telecoms Privatizing after 1990*			
Tele-Danmark	4/27/94	1.08	
Telecom Italia	8/1/94		
Deutsche Telekom	11/1/96		
Telstra	11/17/97		
France Telecom	10/20/97		

Telecoms with more experience in the private sector exhibit higher abnormal returns associated with their foreign investment announcements.

Danmark, Telecom Italia, Deutsche Telekom, Telstra, and France Telecom. As Table 4 shows, average ADR abnormal returns associated with each group differed significantly. The first group of telecoms, with more experience in the private sector, exhibited higher average abnormal returns (1.68 percent) associated with foreign investment events than the second group (1.08 percent). ANOVA model results using the 401 foreign investment events in our sample indicated that differences in abnormal returns between the telecoms in each group were statistically significant at the 90 percent (p<.10) level.

Statistical analyses summarized in table 5 below suggest that private ownership has an even more pronounced impact on the quality of foreign investment decision making by telecoms than privatization experience. Again, we divided the 11 privatizing telecoms into two groups. The first group comprised seven telecoms with majority private ownership at the end of our study period, June 1999: British Telecom, Tele-Danmark, Telefonica, Telecom Argentina, Telmex, Telecom Italia, and SK Telecom. The second group comprised four telecoms with less than 50 percent of their equity in private hands as of June 1999: Telstra, NTT, France Telecom, and Deutsche Telekom. As table 5 indicates, average ADR abnormal returns between the two groups differed signifi-

Table 5.

Private Ownership ANOVA Test Results

TELECOM	Percentage of government-owned equity, June 1999	Average percent abnormal returns (ADR), 1997–1999	Statistically significant difference between groups?
First Group: *Telecoms with Majority Private Ownership*			
British Telecom	0	1.54	Yes, statistically significant at 95 percent (p<.05) level
Tele-Danmark	0		
Telefonica	0		
Telecom Argentina	0		
Telmex	0		
Telecom Italia	3.46		
SK Telecom	17.86		
Second Group: *Telecoms with Minority Private Ownership*			
Telstra	50.1	1.12	
NTT	59.2		
France Telecom	63.6		
Deutsche Telekom	74		

Telecoms with greater private ownership exhibit higher abnormal returns associated with their foreign investment announcements

cantly. The first group of telecoms with majority private ownership exhibited higher average abnormal returns (1.54 percent) associated with foreign investment events compared to the second group (1.12 percent). ANOVA model results using the 401 foreign investment events in our sample indicated that differences in abnormal returns between the telecoms in each group were statistically significant at the 95 percent ($p<.05$) level, which was higher than the level of significance for our previous test.

CONCLUSION

This chapter has demonstrated empirically how shareholder value can be created—and can be destroyed. The results of our analyses support two central propositions regarding the impact of privatization-related factors on the quality of foreign investment decision making. These results have significant strategic and policy implications for research and practice related to telecoms privatization. First, our results indicate that the returns from telecoms privatization are contingent. They do not necessarily materialize the moment telecoms first transfer equity from public (state) to private hands. Privatization is a complex process of institutional transformation, not a discrete financial transaction. Value creation from a shareholder perspective depends on the resolve of the state to press on with successive transfers of ownership and control to domestic and foreign investors. Our results suggest that increases in private ownership lead to small but significant increases in value creation from a shareholder perspective.

The results also suggest that the mere passage of time and the accumulation of experience in the private sectors are important for institutional reorientation and shareholder value creation. Managerial incentives, perspectives, and culture in privatizing telecoms simply do not change easily in the short term. Privatization-related processes may have an evolutionary rather than revolutionary character. Substantial private ownership may speed up these processes by, for example, encouraging faster turnover of key management personnel, and faster shutdown of loss-producing operations. There may be a residual corporate inertia in the privatizing firm, however, that no degree of radical restructuring can overcome. Indeed, moving too quickly to transform the privatizing telecom may lead to substantial management and employee alienation, which in turn could have a negative impact on corporate operations and investment. Organizational stakeholders, including shareholders, managers, and state regulators might benefit from more careful consideration of links between the speed of telecom transformation and the prospects for value creation or destruction.

Our analyses of privatizing telecoms and their efforts to create value in the emerging global Internet economy raise a host of issues for future study. For example, the link between higher abnormal returns for certain privatizing telecoms and their inclination to engage in cooperative foreign investment is a subject requiring further analysis. Further exploration of the link between higher abnormal returns and the propensity of telecoms with more experience in the private sector or higher percentages of private ownership to specialize over time in investments in specific geographic regions may also be suggestive of future industry structures and business strategies. Such follow-on work may provide additional insight on investment strategies helpful to managers seeking competitive advantages for their privatizing firms and greater value creation for their shareholders.

9 THE INTERNET PROTOCOL AND THE CREATIVE DESTRUCTION OF REVENUE

Terrence P. McGarty

The Internet has been a catalyst for the development of an abundant array of new technologies, services, and companies. Firms such as Amazon.com and eBay have created a significant market value generated in part by the ability of the Internet to provide global connectivity in a well-defined and minimalist fashion, using the simplest of networking technologies. But these and other firms have discovered it is much easier to create a business on the Internet, destroying other businesses' revenue streams, than it is to develop a sustainable business model of one's own.

This chapter discusses the architecture and the economics of Internet telephony. How Internet telephony will destroy the business model and revenue stream of traditional telecommunications operators will be highlighted. This author is wagering that a new business model will succeed, after the destruction of prior models. This chapter explains the logic of this bet on the Internet.

The Internet has been evolving into a transaction medium allowing users to purchase certain goods and services, while enabling purveyors of these goods and services to market them. To date, however, the profitability and revenue generated by these approaches have been limited. If the Internet can become a true electronic marketing channel, the normal boundaries of selling may change dramatically, producing significant alterations in the structure of retail selling.

After World War II, construction of highways, suburban developments, and shopping malls resulted in the reduction of urban downtown markets, workforce dislocation, and changes in urban infrastructure. Will Internet retailing create a similar transformation in society, commerce, and industry?

What can the Internet do to become a key element of the economic infrastructure? It must facilitate commerce in the broadest sense, on both a domestic and international basis, and on both commercial and consumer fronts. If the Internet can facilitate trade in goods and services, it may change the current distribution channels, alter the existing barriers to entry, open new markets, and create a new class of competitors.

This chapters first addresses the nature of the Internet protocol, and then considers the security, privacy, and interconnection policy implications of Internet telephony. The strategic alternatives in network architectures and costs of Internet telephony are then considered. The chapter concludes that Internet telephony's creative destruction of revenue promises to create a truly global electronic marketing channel.

As was discussed above, the Internet is a vehicle for facilitating international as well as domestic electronic marketing and distribution channels, thus dramatically altering the means and methods by which people transact. The provision of new electronic media to sell products develops an electronic marketing and distribution channel that has the following characteristics:

Self-segmentation: Consumers may determine for themselves what they want, and control may leave the hands of the purveyor.

Electronic promotion and persuasion: The ability to promote and persuade through traditional advertising and marketing is challenged by having to develop new media interfaces and sensations for product offerings.

Electronic transactions: The ability to perform online real time transactions in a secure fashion.

Displaced selling channels: Sales channels are displaced from the point of sale.

Delayed gratification: Purchasers like to see, feel, and retrieve their purchased goods at the time, place, and point of purchase, but delayed gratification has been shown to have continued acceptance in catalog as well as Amazon.com-type sales channels.

Automation and integration of sales, delivery, and support and service: The customer's ability to order and electronically allow end-to-end delivery may enable a fully integrated process of sales completions, such as is being attempted in Internet auto sales.

In all of these areas, the role of Internet telephony is of increasing significance. Customers and shoppers can talk in real-time to sales clerks while browsing through the products offered at an online store; by clicking on an ad, a casual browser may enter into a transaction; and so on. For all of this to occur, however, reliable, high-quality ways of maintaining an Internet telephony connection must be established. This is the subject to which we now turn our attention.

INTERNET PROTOCOLS

The essence of the Internet is the set of protocols that allows network access by a wide variety of host computers in a complex and fully distributed fashion. The protocols are at the heart of the Internet's success; they are the software and system agreements that allow the disparate machines and software to communicate across equally disparate networks. The current protocols focus on data transactions, with some innovations allowing images and limited voice and video. The future challenge will be the development of new protocols to allow low-end user access to grow while at the same time enriching the capability of the information transferred.

The key underlying protocol structure that makes the Internet function is TCP/IP (transport control protocol/Internet protocol. This protocol allows for easy flow of data from one user to another by agreements at various levels of the network to handle, process, manage, and control the underlying data packets. Protocols such as TCP/IP will remain at the heart of the evolution of the Internet. We will focus later on such protocols as applied to multimedia and new access methods. But one can best understand the protocol evolution of the Internet by looking more closely at TCP/IP. To quote Cerf:

> IP (the Internet Protocol) provides for the carriage of datagrams from source hosts to destination hosts, possibly passing through one or more routers and networks in the process. A datagram is a finite length packet of bits containing a header and a payload. . . . Both hosts and routers in an Internet are involved in processing the IP headers. The hosts must create them . . . and the routers must examine them for the purpose of making routing decisions, and modify them as the IP packets make their way from the source to the destination.

TCP is a protocol designed . . . to provide its clients at a higher layer of protocol a reliable, sequenced, flow controlled end to end . . .[1]

The rationale for many TCP mechanisms can be understood through the following observations:

1. TCP operates above IP and IP provides only best efforts datagram transmission service.
2. End to end recovery . . . leads to sequencing.
3. Flow control requires that both ends uniquely agree.
4. In a concatenation . . . it is possible for a packet to circulate.
5. Termination . . . should be graceful.
6. Every process should be able to engage in multiple conversations.
7. . . . the arrival of information should contain no semantic differences."[2]

TCP/IP protocols have emerged as the standard network interface to the Internet that allows users not only to send messages from one point to another in a reliable form but also to embody in those messages certain characteristics that make them more than just a collection of bits. These architectural and system requirements must be clearly and carefully considered for each new dimension of expansion of the Internet. IP gets the packet across the network, and TCP brings the underlying nature of the packet stream into context as a reconstituted entity. Before we consider how the Internet can be used to provide a near-infinite variety of voice services, we must consider a critical stumbling block to this vision—that is, the inherent insecurity and vulnerability of IP-based communications systems, and what can be done to lessen these risks.

VULNERABILITY OF THE INTERNET

In this section, we consider the types of security threats that are present as the Internet is increasingly relied upon for critical services, such as Internet telephony and e-commerce.

The Internet, as an open network, is vulnerable to electronic attack. It is imperative to determine how best to protect and safeguard users. There are multiple levels of attack to the Internet from two major directions: type of attack and point of attack. Some examples are provided below.

Type of Attack

Active Attack: The active attack is one wherein the adversary intends to inflict direct and measurable harm to a point or set of points in the Internet. The adversary may be covert or overt in approach.

Passive Monitoring: In this approach, the adversary quietly monitors access points for data, transactions, trends, and so on

Active Monitoring: An electronic adversary may actively monitor a transaction point in a network and use the network for their own purposes. Such use may not threaten other users, but it takes advantage of the network assets.

Covert Usage: A covert adversary may use the network assets for covert transactions or simply for transmissions.

Points of Attack

End-Point Attack: This is an attack on an end point of the network such as a router or processor. It may be a covert or overt attack on the system operations software or process control system.

Transmission Attack: This is an attack on the transmission path by causing loss of packets, loss of control, or diversion of packets.

Switching (Router) Attack: This is an indirect attack on the switching. It may result in a duplication or diversion of traffic or packets.

Silent or Embedded Attack: This is the "sleeper" approach, wherein an event may trigger the destruction of resources or interference with available resources.

Technological Imperatives

Given these types of threats, there are several technological imperatives that must be considered by operators and users of Internet telephony networks:

- Router access control
- Access identification and validation
- Authentication schemes
- Monitoring of passive attackers
- Advanced firewalling of intermediate nodes

Policy Issues

Finally, several policy issues in IP network security are as follows:

Government control of networks when they may be under attack. What are the government's rights to "protect" the networks. Does the Department of Defense have a right to demand that network providers "work" with them or other government agencies and add costs to networks to meet government standards for attack protection.

Standards for protection from attack. Who sets them, who pays, and what enforcement rules apply?

Protocols. If an attack takes place, who takes control? Who monitors the networks for overt or covert attack? What are the implications of government surveillance of private communications? At what point does the government have a right to take over control of any network or network element?

Privacy

In addition to the security issues briefly outlined above, Internet telephony carriers and their customers must be concerned with the privacy implications of the new network architecture discussed in subsequent sections of this chapter. Privacy has two embodiments—privacy of action and privacy of identity. Privacy of action means that an individual has the ability to perform certain actions that are deemed personal and private without the intervention of the government. Privacy of identity means that the individual should be able to keep private personal information and that access to it may not be mandated by any governmental authority without just cause.

Currently, there are both advocates and foes of special privacy legislation for online commerce. The European Union has passed a privacy directive that requires that consumers receive "disclosure statements" on how personal information will be used and be given the option of preventing companies from sharing information about them. Further, any company doing business in the European Union is prohibited from sending information to countries that do not meet a threshold of protection. The United States is one of the nations that does not meet the European standard.

The new European requirement for disclosure statements and customer consent is an "opt-in" policy. In an "opt-out" policy , the customer is informed of the intent to collect data and the purpose to which the data is used, but the data is collected unless the customer objects and expressly instructs the company not to do so. The United States so far is favoring a voluntary industry self-policing approach and is more disposed to an opt-out policy.

The European directive also requires companies to give people access to information about themselves, which is not always practical. For example, a company may purchase or collect data for a specific purpose (e.g., a direct mail solicitation) and not retain the data. The United States may be less inclined to grant such unconditional access to information.

Under European law, each member nation is required to implement the directive by enacting its own law. Six nations have drafted or passed such laws so far. It is not clear that all European nations will actually pass the regulations or institute such a policy. In the short term, government and industry officials predict that nothing much will happen. Most countries have yet to implement their own laws to carry out the directive. Also, several countries, including Germany, have had tough laws in place for years, and companies have found ways to deal with the requirement. For example, in 1995 Citibank was challenged but successfully demonstrated to German government officials that its system protected data in the United States, and it has since operated without conflicts.

If sufficient services are available with adequate privacy assurances, and no grievous, well-publicized privacy violations occur, the need for and nature of additional privacy regulation for Internet, over and above already existing consumer protection laws and regulations, are likely to remain cloudy and uncertain.

One type of information disclosure involves the identity of the originator of a message. Notions of privacy suggest to some that there should be a right of anonymity, and anonymity may be particularly important for some types of political speech. But any such right must be balanced with the right to not interact with anonymous parties. For example, if spammers were uniquely identifiable as such, TCP transactions downloading SPAM could abort early, definitively ending SPAM as an issue. Additionally, implementing reliable business transactions with the ability to resolve disputes and meet government regulations (such as taxation and money-laundering reporting) often conflict with the desire for anonymity.

IP ARCHITECTURES

Internet Telephony Strategic Alternatives

This section discusses several IP telecommunications architectures. There are three alternatives that are currently understood and being offered: the clear channel network approach, wherein a dedicated circuit is used; the Internet backbone approach using the current Internet transport mechanism; and an IP backbone, providing a QOS (quality of service) type of IP transport at a price point that can be matched to customer expectations.

Given the architectures that may be made available to the IP telecommunications community, there are four possible extremes, depending on the interface—clear channel or IP backbone—and the fee structure—fixed fee per unit access or fee per transaction (bps, packet, minute, etc.). The first approach is standard Internet telephony using an IP interface but charging a fixed fee per Internet access to an ISP, say $9.95 per month. An alternative approach uses an IP interface but charges on a per transaction basis. In a third approach, companies such as Level 3, Qwest, Zephyr, and others use dedicated clear channel circuits. The interface is at the clear channel basis, namely bit per second, and they do the IP processing on their own network equipment.

Perhaps the most important question in the IP service approach is who will take responsibility for defining common interfaces and standards. No one technological interface or standard dominates, and the field of IP service approaches is as varied as it is entrepreneurial. But this also means that proprietary IP service networks have difficulty linking to one another. A network with one or two IP service approaches would address this difficulty, but it is not likely because of significant regulatory and political hurdles. IP service providers need to work out a

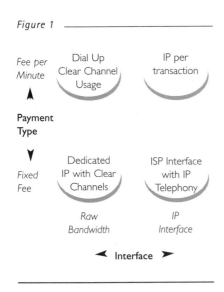

Figure 1

common approach to IP interfaces and standards and then have to persuade hardware and software suppliers, regulators, and other industry stakeholders.

An alternative to this bottom-up approach might be top-down standards setting. An appropriate private player or regulator could go forward on its own to establish standards based on its best guess about the future of IP service. Imagine a private player following an IBM-like strategy of prereleasing its IP service approach on a broad scale in an effort to preempt releases by competitors and move a critical mass of customers to its standard. While possible, this scenario is not likely with IP: There are still several alternative networks that dissident providers and customers can use; there is an increasing availability of bandwidth to support these IP networks; and there are new customers to lock-in to alternative IP service standards around the world. In short, a standards-setting gambit by a private player would be difficult to bring off successfully.

What is the possibility of public regulators going forward with standards before obtaining a consensus among IP service providers? WTO agreements along with national regulatory approaches in the United States and elsewhere are designed to encourage competitive entry in the IP community, not curtail it by forcing entrants to adhere to a single interface. The last thing the IP community probably wants is a third party—public or private—telling it how to build the future network. Neither bottom-up and top-down approaches are likely to emerge in the short-run. Instead, we are likely to see a continuation of proprietary IP service approaches.

THE IP FOOD CHAIN

The provision of telecommunications services via IP consists of several elements. At one end is raw bandwidth that is installed in the ground, under the water, or in the skies above. The next step is leased bandwidth. Then there is the access to a TCP/IP backbone which may be obtained by accessing the Internet. Next there is the provision of voice carriage. Finally, there is the customer or end user. Figure 2 below presents multiple IP players and where they play within this segmented space, also referred to here as the IP food chain.

Figure 2 depicts the disaggregation of the telecommunications industry. Technology and industry have developed in such a fashion that it is possible to effect all elements of a IP-based telecommunications business in a virtual form

Figure 2

The IP Food Chain

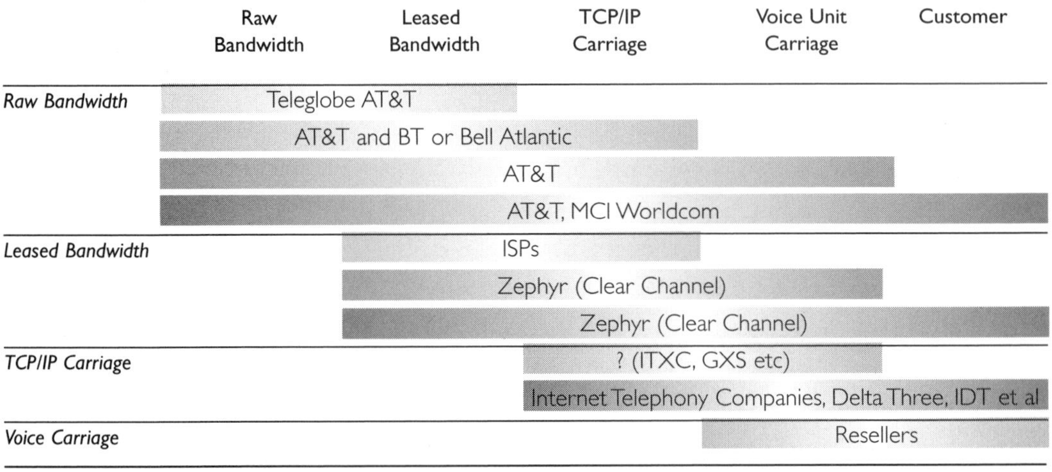

	Raw Bandwidth	Leased Bandwidth	TCP/IP Carriage	Voice Unit Carriage	Customer
Raw Bandwidth	Teleglobe AT&T				
	AT&T and BT or Bell Atlantic				
	AT&T				
	AT&T, MCI Worldcom				
Leased Bandwidth		ISPs			
		Zephyr (Clear Channel)			
		Zephyr (Clear Channel)			
TCP/IP Carriage			? (ITXC, GXS etc)		
			Internet Telephony Companies, Delta Three, IDT et al		
Voice Carriage				Resellers	

by obtaining all functions necessary to deliver a service by purchasing them from third parties, each of whom has similar customers and thus each of whom can deliver their element of the functionality for a minimal marginal cost. In many technologically intense service businesses, thanks to IP's potential as a force for creative destruction, a virtual company can exist wherein all the functions can be purchased from third parties.

INTEGRATION WITH THE TELCO NETWORKS

The standard international telephone connection is shown in figure 3. The local exchange carrier (LEC) customer goes through their local switch, which in turn has access to the signalling data base and system. This then connects to the IXC access tandem switch and then via an international set of circuits possibly to an international gateway switch(s) and then to the access tandem switch and finally to the local switch which has its own signalling system (typically referred to as SS7 or C7), which must convert from one to the other via the gateway switch.

The next variant is with the use of an IP carrier. For example, a dedicated backbone IP network or a shared IP backbone network could be utilized.

The shared is what we typically call the open Internet, whereas the dedicated is the closed user-group Internet, sometimes called an Intranet.

The IP carrier, however, is further characterized by certain elements as illustrated in figure 4, showing the first variant mentioned—that is, the use of leased or owned circuits to create a dedicated IP backbone network.

Figure 4 depicts the routers, the clear channel backbone network, as well as any IP gateways. We also depict a PBX or switch for interconnect to the LEC or PTT, which may or may not be necessary.

An alternative approach is the intermediary services broker. Firms such as ITXC, iBasis, and GXC have taken this approach, assuming the following:

- There are many "naive" and unconnected ISPs that need a clearing house or middleman to effect their transactions.

- Currency transactions and settlements can be done by a multiplicity of third parties.

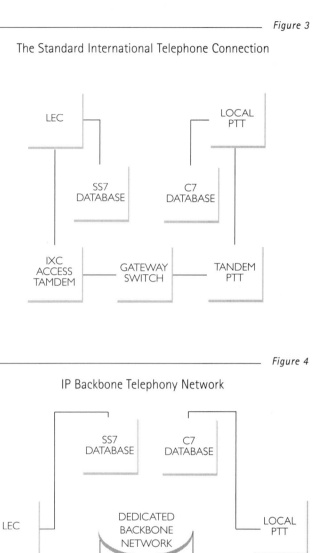

Figure 3

The Standard International Telephone Connection

Figure 4

IP Backbone Telephony Network

• Third-party billing, network management, and infrastructure provisioning can and must be established.

INDUSTRY PLAYERS AND ECONOMICS

Table 1 at right presents the key IP and IP-like competition and contrasts their
approaches, strengths, and weaknesses, seen from the vantage point of the year
2000. Which ones will survive the destruction of revenue for traditional
telecommunications services caused in part by the emergence of Internet telephony? Table 1 presents this author's assessment.

The growth of IP telecommunications companies is expected to be significant. There may be significant changes as each of these carriers evolve and
mature, not to mention the effects of potential mergers that may enable consolidated IP-based carriers to grow more aggressively.

IP economics is the driving factor for its rapid acceptance. The following
two sections present a simple analyses for ILD (international long distance)
and CLECs (competitive local exchange carriers), respectively.

ILD Economics

Table 2 below is an analysis of break-even and full-capacity services using a
dedicated network for ILD using IP. The first analysis is a comparison for a
sub-rate E1 and the second for a dedicated E1 circuit. First, the Polish case is
presented and then the case of Russia.

In the following analysis for Russia, table 3, the margins and breakeven are
better in all cases.

CLEC Economics

The basic economics of the CLEC business are as follows:

• The provider focuses on residential and small or medium-size business customers who are in a ring around a major market.

• The provider will through its own switch offer class and custom calling services as well as basic calling features at a price point that is 10 percent to 20
percent lower than the ILEC (incumbent local exchange carrier) rates. Thus,
a customer using $30 per month in current calling will pay $24 per month.

Table 1

Competitor	Approach	Strength	Weakness
AlphaNet	Start with Fax and become Canadian IRC	Strong regional position	Limited technical expertise
ATT	Global Player	Everything	Few other than inertia and size.
Delta Three/RSL	An Internet player with RSL backing.	Strong financial position	Limited technology, limited technical expertise, and risky business strategy of contracts. Uses Internet as transport.
Esprit	Major player now merged with GTS	See GTS	See GTS
GTS	Dominant European player with many assets in play.	Great position as carrier. Good ops and marketing.	No IP experience and management dominated by old-time telco types.
GXC	A group attempting to be a broker in IP telephony. Focus is in creating a clearinghouse.	Some funds and contacts with international ISPs.	No telecom or significant international experience and no infrastructure.
IDT	An aggressive telecom reseller.	Great sales and great motivation. Experience in telecom.	No significant experienced staff for international.
ITXC	A group from Microsoft with no telecom experience trying to be a clearinghouse.	Have raised about $10 million and have no revenue.	No telecom capability and no international capability. Devoid of significant IP experience.
OzMail	Australian player with IP experience.	Great execution and coverage.	Limited international exposure and company ownership problems.
Primus	Well-financed international carrier.	Good presence and telecom capability.	Limited IP competence and focusing on selling capacity.
Star Telecom	Global telecom carrier.	Good network experience and presence.	Limited IP experience.
StarTec	Ethnic reseller.	Good sales and some telecom capabilities. Well motivated.	Limited IP and international operations experience.
iBasis	A small start-up; they are software people with money raised successfully.	Financing and network performance monitoring.	Limited experience internationally or in telecom. Uses Internet as backbone network.
Zephyr Telecommunications	A start-up telecommunications company focusing on international and some local domestic CLEC opportunities.	Small but growing international presence.	Strong IP capabilities with first dedicated channel services started in 1996.

Table 2

IP-Based International Long Distance: The Polish Case

	Breakeven Sub-Rate	Fully Loaded Sub-Rate	Breakeven EI	Fully Loaded EI
Circuit Capacity MOU/Month	960,000	960,000	4,800,000	4,800,000
Capacity %	**45%**	**95%**	**15%**	**88%**
Minutes of Use/Month	431,175	912,000	730,425	4,200,000
Revenue	$75,456	$159,600	$127,824	$735,000
COS:				
International circuits	$29,075	$29,075	$55,000	$55,000
Foreign termination	$32,338	$68,400	$54,782	$315,000
Foreign local EIs	$2,000	$6,000	$6,000	$8,000
Gross Margin	$12,043	$56,125	$12,043	$357,000
GM %	**16%**	**35%**	**9%**	**49%**
Allocation:				
Salaries	$7,084	$7,084	$7,084	$7,084
Operating expenses	$4,959	$4,959	$4,959	$4,959
Net Operating Income	$0	$44,083	$0	$344,958
NOI %	**0%**	**28%**	**0%**	**47%**

Table 3

IP-Based International Long Distance: The Russian Case

	Sub-rate Breakeven	Fully Loaded	Fully Breakeven EI	Loaded EI
Circuit Capacity MOU/Month	640,000	640,000	4,800,000	4,800,000
Capacity %	**49%**	**94%**	**11%**	**88%**
Minutes of Use/Month	310,750	600,000	514,200	4,200,000
Revenue	$40,398	$78,000	$89,985	$735,000
COS:				
International circuits	$22,500	$22,500	$65,000	$65,000
Foreign termination	$7,769	$15,000	$12,855	$105,000
Foreign local EIs	$2,000	$4,000	$4,000	$8,000
Gross Margin	$8,129	$36,500	$8,130	$557,000
GM %	**20%**	**47%**	**9%**	**76%**
Allocation:				
Salaries	$4,781	$4,781	$4,781	$4,781
Operating expenses	$3,347	$3,347	$3,347	$3,347
Net Operating Income	$0	$28,372	$2	$548,872
NOI %	**0%**	**36%**	**0%**	**75%**

• The provider will bundle long distance and other services.

• The provider will sell services, typically at 20 percent less than current rates averaging $3.00 per month, thus adding another $7.20 per month on the average bill resulting in a $31.20 per month per residential services. The provider also provides its own voice mail platform for both the reseller and facilities-based elements of the business.

• The provider will pay on a per access line basis $9 per month per access line to the ILEC. It is assumed that there are 1,200 minutes per month per access line so that this is approximately $0.0100 per minute.

• The provider will target central offices, such that the provider will connect a T1 carrier from the targeted CO to its switch. The T1 will cost $325 per month. Assuming a 50 percent loading, and an Erlang load of 10 percent per customer per month, this means that a T1 can handle 120 customers per month, or approximately $3.00 per month per customer. Greater loading is possible and that will reduce the cost. This is approximately $0.0025 per minute.

• The provider's switch is leased at approximately $8,000 per month. The switch can handle 10,000 access lines at that rate. That is $0.80 per access line per month or $0.0070 per minute per access line. At 50 percent loading, this is $1.60 per access line or $0.0140 per minute.

• The sales costs are approximately 15 percent of the gross revenue. This is $5.00 per month per access line or approximately $0.0020 per minute.

• The operations costs are the combined leased costs of the operations support systems of $0.080 per access line or $0.0070 per minute. In addition, the billing is $2.40 per bill per month per access line or $0.0020 per minute.

The net margin is shown below. Assuming no additional revenue from other services, this is a 10 percent net margin on a 20 percent discount. If the discount is less than 20 percent then the difference basically goes to the bottom line. The following table depicts the differences between the pure reseller market and the facilities-based market.

The facilities-based market is shown as described above. In the reseller approach, however, the rate reduction is 5 percent rather than 20 percent, the dominant costs factor is the cost of service, which is 81 percent of the gross ILEC revenue, and billing and operations still must be dealt with as fixed costs.

Table 4

CLEC Margins

Element	FACILITIES BASED			RESELLER		
	Per Access Line	Per Minute	Percent	Per Access Line	Per Minute	Percent
ILEC Revenue	$39.00	$0.0325	125.00%	$39.00	$0.0325	105.26%
Revenue	$31.20	$0.0260	100.00%	$37.05	$0.0309	100.00%
Local Loop	$12.00	$0.0100	38.46%	$0.00	$0.0000	0.00%
Transport	$4.00	$0.0033	12.82%	$0.00	$0.0000	0.00%
Switch	$1.60	$0.0013	5.13%	$0.00	$0.0000	0.00%
Operations Support	$0.80	$0.0007	2.56%	$0.80	$0.0007	2.16%
Billing	$2.40	$0.0020	7.69%	$2.40	$0.0020	6.48%
Service	$0.00	$0.0000	0.00%	$31.59	$0.0263	85.26%
Net Operating Expense	$20.80	$0.0173	66.67%	$34.79	$0.0290	93.90%
Gross Margin	$10.40	$0.0087	33.33%	$2.26	$0.0019	6.10%
Cost of Sales	$6.24	$0.0052	20.00%	$7.41	$0.0062	20.00%
G&A	$2.40	$0.0020	7.69%	$2.40	$0.0020	6.48%
Net Expenses	$29.44	$0.0245	94.36%	$44.60	$0.0372	120.38%
Net Margin	$1.76	$0.0015	5.64%	($7.55)	($0.0063)	-20.38%

We can now do the same analysis for a comparison of three options: a fiber-based system using a dedicated fiber to a co-location chamber in a central office; a concentrator using a RSM (remote switch module) and a concentrated leased T1 one; and finally the IP-based solution. We do this analysis for both the local service as well as the long-distance service. The final measure for comparison is the effective cost per minute.

The bottom line is as follows:

Fiber-Based System: This has a local cost per minute of $0.0233 and a long distance (LD) cost of $0.1087. We have used 5 percent loading for local and 20 percent loading for LD.

RSM-Based Design: This assumes that the remote switch module (RSM) has a local switch module in the co-location site and uses 10:1 concentration. The local cost is $0.0009 and the LD is $0.0078. This is a dramatic difference. It says that putting a concentrator reduces the costs about 10:1 for the local as expected and much more so for the LD costs.

Table 5

Cost Advantage of IP-Based Telephony

Cost Element	LOCAL SERVICE			LD SERVICE		
	Fiber Based	RSM Based	IP Based	Fiber Based	RSM Based	IP Based
Co-Location Space Lease per Month	$500	$500	$500	$500	$500	$500
Fiber Cost per Mile	$150,000	$150,000	$150,000	$150,000	$150,000	$150,000
Miles to CO	4	0	75			
Fiber Cost	$600,000	$0	$0	$11,250,000	$0	$0
Fiber Cost per Month	$12,000	$0	$0	$225,000	$0	$0
Number Effective TIs per Fiber	$360	$360	$360	$360	$360	$360
Effective Fiber Loading	5%	5%	5%	20%	20%	20%
Monthly Fiber TI Costs	$667	$0	$0	$3,125	$0	$0
Switch Line Card Cost/Line	$150	$150	$150	$150	$150	$150
RSM Cost per Line	$50	$50	$50	$50		
Lease Rate Line Card per Month	$3	$4	$4	$3	$4	$4
Mux Costs per TI Bank	$125	$125	$125	$125	$125	$125
Mux Cost per Month	$3	$3	$3	$3	$3	$3
TI Costs per Month	$250	$250	$2,250	$2,250		
IPN Capital Costs per TI Unit	$0	$20,000	$20,000			
Monthly IPN Costs	$0	$0	$400	$0	$0	$400
RSM Concentration Ratio	1	10	10	1	10	10
IPN Compression Ratio	1	1	8	1	1	8
Number of AL per TI	1	10	80	1	10	80
Total Costs per Month per TI	$672	$257	$657	$3,131	$2,257	$2,657
Number of Minutes per AL per Month	1,200	1,200	1,200	1,200	1,200	1,200
Total Minutes per Month per TI	28,800	288,000	2,304,000	28,800	288,000	2,304,000
Effective Cost per Minute	$0.0233	$0.0009	$0.0003	$0.1087	$0.0078	$0.0012

IP-Based: This is the most efficient option. It has the lowest local costs and
low, almost inconsequential costs for long distance.

The conclusion to be drawn is that IP telephony will drive all costs down to
a minimal costs base. This is why AT&T has recently announced the elimina-

tion of circuit switches in their domestic network. IP will change dramatically the costs of service and will drive usage up and drive costs down.

PRINCIPLE OF COST-BASED PRICING: ACCESS AND INTERCONNECTION

The interconnection issue is a major factor in the deployment of any telecommunications system under the domain of the 1996 Telecommunications Act, which provides a significantly changed platform for new entrants. This section provides an analysis of the interconnect problem from the CLEC's facilities to the ILEC (incumbent local exchange carrier). The interconnect issue for a wireless carrier falls into two categories: intra-plant and inter-plant. The intra-plant interconnect is between cell sites and the carrier's own switch, and the inter-plant interconnect is between the carrier's switching facilities and the ILEC's facilities. Interconnection is the physical process of connecting two discretely owned telecommunications facilities. Access is the process of compensating any carrier involved in the interconnection process. The nature of this is shown in figure 5 below.

The figure depicts three issues. First, the intra-plant facilities are generally

Figure 5

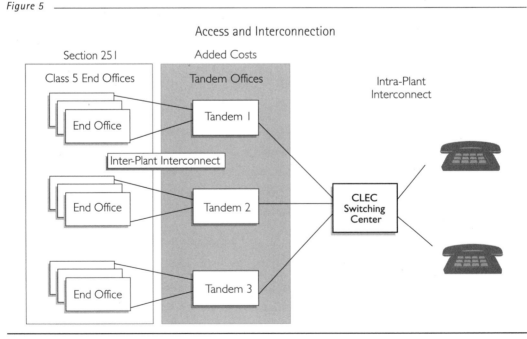

Access and Interconnection

under the total control of the carrier. Second, the end office ILEC interconnect is clearly under the control of the Section 251 reciprocal compensation rule in the United States. Third, the real problem is how to get from a single switching center, to several access tandems, and ultimately to dozens of end offices. Any new carrier must be aware of these options before they interconnect, because these interconnection options present significant fixed costs to the carrier and there may be ways to move these monthly fixed costs into some variable form or to move them into a form of carrier-owned facilities.

A CLEC is a non-incumbent LEC. An incumbent LEC is generally a RBOC. A LEC is defined by the 1996 Telecommunications Act as follows:

> The term "local exchange carrier" means any person that is engaged in the provision of telephone exchange service or exchange access. Such term does not include a person insofar as such person is engaged in the provision of a commercial mobile service under section 332(c), except to the extent that the Commission finds that such service should be included in the definition of such term.

The definitions of exchange access services and telephone exchange services are as follows:

> As per the Act, Sec.3(b)(2), the term Exchange Access means the offering of access to telephone exchange services or facilities for the purpose of the origination or termination of telephone toll services.

and,

> Telephone Exchange Service as defined in 47 U.S.C. Sec. 153 (r) means service within a telephone exchange or within a connected system of telephone exchanges within the same exchange area operated to furnish to subscribers intercommunicating service of the character ordinarily furnished by a single exchange, and which is covered by the exchange service charge.

Exchange services is generally the provision of toll telephone services, whereas telephone exchange services is local services directly to the end user or customer.

Rates for interconnection have been established by the FCC, but as of mid-1999 were still under judicial review. Even so, many of the RBOCs have entered into interconnect agreements or are currently negotiating them based on these proposed rules.

The proposed rules relate primarily to local termination traffic, which is defined as follows:

> Local Telecommunications Traffic means: (1) telecommunications traffic between a LEC and a telecommunications carrier other than a CLEC provider that originates and terminates within a local service area established by the state commission; or (2) telecommunications traffic between a LEC and a CLEC provider that, at the beginning of the call, originates and terminates within the same Major Trading Area.

An Analogy

To understand the issues involved in intercarrier interconnection, we start with the principle of cost-based pricing:

The consumer of a service should pay for each element or link of service provided and purchasable separately and they should pay only for those links for which they are customers of that link provider. The payment the customer makes should reflect a price that is in turn based on the costs of only that link. There expressly should not be any element of a link price that reflects an externality that results from interconnection, interface, or similar inter-operability.

We now can apply the principle of cost-based pricing to the case of ILEC interconnection. This principle will be a key element in the pricing of access and interconnection and can be understood by the following analogy:

Consider the case of two towns separated by a river. A single company, River Transport and Travel, known at RT&T, owned docks on each side of the river and the boat that crossed between them. RT&T rented out space on the docks, which was deemed in the public good, and charged a premium to rich people of the towns for the boat crossing. That premium was used to subsidize the local docks and provide free Sunday entertainment.

After many years RT&T became so large that the governments of the two towns decided to break it apart. They let RT&T keep the boats but insisted that a new company, New Crossing Inc. (NCI), be allowed to operate a boat system in competition with RT&T. The governments then split the two docks into regional docks, called RDOCs. The RDOCs said they must charge for the Sunday entertainment unless they received a fee from the inter-crossing carriers, called the IXCs. To keep the people happy, the governments established a fee, called the access fee, that the RDOCs charged the IXCs for the "right to access" the docks. This fee was used to support the local services and to allow anyone to come to the free Sunday concerts. This was called Universal Service.

The RDOCs argued that owning a dock was a natural monopoly and that only one such dock operator could be in existence to provide services. They argued that because the docks were made of hand-cut stone and there were so few stonecutters, the law of economy of scale demanded a single monopoly. About a year after this breakup, however, a young inventor came up with the idea of using plastics and cement instead of stone. Now anyone could build a dock, and the costs of entry were small. After ten more years, the governments agreed to allow other competitive dock providers, called CDOCs, to enter the business. The RDOCs argued, however, that all players now had a duty to support the free Sunday concerts, and the governments agreed. They forced the CDOCs and the IXCs to pay the RDOCs for this service.

After several years, the CDOCs banded together and said they should be able to charge their customers a fee that represented a fair market price for the dock service, and that if people wanted to go to the concerts, then they would have to pay a concert fee. In fact, very few people wanted to go the concerts now, because the band was playing John Phillip Sousa music and most people liked heavy metal bands better. The CDOCs after much litigation were allowed to charge a fee based on the free market, the IXCs were allowed to pay a fee based on what the free market allowed and the CDOCs and IXCs prospered. The two towns then had great growth.

Then a new inventor came up with the idea of a bridge. It was called the intertown network—Internet for short—and went across the river without using the boats. Anyone could now cross without delay, and the capacity of the bridge was much greater than the boats. The governments were very confused. The knew that their role was to regulate, and they had regulated the boat and dock businesses very well. Almost immediately they moved to regulate the bridge business in the same way.

But in a small room, another inventor was developing something she called wings . . .

This little story illustrates the elements of regulation, new technologies, and access fees. The issue is that interconnection should where possible be open and "free"—the costs carried by the end user in some express fashion, and alternatives available based on a free open market.

CONCLUSIONS

Three observations can be made regarding Internet telephony:

• There is a convergence of networks that allows for any one network to be integrated with any other network.

• The use of IP and the ability to integrate with existing networks allows for the full global integration of multimedia, voice, data and other similar services-based telecommunications facilities. It pushes the intelligence to the edge of the network and establishes a minimalist approach to network design and execution.

• This creates an openness of networks and markets allowing for inter-border and inter-country exchanges, facilitating a global electronic marketing and distribution channel.

The IP-based system creates a true open market that is essentially borderless and allows for the growth of new electronic marketing channels. This means the ways of viewing transactions and even tariffs changes dramatically. The issues then become where and in what country does the transaction occur, whose taxes, whose laws, and what consumer protections are in place?

The disaggregation of services and systems lowers a barrier to entry and dramatically expands the Internet market for new entrants. The lower barrier to entry for new entrants means increased short-term efficiencies that may become reflected in long-term price reductions and the introduction of new services, products, and communications. The creative destruction of the revenue base of incumbent telecommunications firms, then, promises many new benefits and new services for users.

PART5

CREATIVE BUSINESS
SURVIVAL STRATEGIES

10 A NEW THEORY OF THE INTERNET FIRM

William Lehr

The Internet industry is undergoing rapid change as a consequence of telecommunications deregulation, growth in the demand for and supply of IP-based services and products, and the need and desire to provide integrated voice, video, and data services on a single network platform. Currently, the public Internet runs on infrastructure that is owned by a combination of Internet service providers (ISPs) and traditional telephone companies. In North America, there are more than 7,000 ISPs, ranging in size from small "mom and pop" operations that provide basic Internet access services to large international backbone providers (*Boardwatch Magazine, 2000 Directory of Internet Service Providers,* 12th Edition). By 1999, there were 42 national backbone ISPs in North America (table 1). These ISPs rely on transport services provided by more than 1,700 traditional facilities-based local and long-distance telephone service providers (table 2).

The telecommunications industry structure in the United States, as is the case in other countries, is largely a consequence of legacy regulation and network design. Historically, telephone service providers were subject to rate regulations and

Table 1

National Backbone ISPs in North America

@Home Network	Intermedia Business Internet
1 Terabit	Internet Access/GetNet
Abovenet	Internet Services of America
Apex Global Info Services (AGIS)	IXC Communications, Inc.
	Level 3
AT&T Networked Commerce Services	MCI WorldCom– Advanced Networks
Cable & Wireless USA.	MCI WorldCom–UUNET
CAIS	NetRail
Concentric	PSINet, Inc.
CRL Network Services	Qwest/Icon CMT
Digital Broadcast Network Corp	Rocky Mountain Internet/ DataXchange
Electric Lightwave	
EPOCH Networks, Inc.	Savvis Communications Corp
e.spire	ServInt
Exodus	Splitrock Services
Fiber Network Solutions	Sprint IP Services
Frontier Global Center	Teleglobe
Globix	Verio
Genuity Inc.	Visinet
GST Communications	Vnet
ICG/Netcom Online	Winstar/Broadband
IDT Internet Services	ZipLink

Source: *Boardwatch Magazine's Directory of Internet Service Providers*[1]

line-of-business restrictions, on the presumption that they were a natural monopoly. Traditional telephone networks were optimized to support a single-service: 4KHz circuits for voice telephony. The need to support universal service in a network comprised of multivintage, long-lived infrastructure deterred anything more than incremental service innovation. Although the quality and reliability of telephone service have increased dramatically while the real price of service has fallen dramatically, the basic functionality of plain old telephone service remains largely unchanged. Telecommunications deregulation and the development of new wireless and local access technologies—such as LDMS, xDSL, wireless fixed loops, and cable modems—enhance prospects for increased local telephone competition and an expansion in the range of services offered by traditional infrastructure providers. Some examples of service expansion are cable systems operators adding telephone service; local telephone companies adding video and Internet access services; and long distance companies offering local telephone service.

This changed environment has promoted significant restructuring in the participating industries. In addition to new entrants at all levels within the value chain, there have been numerous horizontal and vertical mergers, divestitures, and restructurings (table 3). The goal of this chapter is to present an analytical framework to address the following kinds of questions:

Table 2

Telecommunications Carriers in the United States

Facilities-based carriers[2]

Carrier Type	Number in 1998
Competitive Access Providers (CAPs) and Competitive LECs (CLECs)	276
Interexchange Carriers (IXCs)	171
Local Exchange Carriers (LECs)	1,348
Total	1,795

Major U.S. Telecommunication Carriers

Company	Carrier Type	Operating Revenues[3] ($billion 1998)
AT&T	IXC and LEC	40.6
MCI Worldcom	IXC	24.1
Sprint	IXC and LEC	14.8
Verizon	LEC and IXC	25.6
BellSouth	LEC	15.8
SBC (merged with PacTel, SNET, Ameritech)	IXC and LEC	21.2
QWEST	LEC & IXC IP-based	10.7

- What are the incentives of firms at various stages in the value chain to vertically integrate?

- What does this imply for Internet industry structure today and in the future?

- Is the market for a commodity IP bearer service sustainable?[4]

The focus is on residential, dial-up subscribers to simplify the analysis.[5]

Table 3

Some Significant Restructurings of Communications Firms

Date	Event
1996–1997	Worldcom acquires MFS and UUNET. Worldcom acquires CompuServe, divests retail business to AOL in return for AOL network and service contract
1996	Qwest Communications is incorporated
1997–1998	British Telecom tries to acquire MCI, GTE bids for MCI, Worldcom acquires MCI
2000	Qwest acquires US-West. Deutsche Telecom trying to acquire Sprint, and/or Qwest, and/or Voicestream, and/or US West
1998–2000	AT&T acquires Teleport, Telecom Inc., MediaOne, TCI
1999–2000	GTE divests BBN Networking. Becomes Genuity. Bell Atlantic/Nynex acquires GTE/Verizon
2000	Proposed Sprint-Worldcom merger nixed by EU and US authorities

Section I introduces a framework for evaluating industry structure; Section II reviews the economics of vertical integration; and Section III uses this framework to evaluate incentives to vertically integrate in the Internet.

A FRAMEWORK FOR ANALYZING INTERNET INDUSTRY STRUCTURE

Following Coase, we can investigate the boundaries of firm structure by considering the advantages of integrating production stages within a single firm relative to the alternative of using market exchange to transfer intermediate goods. The value chain for Internet services may be divided into the four essential elements that must be present to offer end-to-end Internet services:

- Retail-level Internet access provider (IAP)
- Local area transport services (LAT)
- Backbone Internet transport services (ISP)
- Wide area transport services (WAT)

In providing Internet services to the consumer, the retail-level IAP is the farthest downstream. To deliver its services, the IAP relies on the LAT to deliver traffic from the customer's premises to the IAP's POP (point of presence) and from the IAP's POP to the backbone ISP's network. The backbone ISP provides the IAP with connectivity and transport services to the rest of the Internet. The ISP may lease bulk transport capacity from WAT providers. These services may be combined within a single fully-integrated firm,[6] provided by four independent firms,[7] or furnished by some combination of partially integrated firms. Considering all possible combinations, there are 13 different types of firms that might exist (table 4). An industry structure would consist of some combination of these 13 firms.

Table 4

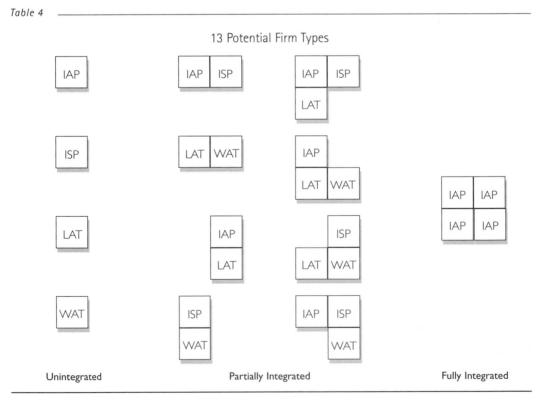

13 Potential Firm Types

Unintegrated   Partially Integrated   Fully Integrated

The value chain described above gives rise to five potential types of market transactions between activities (see table 5a and table 5b):

Customer – IAP   IAP – ISP   ISP – ISP   IAP – LAT   ISP – WAT

―― *Table 5a.*

Internet Industry Structure—Market Interface

Buyer	Seller	Market/Good Purchased	Comment
Customer	Internet Access Provider (IAP)	Internet access and web hosting service for small businesses and residential customers. Could be transaction or monthly purchase.	Pricing interface between final demand and supplier value chain. This is source of all revenue which flows into the network. Note, this is logical interface because possible to imagine separate contractual arrangements with each of the providers in value chain.
Internet Access Provider (IAP)	Internet Service Provider (ISP)	Bilateral interconnection agreements to provide wide area Internet transport and universal termination	Retail-wholesale relationship. IAP provides all customer interface functions and ISP provides wide area transport and ubiquitous connectivity. Potential for vertical integration.
Internet Service Provider (ISP)	Internet Service Provider (ISP)	Interexchange points and bilateral interconnection agreements to provide wide area Internet transport and universal termination.	Wholesale-wholesale relationship between peer ISPs. Potential for horizontal integration to expand scope of service.
Internet Access Provider (IAP)	Local Area Transport (LAT)	Regular tariffed business line service from LEC for dial-up access and leased lines to ISP POP	Pricing interface for essential input for IAP to provide service. Today, ISP typically leases local access facilities from regulated monopoly LEC. Potential for vertical integration.
Internet Service Provider (ISP)	Wide Area Transport (WAT)	Leased lines and VPN services purchased in wholesale toll market for wide area transport	Pricing interface for essential input for ISP

Table 5b.

Examples of Internet Industry Market Interface Transactions

Buyer Example	Seller Example	Market/Good Purchased	Comment
Residential consumer	TIAC, Barnet	$20/month unlimited usage for dial-in Internet access. Implicitly, this is end-to-end service for Internet applications.	Customer purchases flat rate local telephone service and uses 28.8 modem to access IAP with local dial-up.
TIAC, Barnet	MCI	DS-1 or DS-3 interconnection	Capacity-based pricing for interconnection; may include traffic sensitive component. This is hierarchical relationship.
MCI	UUNET	DS-1 or DS-3 interconnection	Revenue-neutral peering relationship
TIAC	NYNEX	Regular tariffed business line service from LEC for dial-up access and leased lines to ISP POP	IAP avoids paying access charges for traffic.
MCI, UUNET	MCI, AT&T	Leased lines and VPN services purchased in wholesale toll market for wide area transport	Bulk transport services purchased in competitive wholesale market for $0.01–$0.03 per minute.

Each of these transactions involves different types of participants, yet all are related in that the customers are the ultimate source of revenue that can be captured by the suppliers at successive stages in the value chain.[8] While the aggregate willingness-to-pay or final demand of the customers sets an upper bound on the total revenues that can be transferred from customers to suppliers, the aggregate costs of suppliers set a lower bound on the amount of revenue that must be extracted to make the service viable. The difference between these two sets is the amount of surplus that can be generated in these markets. Each of these transactions could take place either in an open market between independent firms or as an internal transfer within an integrated firm.

If each of the supplier markets is competitive, then all of the surplus will be captured by consumers and prices will be no higher at each interface than is

Table 6a

Internet Industry Structure—Participant Characteristics, *continued*

LAT
- sell local area access, termination and transport services to IAPs
- inherently local
- large regional RBOCs, currently seeking to expand into interLATA service

WAT
- sell wide area transport services to ISPs
- inherently regional, national or global
- large national IXCs, currently seeking to expand into local access service

Table 6b

Internet Industry Structure—Costs

Customer
- **Zero incremental cost for usage** under current regime beyond opportunity cost of user's time. Significant adjustment costs to change interface (learn, purchase new CPE). Potential for large congestion costs in aggregate.
- Largest usage-sensitive cost is opportunity cost of consumer's time (and negative impact of congestion). Fixed cost small, sunk cost may be significant (first-mover advantage).

IAP
- **Retailer cost structure.** Operating expenses include corporate overhead, sales & marketing, customer service, and telco and ISP service fees for transport. Capital equipment includes modem banks and servers.
- Most costs variable with customer count, including capital costs that scale with modems. Modem costs vary with usage, but retail-level costs are not usage sensitive.

ISP
- **Wholesaler cost structure.** Operating expenses include corporate overhead, network operations (maintenance), and telco service fees for leased lines. Capital equipment includes routers, gateways, and backbone transport facilities. Network operations and maintenance.
- Capital costs vary with capacity, but not usage. Large share of costs are sunk or fixed. Potential for significant variable costs if usage-sensitive termination fees charged for settlements.
- Gateways and shared transport, e.g., international undersea cable plant when ISP-ISP interface, which need to be recovered.

LAT
- **Cost structure of RBOC.** Operating expenses include corporate overhead, retail-level costs, and network operations. Capital costs include local distribution plant and switches, but former dominate.
- Large fixed and sunk costs. A significant share of costs is NTS and customer-specific. Large scale economies and expectation of no more than a few facilities-based carriers in any locale.

WAT
- **Cost structure of IXC.** Operating expenses include corporate overhead, retail-level costs, network operations, and local access charges. Capital costs include POPs, switches, and long-haul transport facilities.
- Large fixed and sunk costs, however, much less capital intensive than RBOC. Large scale economies. Retail-level costs more significant because of increased competition (includes customer churn). Inherently national.

required to recover costs. In the more realistic case where firms in one or more of these supplier markets possess market power, we may observe a much more complex array of strategic interactions. Firms may have incentives to exploit their control of bottleneck facilities (e.g., LAT providers) to extract additional surplus. Any kind of entry barrier (e.g., regulatory restrictions, scale economies, sunk costs, customer switching costs) can provide the basis for market power. Generally, firms prefer suppliers in other stages of the value chain to face as stiff competition, because this weakens their relative bargaining position.

To understand incentives to vertically integrate in the Internet industry, one must consider the characteristics and cost structure of each of the production activities in the framework. These may be summarized as follows (table 6a and table 6b):

Tabl

Internet Industry Structure—Participant Characteristics

Customer	• residential subscriber (commercial customers much more complex because they have many more options to self-provision and contract at different stages in value chain) • buyer of Internet access services and CPE • inherently local • very heterogeneous willingness-to-pay. Many subscribers. Diverse QOS requirements an tolerance for congestion • often risk averse so prefer flat rate pricing. Demand is multidimensional, defined over multiple applications (WEB, telephony, e-mail, etc.). • no market power. Each small relative to market. Demands are not coordinated. • demand of individual customer is very bursty and hard to predict, but application deman in aggregate may be relatively easy to predict, depending on application.
IAP	• sell Internet access services to residential subscribers and buy network equipment, local transport services, and ISP services • inherently local, although may be active in multiple local markets • diverse size ranges from quite small to large. Large are typically vertically integrated with ISP to provide national access and possibility of improved congestion control (e.g., by segregating traffic).
ISP	• sell Internet backbone/termination services to IAPs and buy network equipment, wide an transport services, and backbone/termination services from other ISPs • inherently regional or national. May be integrated forward into IAP services. • medium to large size ranging from regional to global backbone providers. In most cases, single interconnection between ISPs is sufficient to connect source and destination. • offer transport and universal termination services to enable IAP to sell end-to-end access to final consumer

continues on page 198

Internet Access Provider (IAP): Internet service retailer

The IAP is the service provider of dial-up access to the residential consumer.[9] The IAP provides basic Internet access, e-mail, and Web hosting services that are delivered over facilities leased from the telephone company (the LAT) and from ISPs or WATs (the Internet cloud). The IAP is the downstream retailer or reseller of ISP transport services. There are a wide array of IAPs, ranging from "mom and pop" operations offering service to a small number of subscribers in a specific locale to national IAPs that offer access across the country (e.g., AOL, MindSpring), and are typically vertically integrated ISPs (or even facilities providers, such as AT&T).

The IAP has the cost structure of a retail firm. Operating expenses include corporate overhead; sales and marketing; customer service; and telco and ISP service fees for leased transport services. The capital equipment owned by the IAP includes modem banks (to support dial-up access) and the servers (Web hosting, e-mail, file server).

Entry costs to become a local IAP are low, and this is the least capital intensive of the activities considered. There are only limited opportunities to realize capital scale economies (i.e., modems and servers reflect constant returns to scale).

Internet Service Provider (ISP): Internet service wholesaler

The ISP offers IP connectivity to the Internet cloud for the IAP and provides backbone transport (this includes routing and basic transport). The ISP is the upstream supplier of Internet services to the IAP. Most of the ISPs are integrated forward into IAP services. These may be regional or national service providers, such as UUNET.

The ISP has the cost structure of a wholesale facilities provider. Operating expenses include corporate overhead, network operations (maintenance, network planning), and telco (and perhaps other ISP) service fees for transport.[10] Capital equipment includes the Internet routers, gateways, and some backbone transport facilities.

The ISP is more capital intensive than the IAP, but less so than the facilities-based providers (i.e., LAT and WAT). Setting up and operating a national IP network (even on leased WAT facilities) and managing the interconnection arrangements to IAPs and other ISPs present significant entry barriers.

Local Area Transport (LAT): local access facilities provider

The LAT is the upstream supplier of the underlying physical infrastructure to support IAP access. For dial-up access, this is usually the telephone LEC (local exchange carrier).[11] The existing physical access infrastructure supports other types of service besides Internet access (telephone calling, cable television).

The LAT has the cost structure of a wholesale facilities provider, such as an LEC. Operating expenses include corporate overhead, network operations, retail-level costs (e.g., for telephone service). Capital costs include local distribution plant and local switching, as well as the billing and signaling network infrastructure.

The LAT is the most capital-intensive activity in the value chain. Today, LAT services are provided by monopoly LECs, whose core business is providing local telephone access and calling services in a contiguous geographic area. As a consequence, the interconnection policies, prices, and market participation of the LECs remain heavily regulated. Regulatory policy is seeking to promote competition in local services and, if successful, deregulation. In the future, cable TV companies and wireless providers may provide competitive local access alternatives.

Wide Area Transport (WAT): wide area transport provider

The WAT is the upstream supplier of the underlying physical infrastructure to support the ISP. Typically, these are long-distance carriers. The WAT are the wide-area analog to the LAT firms.

The WAT has the cost structure of a wholesale facilities provider, such as a telephone interexchange carrier (IXC). Operating expenses include corporate overhead, network operations, and retail-level costs (e.g., for telephone service). Capital costs include long-distance switching and transport plant, as well as the billing and signaling network infrastructure.

The WAT is also quite capital intensive, but significantly less so than for a LAT. Because WAT markets are much larger geographically[12] and less capital intensive, effective competition already exists in U.S. long-distance telephone markets. Consequently, long-distance carriers are subject to significantly less regulatory oversight.

REVIEW OF THE ECONOMIC THEORY OF VERTICAL INTEGRATION

Much of the discussion will proceed as if the choice between vertical integration and market-based transactions is dichotomous; in reality, there is a continuum of organizational forms. The forms range from arm's length, anonymous, "take-it-or-leave-it" market transactions (e.g., as in competitive markets) to term commitments to complex bilateral contracts to full vertical integration (i.e., consolidated ownership). The more likely it is that the buyer and seller interact in a non-anonymous fashion, the more likely their interactions will be constrained by implicit or explicit contracts that will reflect vertical integration.[13]

There are a number of motivations for vertical integration:[14]

Scale and scope economies: Average costs are reduced through vertical integration because of the existence of fixed shared costs.[15]

Transaction costs: Internal transfers may be less expensive than market-based transactions (e.g., because of metering or contracting costs).

Coordination and control: There are co-specialized assets in the multiple stages that are more valuable if used together in a coordinated fashion.[16]

Product differentiation or price discrimination: Downstream integration to facilitate price discrimination may be necessary for cost recovery (e.g., the market for an undifferentiated upstream IP bearer service may be unsustainable).[17]

Innovation and strategic positioning: A firm may need to vertically integrate if new product and upstream (downstream) firms do not exist.[18] Or, a firm may vertically integrate to develop complementary skills to enhance its strategic position.[19]

Market power: Integration to protect or extend (leverage) market power is a common motivation hypothesized for vertical integration. This may also include a desire to protect quasi-rents associated with sunk investments (e.g., to guarantee cost recovery of facilities investment).

The first five motivations enhance efficiency and reduce costs, and public policy should wish to encourage vertical integration that can be justified on these grounds. The last motivation is likely to be opposed by public policy.[20] Historically, U.S. antitrust policy proscribed a number of vertical relationships as inherently anticompetitive (e.g., exclusive franchises). Subsequent economic theory has raised serious doubts about per se restrictions against vertical integration by identifying efficiency-enhancing motivations that are not anticompetitive (see above), and by calling into question the effectiveness of vertical integration as a strategy to extend market power. For example, if the downstream (or upstream) market is already competitive, then vertical integration to extend market power may not make sense.[21] Potential rationales for vertical integration to extend market power include the desire to avoid regulation[22] or to protect market power in a core market.[23]

In the following discussion, we will examine the costs and benefits to each of the suppliers in the value chain to vertically integrate with adjacent stages.

With this industry taxonomy, we can explore opportunities to both vertically and horizontally integrate. The natural question to ask is what types of firms exist today and what types of firms may exist in the future.

The industry analysis discussed above partitions the Internet service function into retail (IAP) and wholesale (ISP) services that use the capacity of local (LAT) and wide area (WAT) facilities providers. With these four types of activities, there are 13 possible types of firms, and it is possible that multiple types will coexist simultaneously (table 4).[24] In the future, we expect to see an even larger number of possible firm configurations. The overall conclusions or predictions that emerge from this analysis include (see table 7):

VERTICAL INTEGRATION IN THE INTERNET

1. Incentives to vertically integrate in the Internet

There are strong incentives to vertically (and horizontally) integrate for each of the participants in the service provider value chain. Consideration of the motivations discussed above indicates that there are efficiency incentives to vertically integrate.

Scale and scope economies. These economies exist whenever there are large fixed or shared costs. Fixed costs do not vary with the volume of traffic actually handled (or number of customers served). Therefore, increasing the volume of traffic (or expanding the subscriber base) will decrease

Table 7

Vertical Integration and Industry Structure

Type of Firm	Today?	Future?
IAP	Yes, low entry costs. Small (e.g., TIAC)	Yes. Small in future. Large are national.
ISP	No. If ISP, then also IAP.	No (?? maybe if sufficient market of standalone IAPs. Could avoid retail-level costs).
LAT	Yes, regulation and economic entry barriers (e.g., RBOCs–Bell Atlantic)	No. Incentives to integrate forward.
WAT	Yes, regulation and low entry costs because of active reseller market (e.g., AT&T)	No. Incentives to integrate forward.
IAP-ISP	Yes (e.g., UUNET, AOL)	Yes, taking advantage of wholesale bearer service market.
LAT-WAT	No (exceptions GTE, International)	Yes (??), because of Telco Act and technology
IAP LAT	No, regulation.	Yes (??)
ISP WAT	No. If ISP then also IAP.	Yes (??). If WAT then why not ISP.
ISP LAT-WAT	No	No (??). If ISP then why not IAP also.
IAP LAT-WAT	No	No. If WAT and IAP then why not ISP also.
IAP–ISP WAT	Yes (e.g., MCI)	Yes (??)
IAP-ISP LAT	No	Yes (??)
IAP–ISP LAT-WAT	No (but GTE, international yes)	Yes

average total costs (scale economies). Shared costs are costs that cannot be uniquely assigned to a single product or customer. Therefore, expanding the number of customers served or products offered can reduce average total costs (scope economies). For all of the participants in the value chain, there are significant fixed and shared costs, giving rise to scale and scope economies that will encourage vertical integration. This can be best understood by reviewing the cost characteristics of each of the major cost categories.

Network capital and operations costs

• There are significant increasing returns to scale associated with capacity expansion costs. Because of the costs of installing outside plant, it is typical to install excess capacity to provide room for future growth.

• Because of the need to size the network to accommodate peak demand, and because peak network demands are not perfectly correlated across domains, there is generically excess capacity in the network (although local bottlenecks may exist at different places and times in the Internet).

• Network operations expenses (planning, maintenance, management) are driven more by the network capacity than by the actual traffic handled. Also, network operations expenses may reflect increasing returns to scale (i.e., it does not cost twice as much to manage a network twice the size).[25]

• Off-peak traffic shares peak capacity, so assignment of costs is somewhat arbitrary and depends on classification of peak.

• End-to-end services share backbone capacity, especially in Internet where route may vary with each packet.

• Large shared and fixed costs mean there are large scale and scope economies.

• These economies are likely to be largest for LAT providers, because these are more capital intensive than WAT. Similarly, network-related scale and scope economies are likely to be larger for ISPs then for IAPs.

• There are likely to be some scale and scope economies from integrating local and long-distance access network facilities. For example, these may come because some of the facilities used to support wide area transport services will be shared by local services (e.g., tandem switches, signaling networks, intermachine trunks).

Retail-level costs

• Advertising costs show significant scale economies, and brand advertising yields scope economies. Brand advertising of a specific firm's name is likely to be especially important when reputation effects are important, as they may well be until consumers are more experienced and knowledgeable about Internet service options.

• Customer service costs yield moderate scale economies and need to be sized for peak usage.

• Bad debt yields moderate scale economies (because of diversification).

• Product innovation and management costs are fixed.

• Sales costs (customer acquisition costs), including original contact and setting up or modifying the customer account, include a number of nonrecurring charges that do not vary with the number of services sold to the customer. This is the retail-cost side of providing one-stop shopping. These costs become more important as competition heats up and customer churn increases (reducing the amount of time over which nonrecurring customer costs can be recovered).

• Billing costs include a significant non-traffic-sensitive component that does not vary when the customer is sold multiple services.

• It is unclear whether there are significant scale and scope economies.

• Retail-level scale and scope economies are perhaps not as large as network-level economies in absolute terms, but they are likely to become more important strategically as non-facilities-based providers become more important and as network-related costs become a smaller share of total costs.[26]

Corporate overhead

• Corporate overhead, associated general support services, and headquarters operations are largely fixed and shared across multiple services.

• Scale and scope economies can be realized through vertical integration.

Closely related is the demand-side driver of network externalities (i.e., it is more valuable to be connected to a larger network). In the absence of market power considerations, networks would choose to interconnect to expand the value of their networks.[27] The Internet promotes ubiquitous interconnection, which means that smaller networks can share in the benefits of universal termination supported by larger networks.[28] Because these interconnection policies and settlements arrangements are currently in flux, smaller networks may be at a disadvantage if larger networks seek to exploit the advantages that network externalities yield to larger incumbents.

Therefore, an analysis of the cost structure reveals significant scale and scope economies that can be exploited through vertical integration.

Transaction costs. The costs of metering traffic is one of the justifications for not employing usage-sensitive pricing in the Internet today. The costs include administrative overhead and creating the appropriate infrastructure (modifying existing routers and servers) to meter traffic.

Coordination and control. The local access network and wide area transport facilities may be regarded as co-specialized assets in the sense that demand forecasting and management, capacity planning, and network management may be easier for end-to-end services if the underlying facilities are controlled end-to-end.

The importance of this motivation for integrated ownership of facilities is less today than it was before the development of equal access capabilities in the telephone network and the development of open interface standards. The reliance of the Internet on open interface standards makes this rationale for integrating network facilities end-to-end less important than it was before divestiture of the Bell System.

An important driver for end-to-end integration, however, may be associated with the need to provide integrated, quality-of-service differentiated services. This may provide a powerful incentive for an IAP to integrate into ISP services to assure reliability, customer security, and to support quality-of-service guarantees for Internet services. An IAP that does not have end-to-end control over Internet services may be constrained in the kinds of services it can offer. This motivation for integration is logically separable from the motivation to integrate facilities end-to-end, or for an Internet service provider to own its own facilities.

Product differentiation or price discrimination. The need to recover the sunk and fixed costs of constructing network facilities will provide a powerful inducement for facilities-based providers to integrate forward to permit product differentiation and price discrimination to offer value-added services.

Because there is likely to be excess capacity and because short-run incremental costs are significantly less than long-run average costs (which include fixed and shared costs), it will be difficult for facilities-based providers to avoid aggressive "Bertrand-like" price competition. This argument is explained at greater length in Srinagesh and Gong.

To price discriminate, facilities-based providers will have a strong incentive to offer bundled services (one-stop shopping and services that bundle transport with value-added features such as enhanced billing and new features). Creative bundling will facilitate a wider range of targeted discount programs that can be used to more narrowly target customer groups. Moreover, one-stop shopping bundles provide opportunities to offer forward-discounts (rebates to customers who stay with a provider, or volume discounts over multiple services) that reduce customer's incentives to switch to a competing carrier.

While this will provide an extremely powerful motivation for facilities-based providers to integrate downstream into services, it will not preclude the existence of non-facilities-based service providers, as I will discuss further below.

Innovation and strategic positioning. In technologically advanced markets, the need to vertically integrate to fill a new opportunity (no current supplier upstream, no distribution channel downstream) is often an important motivation. Similarly, vertical integration may be needed to develop complementary skills.

Vertical integration seems less likely to be important for integration of local and wide area facilities providers, because these services already exist and the skills associated with each are not substantially different. However, this may provide a motivation for IAP-ISP integration or for facilities integration into IAP or ISP services. In both cases, integration may result in an expansion of firm-specific skills. Moreover, IAP-ISP integration may be required to offer quality-differentiated services as noted above.

Market power. As noted above, vertical integration is often pursued or considered as a strategy to protect, exploit, or extend market power.

Because this is harmful to competition, antitrust policy scrutinizes the effects of vertical mergers for their effect on competition.

Although this is an important motivation, discussion of its impact is beyond the scope of this chapter.

2. Viability of wholesale market for IP bearer service

The existence of non-facilities-based providers requires the existence of a wholesale market for an IP bearer service. I am assuming that there will be an IP bearer service as suggested in the Open Data Network (ODN) model described in the National Research Council (1984) report. According to this model, multiple technologies will be able to support an enhanced version of IP services flexibly and interoperably across a wide array of applications at higher protocol levels.

As noted above and discussed in Srinagesh and Gong, facilities-based providers will have a powerful incentive to integrate forward into product services to differentiate their products and price discriminate. Kavassalis, Lee, and Bailey argue that such differentiation will be possible even at the facilities level because of differences in the ability of applications to support the full spectrum of applications. They argue that the bearer service market will not be a commodity market, and hence will support multiple types of organizational structures. The analysis presented here complements their work and reaches a substantially similar conclusion.

Moreover, even if Kavassalis, Lee, and Bailey are incorrect in arguing that bearer-services will be differentiated, it is likely that there will exist a wholesale bearer service market. Such a market already exists in long-distance telephone services. The factors that will contribute to the existence of such a market are as follows:

Excess capacity: As argued above, there are fundamental cost and demand drivers that will result in excess capacity. This will include capacity that was installed for future growth (e.g., dark fiber) as well as capacity on different vintage networks.[29] Moreover, competition will imply churn and excess capacity inventory to accommodate uncertainty in market shares.

Free-rider problem of disciplining competition: Unless facilities-provisioning is a natural monopoly, there will be multiple facilities providers from which potential non-facilities-based resellers can lease capacity. Even if reseller competition harms facilities-based providers as a whole, it will be difficult for them to collude on an anticompetitive strategy to resist competition (it will always be privately profitable to defect from the high "bearer service" price strategy to capture reseller business at the margin).[30]

Open interface standards and architecture of the Internet: Because IP can run on many technologies and can be used to flexibly interconnect heterogeneous networks, it will be relatively easy for competing facilities based on competing transport technologies (e.g., ethernet, frame-relay, ATM, etc.) to support competing versions of an IP bearer service.

It is likely that bearer services will be available under a variety of terms and conditions. These will range from relatively short-term contracts (approaching spot markets for wide area transport) to longer-term capacity commitment contracts. These latter kinds of contracts may approach full vertical integration as the reseller assumes a greater proportion of the capital risks and residual control rights associated with the underlying capacity.

3. Integration downstream more likely than upstream

As noted above, the incentives to vertically integrate are strongest for the facilities-based providers. Moreover, the economic barriers to entry are greater for upstream integration.[31] Therefore, it is more likely that upstream firms will integrate downstream—ISP into IAP, LAT into IAP, WAT into ISP, and LAT into WAT—rather than the reverse.

4. ISPs will integrate into IAP services

National IAPs are likely to have important advantages in a number of markets, and it seems unlikely that a national ISP would not seek to exploit this opportunity by offering retail-level services. As discussed above, therefore, it is expected that most ISPs will also offer IAP services. A standalone ISP seems unlikely in the future because it would compete as a wholesaler and would be at a disadvantage relative to a facilities-based reseller.

A competitive fringe of standalone IAPs will continue to exist, because entry costs are quite low as long as there is a viable resale market for IP bearer services offered either by IAP-ISP facilities or non-facilities-based carriers.

These IAPs will be both pure resellers (reselling bulk services purchased from other IAP-ISPs) or facilities-based resellers that lease the capacity from LATs. These service providers will continue to survive because of their strategic advantage in providing retail-level services to niche customer groups, but they are not expected to earn excess profits. Examples of niche opportunities include vanity credit cards and "mom and pop" operations. A potentially rich source of such firms are firms that have local access capacity installed for another reason that can be expanded to support IAP at a low incremental cost. This may include shared-tenant services networks in apartment buildings or malls that could be extended to offer IAP services to the surrounding community, or even private intranets.

5. Facilities-based providers will integrate into Internet services

LAT entry into IAP or WAT entry into ISP would involve a relatively small incremental cost, especially because these providers are already providing retail-level services to consumers. Adding Internet-level services would provide them another opportunity to offer one-stop shopping and to respond to competition from ITel. In the near term, entry by a LAT into IAP may be limited by regulatory considerations.[31]

LAT entry into WAT faces significantly lower economic entry barriers than does the reverse, because LAT entry is more capital intensive.

CONCLUSIONS

1. Incentives to vertically integrate in the Internet

Incentives to vertically integrate are strong at all stages within the value chain, and we should expect to see the emergence of fully integrated facilities-based service providers.[33]

2. Viability of wholesale IP bearer service market

Availability of wholesale IP bearer services from these and other facilities-based providers will permit the continued existence of non-facilities-based Internet service providers, implying that the industry will consist of a variety of different types of firms.[34]

3. Integration downstream more likely than upstream

Incentives to vertically integrate are asymmetric and are stronger for upstream firms to integrate downstream.

4. ISPs will integrate into IAP services

Standalone ISPs are unlikely because ISPs have a strong incentive to integrate into IAP services, and national IAPs have a strong incentive to maintain backbone facilities.

5. Facilities-based providers will integrate into Internet services

Standalone facilities-based providers (LAT, WAT) are unlikely because they have incentive to offer Internet services to complement existing offerings (e.g., telephone service) and to respond to competition from resellers (i.e., ITel offered by non-facilities-based providers in competition with traditional PSTN offerings).

The preceding conclusions are based on an assessment of key underlying trends and rely on several important assumptions. The key trends/factors are as follows:

One stop shopping: Consumers will demand and service providers will seek to offer one-stop shopping services that bundle multiple communication services into a single bill. One-stop shopping services will appeal especially to risk-averse (reputation-sensitive) and convenience-minded (less cost-sensitive) consumers who will value the simplicity of consolidating multiple electronic bills. This will provide a strong market demand driver for vertical integration.

Scale and scope Economies: There are significant retail-level scale and scope economies that encourage suppliers to offer one-stop shopping services. This is the cost-side driver for vertical integration. In addition, there are scale and scope economies associated with expanding nationally, or even internationally, that will also encourage vertical integration.

Open interface standards: The Internet is distinguished, in part, by its reliance on and promotion of open interface standards that allow heterogeneous network environments to be flexibly interconnected. This means that it is not essential to be vertically integrated to provide service, especially with respect to the network-related cost economies. Without such standards, vertical integration would be even more important and the viability of non-facilities-based providers or partial facilities-based providers would be suspect. The prevalence of such standards increases the relative importance of non-network cost economies (i.e., retail-level costs, overhead costs).

Pro-competitive regulatory policy: Public policy would like to promote competition at all stages in the value chain. To the extent such policies are successful, they will promote the coexistence of both vertically integrated and non-integrated types of firms. The viability of these programs is most suspect with respect to the promotion of competition for local access facilities.[35] If competition is not successful here, then it is likely that local access will continue to be regulated as a bottleneck facility, with the potential for continued restrictions on access pricing, interconnection policies, and participation in adjacent markets. If facilities-based local access competition is not sustainable, then regulatory policy will be required to sustain non-fully-integrated firms (e.g., equal access, common carriage, etc.). In this chapter, however, I have assumed that local competition will be viable.

Availability of bandwidth: The viability of an active reseller market for non-integrated carriers presumes the existence of a competitive wholesale market for facilities-based transport. This presumes that, generically, there will be excess capacity.[36] For WAT services, this already exists and will continue to exist in the future because of the relatively low entry costs and excess capacity in wide area transport.[37] For LAT services, today, access pricing is regulated and will continue to be regulated until there is effective competition. Because of the costs of installing local outside plant, when competition comes there is likely to be excess capacity.

This chapter has developed a new theory of the Internet firm, explaining the economic factors that will lead to continued creative destruction of telecommunications and Internet service provider firms.

11 SUSTAINABLE OPEN SOURCE SOFTWARE BUSINESS MODELS

Jean Camp

Cooperation and the blurring of the distinction between software developer and software user always seemed to be the most important aspect [of free software] to me.

Stig@hackvan.com
http://www.hackvan.com/

I have always depended on the kindness of strangers.

Blanche DuBois, in
A Streetcar Named Desire
Tennessee Williams

Joseph Schumpeter's idea of the "creative gales of destruction" surely describes how the Internet is upending traditional business-to-consumer relationships and challenging them with new relationships made in cyberspace. This technology-led dynamic leads to several interesting questions: Who or what is the Internet consumer? An automaton? A search engine? A popular bot? A corporate or governmental agent? Or an active, thoughtful individual browsing an electronic marketplace?

First, the Internet consumer is a "who" not a "what." Whether shopping on the Internet or at the mall, the consumer is looking for high-quality, low-cost goods. In resorting to the Internet, the consumer's choice of merchants broadens and accords her or him more leverage.

The level of control between business and consumer has changed. In the second quote above, Blanche DuBois is an individual caught in a situation beyond her control. At the moment she acknowledges her lack of control, she begins the process of regaining her balance. Similarly, businesses affected by the forces of creative destruction engendered by the Internet, are thrashing about through the courts, legislation, and law enforcement in a situation beyond their control.

Many Internet merchants have been focused on extending control over the consumer, and as a result the stock market is littered with failed electronic "communities" that were tourist traps on the information highway. The traditional merchant-consumer relationship is based on the difficulty and costs for the consumer of switching—whether that be locating a new supplier, establishing a new business relationship, or driving to a new location. With the explosion of connectivity and information, however, switching difficulties and costs are plummeting.

In the Internet-mediated business-to-consumer relationship, customer information is often sketchy, incomplete, and unreliable. The two responses to this situation are not mutually exclusive. The first response is to track customers and attempt to target them exactly. This approach is referred to variously as an ideal (Hagel and Armstrong), a moral wrong (Johnson and Nissenbaum), or an information pathology (Camp and Tsang). The second response is to trust customers to know themselves and provide useful information directly. Merchants will have to depend on customers—"on the kindness of strangers"—to compete with traditional rivals.

Merchants have the opportunity to thrive in this environment by delegating to the Internet-mediated consumer (rather than soothsayer-market analysts) a critical role in the design of goods. Open, interactive systems; consumer-centered, consumer-designed products; and self-executing sales arrangements will define business survival and success. In sum, merchants in the Internet economy will cede authority to their sometimes-anonymous consumers and succeed by relying on the kindness of these strangers. Note that it is not the anonymity but the change in the locus of control that is critical.

CONSUMERS AS PRODUCERS

The consumers-as-producers model is the core of the success of the Internet over closed proprietary systems. Consumers as producers is also the core of several business models: portals, auctions, and communities

Amazon is an excellent example of consumers as producers. At Amazon, consumers furnish information that would be impossible for Amazon itself to provide. Consumers identify connections between products (books, videos, recordings, etc.) by bundling their orders. Consumers review products. Consumers comment on other consumers' reviews. This is the open source model of evaluation. The description of open source in the Harvard Business School case study of Red Hat identifies the input of thousands of programmers as the critical component of open source and free software success. Similarly, Amazon does not simply provide services to purchasers—it provides the reviewing and sorting services of all its customers to other customers. Amazon has mastered the open source book stall.

A recognition of the changed consumer-merchant relationship is at the heart of many of the popular Internet business models—electronic communities, portals, and personal news agents to name but a few. This chapter will explore the implications for all businesses utilizing the Internet of their increased reliance on the kindness of strangers, and specifically on the role of "strangers" in creating sustainable open source software business models.

CONSUMER AS DESIGNER

The greatest waste in the information age is that consumers cannot take part in design at a sufficiently early stage to provide useful feedback. This is changing in high-end markets—e.g., blue jeans designed for me—but such practices do not yet extend through all economic sectors.

The common objection to consumer-centered design is that consumers simply do not know what they want. For example, if asked at the turn of the century about improvements in plowing, a farmer would have requested a stronger, healthier mule—not a tractor. The observation is clearly true for genuinely revolutionary products, but there are few revolutionary products on the order of the internal combustion engine, the Internet, the stirrup, or the printing press. The vast majority of products incorporate only incremental improvements over previous products.

The new model is consumer as designer. Customers have ideas, and the company that can separate the wheat from the chaff in the flow of ideas will move and adapt at speeds untouchable by companies connecting to their market only through mediating agencies based on a broadcast model of consumers.

Because the Internet has been the driver of consumer-to-designer convergence, this chapter focuses on the quintessential post-convergence area in which the customers create the product: open code. The customers are the producers and the merchants provide insurance, trust, certification, and filtering services. First, open source and free software models will be introduced. Auctions and electronic communities are two other areas in which consumers are explicitly producers. In all three cases, consumers both create the value and consume the value.

By integrating into the iterative design process the ability of consumers to organize and express preferences and opinions, companies can dramatically increase both the creativity and the suitability of offerings. In computing, designing the system with the user's input is referred to as user-centered design. In the future, product design will be user-centered or not competitive.

In open source and free software communities, there is a saying: "Every program begins as a programmer's itch." (Dibona, Ockman, and Stone). That is, a program originates when someone recognizes the need from his or her own experience. Extremely successful programs meet that need and category killers meet the need extremely well—so well that no other program is needed for a particular purpose. But it all begins with a programmer's intuition and code.

FREE SOFTWARE

Democracy needs information that is truly available to its citizens—for example, programs that people can read, fix, adapt, and improve, not just operate. But what software owners typically deliver is a black box that we cannot study or change.

Society also needs freedom. When a program has an owner, the users lose freedom to control part of their own lives. And above all society needs to encourage the spirit of voluntary cooperation in its citizens. When software owners tell us that helping our neighbors in a natural way is "piracy," they pollute our society's civic spirit.

This is why we say that free software is a matter of freedom, not price.
—Richard Stallman, MIT computer scientist, 1984

We can—we must—choose what kind of cyberspace we want and what freedoms we will guarantee. These choices are all about architecture:

about what kind of code will govern cyberspace, and who will control it.

—Larry Lessig, Harvard Law Faculty, 1999

The Free Software Foundation was founded by MacArthur "genius award" Fellowship winner Richard Stallman to promote free ("free as in speech, not free as in beer") software. Free software is first and foremost a political movement, originally based on a particularly cogent observation of computing trends in the eighties. Software was poised to become licensed closed property; programming was moving to Dilbert's cubicle, away from the world of research and experimentation. In 1984, Stallman observed that "programming is just a way of making money."

The free software paradigm is fundamentally about freedom, but the end result is readable code and shared programs. Despite the reliability and widespread use in the industry of free software (particularly GNU Emacs), the emphasis on freedom apparently makes some businesspeople nervous. Note that the Free Software Foundation is not opposed to selling or profiting from programming, other than preventing the redistribution of the code itself. Yet free software remains fundamentally at odds with classical economics.

> In the long run, making programs free is a step toward the post-scarcity world, where nobody will have to work very hard just to make a living.
>
> *The GNU Manifesto*

Economics remains fundamentally the study of scarcity and of conflict for goods. The economics of air were not interesting until clean air became scarce. Thus a post-scarcity world is a world that can not be built entirely on today's economic foundations. Of course, many observed human actions are fundamentally at odds with economics (like voting), and others only coexist with economic theory by the astounding flexibility of the concept of utility. Holding an ideological position in stark conflict with an underlying tenet of classical economics has tended to limit the popularity of free software as a movement (as opposed to the success of free software products) in the business community. Thus, to change the perception of the free software movement as antibusiness, the open source movement was born.

In addition to ideological packaging, licensing is a consistent substantive difference between open source and free software. The free software license requires any software that includes code under that license to be free as well. The free software license is genuinely revolutionary in the way that any paradigm-shattering idea is revolutionary. Free software is all open, but all open software is not free.

THE FREE SOFTWARE REVOLUTION

Convergence on the packetized network is a result of the first free software revolution. The very interoperability and innovation that characterize the Internet is a function of free software. In this new century, it is easy to forget that the Internet is very unlike the original public and private visions of a national information infrastructure.

The free software revolution overthrew the proprietary model of networks—whereby AOL and MSN have their own networks. All of these networks exist now as part of the Internet—not as separate and wholly controlled distinct networks. The free software revolution was the radical, pervasive deployment of an open, bottom-up, user-empowering National Information Infrastructure. The first free software revolution initiated the creative destructive that is the focus of this book.

In the early nineties, cable television was the model for the then-emerging broadband information superhighway. While the vision from the top down was of hundreds of channels, what has emerged from the bottom up has been a construction with millions of Web pages. The Internet has been widely adopted, no doubt in part because of the ability to innovate at the endpoints as opposed to concentrating control in the center. When people were provided a choice between adopting an open TCP/IP[1] based system over the closed cable and telephony standards, the open system won out. With the adoption of different protocols over the same wires, the information infrastructure became fundamentally different in terms of speech, consumer choice, merchant options, and commerce than the original broadband vision. Individuals could more easily adopt the protocol because it was an open standard. Freeware and shareware implementations of the software necessary to connect to the Internet were widely available. By choosing to connect to the Internet as opposed to using the disks sent by AOL—proprietary software connecting to a closed network where AOL chose all merchants—people chose an open network where anyone could join as a merchant or producer for the information infrastructure. Even the six-hundred-pound gorillas of proprietary networks at the time—AOL, CompuServe, and Microsoft—had to connect users to the Internet.

The original information superhighway vision suggested a service composed of hundreds of television channels with the citizen as passive viewer, active only to make a purchase. On the Internet, however, the consumer is active: as a neighbor in chat groups, as a participant in political debates, and as an empowered consumer in Internet commerce. The same cable wires, the same phone wires, and the same physical realities of microelectronics that would have provided the 500-channel mall in fact provide Internet connectivity. The critical difference is that people chose open protocols in which the consumer is simultaneously the producer of information goods. Consumers chose the medium in which everyone could speak—chose to communicate as well as consume, to speak as well as listen, to sell as well as buy, and to design as well as judge designs. Instead of being a passive consumer—whose only opportunity to provide feedback is a button labeled "Buy"—today's Internet user is chatting, posting, authoring, arguing, and contributing. The freedom to choose between alternate versions of code has played a critical part in the construction of the information infrastructure and the information society.

OPEN SOURCE

Open source may or may not be simply free software with another name, depending on the questions asked. The business models of many of today's open source companies were originally proposed in the GNU Manifesto: providing support from hand-holding to customer programming, building price through reputation, and the code itself as an advertisement for its programmers. The end result of the application of either philosophy is the same: open code. Yet the open source movement is explicitly procapitalist where free software is incidentally capitalist. With free software, economics is a powerful part of the argument, but the core is freedom. With open source, economics is the argument.

Does it matter if the Soviet Union fell because the people wanted free speech or better beer? Or does it matter only that liberal democratic capitalism was dominant in the end? This is essentially the free software versus open source debate: the end point for both is open code. While the open source and free software movements have fundamentally different motivations, it is critical to understand that closed code cannot compete with open code over the long term.

In both open source systems and free software, the code is given away, but the licensing in open source systems is fundamentally different from the licensing in free software. Free software is protected by the Gnu Public License (GPL). The GPL prevents organizations from taking free software and using it to build a proprietary product. The open source products do not have that prevention built in. As a result, most Linux distributors offer a proprietary Graphical User Interface as part of their package. Notice that from either the free software or the open source perspective, the open installer would be improved at a faster rate. Thus according to either theory, it should not matter in economic terms that it is feasible to graft inferior closed software onto superior open code. (Open code is superior in traditional business terms: more robust, more efficient, faster, and more secure.) However, because free software is about freedom, it would be morally wrong to allow the software to be closed. With open source, it is merely stupid.

An alternative argument is that open code only works close to the wire. That is, problems at the higher layers—particularly in the case of interfaces—are not sufficiently interesting to hackers for the hackers to solve them. For an open source project to be useful, it must have users who are programmers. A counter observation, however, is that for many interface problems, the programming can occur at such a high level that the users need not truly be programmers. If one considers the Web to be fundamentally about user interfaces—after all Gopher and Archie could do many of the same things with an inferior interface—then clearly the largest cooperative effort in history is being made to define useful user interfaces.

THE OPEN SOURCE REVOLUTION

Convergence has happened, and the post-convergence network was created by free software. Now businesses are coming to the next revolution—open source.

Unlike the free software revolution, the open source revolution has yet to occur. High stock market valuations are only a bet that the open source revolution will happen. Open source is not free software. Open source is expressly pro-business. Charging for open source is inherently reasonable.

The potential of open source depends entirely upon the question asked. To ask, "how can anyone make money selling something free?" suggests inevitable failure. The alternative, "Why would any consumer lease closed source when they can buy open source?" suggests the inevitability of success.

The open source model has proven a mystery to many traditional businesses. The open source business model starts with the assumption that open source can provide real value to customers. The founders of open source recognized the value that source brings to a customer's business. Unlike traditional businesses, the current open source businesses were founded primarily by programmers who understood the existence of customer value and had no business plan set in stone. The open source business plans are evolving as customers provide feedback for what they want.

Compare Dell and VA Linux. Dell will ship the consumer exactly what the consumer wants in terms of RAM and disk size. VA Linux can be provided with a description of expected load and provide specifications for a machine. In both cases the companies are responding to the customer's specifications. In the open source case, the company actually listens to the customer's problem and then offers a solution. Both companies have the expertise internally to translate load specification and uncertainty to machine specifications. Only one of these companies uses that expertise to listen to the customer and scratch the customer's itch.

In general the value in open source companies comes in two basic forms: solutions and options.

Software customers, of course, do not want code, just as home buyers do not want a random collection of studs and doorframes. Customers want solutions to specific problems—serving their own customers better, staying ahead of the competition. Open source provides far faster evolution and innovation and better reliability. System administration can be cheaper in the near term as the market for open source programmers is better and cheaper in the long term as there will be no requirement for companywide upgrades. Upgrades in the virtual working space can be as independent and appropriate to each particular business as upgrades to physical spaces are today. System upgrades and maintenance can be handled by a larger number of companies on equal competitive footing, because all the companies have access to the code. Open source systems also offer superior security.

The other primary component of open source is the options offered. When purchasing a closed package, the customer is trusting that the owner of the software continues to evolve in a manner and at a speed compatible with the company. (As a side note, what is purchased when closed software is purchased is a license to use the specific software under given terms, not the code itself.) In open source, the company purchases the specific code. The company owns the software and can alter it as necessary. The customer retains the option of embarking on a completely separate strategic path than that envisioned by the software merchant for its customers. That is, the software consumer has not been captured or bound to the software provider over the long term. The software consumer maintains all strategic options. The next section describes how both merchant and customer use of open source can increase the information on customer's needs for merchants, and the merchant's options for customers.

THE OPEN SOURCE CONSUMER

What does open source have to do with the average computer user? Does the average user care about code? No. He or she wants reliable software that does not lock up or crash, a system that finds the printer and prints without active management, a computer fast enough to do what he or she wants, all at a reasonable price. The open code model is to provide examination, customization, and verification for income while giving the code away for free.

The argument that the value of open source most certainly ends before the user interface is accepted by the majority of open source businesses, as illustrated by the popularity of proprietary GUI installers.

The argument for the post-convergence open source consumer is presented through two core arguments. These both contradictory and complementary arguments are that when consumers know what they want they will first speak and then act. The action may be to address the need themselves (as with privacy-protecting software discussed in the following section) or to cease doing business with a specific company. Open source provides the ability to take action, or to hire an individual to have action taken without the permission of the original software merchant. The model for open source companies as responsive listening companies is best illustrated by the discussion of protocols of code as choice in privacy and code as choice in pricing. The model of open source companies as resellers of information made freely available is illustrated in the discussion of auctions and online communities.

CODE AS CONSUMER CHOICE: PRIVACY

Trust has three components: privacy, reliability, and security. When a consumer comes to a company, that company asks for a certain amount of trust—trust that the company is an authentic company and not a corrupt merchant; trust that the merchant is reliable in the ability to provide service as well as honest in the intent to do so; trust that data provided by the consumer to the company are not reused in a manner that will harm the consumer. Privacy is a part of that trust; asking for more privacy implies providing more reliability.

Open code alters consumer options. The Anonymizer was originally a project of Justin Boyan, a Carnegie Mellon computer science student. (The difficulty of imagining a student tweaking SS7—the signaling system for traditional telecommunication networks described in Terry McGarty's chapter earlier in this volume—and the importance of the open network is apparent.) Justin created a proxy for anonymous Web browsing.[2] He also created a script to tell each browsing person what information was available about them—usually machine, site previously visited, and domain.[3] Most users simply cannot see the footprints they leave across cyberspace, and tools such as the Anonymizer provide more information to nontechnical users.

Users who install Web proxies or other identity-protecting software are using code to limit the extensions of trust required by Internet merchants. The terms on which consumers and citizens extend trust on the Internet can not be negotiated face-to-face or in contracts, because of the number of websites visited and the relative bargaining power of site producer and consumer. Privacy-protecting software allows individuals to opt out of the privacy bargain proffered by politicians, merchants, and network service providers. There is no other way for most consumers to have a meaningful debate with those who design websites, other than to stay away. Exhibiting a desire for privacy, while also showing a desire for the content or goods offered is a way of being heard—

less active than other direct actions, such as writing a letter of complaint or going in silence to another site. Privacy-protecting code is a demand for autonomy, a refusal of surveillance.[4] It is the choice of a consumer who is altering the terms of service. The consumer who refuses cookies or offers an anonymous browser profile is clearly stating design requests and requirements of every site visited. This information, offered through explicit consumer action, is arguably more valuable than the consumer detailing of preference on a survey filled out by an unrepresentative population.

Compare this to the privacy choices provided both consumers and companies with Microsoft Office. There is a unique user identifier for each copy of Microsoft Word purchased. Thus, Microsoft has the ability to track all documents produced by an individual owner or by an employee of a company. If, for example, attachments are frequently made in Microsoft Word to an anonymous investment discussion area, only Microsoft could track which employers and individuals were making which comments. This is a choice available only to Microsoft, not to the consumer or to the merchant offering the discussion area.

The choice of closed code limits information from customer to merchants, because customers have no way of expressing their desires in their settings. The choice of closed code limits the merchant's options in providing customer services to the privacy-valuing customer, because the merchant may be unable to serve the stated customer desire (e.g., removing a unique identifier). One example is of how code may create new possibilities for pricing Internet services.

CODE AS PRICING

There are many and varied proposals for charging for different quality services on the Internet. All of these proposals have different assumptions about equity, resource allocation, and efficiency. In this section we will describe two such protocols and how they would differ.

The dynamic auction (see Mackie-Mason and Varian) optimizes for economic efficiency. In this case, there is a bid attached to every packet. Nothing need be free; there is no need for social surplus. We would all pay what we would for each packet. In contrast, technologists prefer the expected capacity system (Clark, 1996), which optimizes network resources rather than prices, and has two levels of service. The expected capacity system has people guess their demand, and calls this prediction of demand a profile. Each user would be billed for his or her (guessed) profile, not actual use. Use within any profile would be given a higher priority than use outside of a profile. Use outside of the guessed-use profile would be served at a lower priority, called best effort. (Currently all data on the Internet uses best-effort services.) This proposal is compatible with flat-rate service.

The design goals for the two systems are, respectively, economic efficiency and technical efficiency, clearly two very different models of efficiency. Choosing to use one system or another, choosing to install code based on its functionality, means making value choices about efficiency. Efficiency includes the time it takes to evaluate a choice. Flat-rate pricing has proven its popularity with consumers, because the consumer concept of economic efficiency includes the consumer's attention span and consumer aversion to a sudden spike in a network services bill.

WEB AUCTIONS: BUYING FROM STRANGERS

In the domain of Web auctions, there are business-to-business, consumer-to-business, and consumer-to-consumer transactions. The archetype of a consumer-to-consumer Internet auction site is eBay. At eBay consumers buy and sell, but they also participate in other critical actions that underlie any information business. Customers rate sites, prices, deals, customers, and categories.

Consider a walk through eBay as a model for the active consumer. First, consumers are self-directed to auctions presented by other consumers. eBay is a community that includes an auction option, and this is as much a part of its success as the first-mover advantage, because it is important not only to move first but also to move in the most appropriate direction.

When first logging on, there is an option to evaluate the eBay community. Each eBay user has a profile related to their name—the user's reputation. Every user can comment on every other user; however, the reputation of the commentator is also available.

Thus, users provide the following on eBay:

- the goods themselves (the supply)

- the demand

- the evaluation of users as both customers and merchants

- information about the widespread willingness to pay for an item.

Compare this to other auctions where the users provide only three of the four. The most critical information for an online auction is the reliability of the seller. The customer's question is not simply, "Can I buy this online?" The customer's real question is—"Can I buy this online from a reputable source?"

Consumers could make blind purchases online from strangers with old-fashioned news groups. In newsgroups, markets functioned for specialty goods, because in the early online community specialty goods represented a small enough market that informal reputation systems worked. The brilliance of eBay is not that it allowed bidding, because there was no impediment to online bidding in newsgroups. The genius of eBay is harnessing the consumer to rate the merchants. In effect, First Virtual tried to perform the same service for the entire Internet, but this required a concentration of merchant and customer trust in an infant corporation. First Virtual failed. eBay offers the same low level of certainty that money will not be stolen as First Virtual, but eBay does not ask each consumer to trust corporate judgment of appropriate consumer risk. It allows each user to evaluate a collective judgment of risk.

THE ELECTRONIC COMMUNITY

What ingredients are necessary for an electronic community? The only critical ingredient is committed users. Electronic communities exist in role-playing environments, shared-value environments, and environments that seem to exist solely for the purpose of venting spleen (see alt.politics.abortion or alt.flame for examples of spleen-venting forums).

Electronic communities and portals are particular versions of open source communities, because each user input creates value for themselves and for others. The loyalty of each consumer will be some function of the amount of time the consumer invests in the community. As the consumer begins to build the community, the consumer will feel, and reasonably so, ownership. The more input the consumer provides, the more responsive the electronic community organizers should be to the specific consumer (see Horn, 1997; Hagel and Armstrong, 1997).

Electronic communities depend on open content, which is analogous to open code. The more users contribute to the content, the more valuable is the content. However, the same concerns that exist in open source exist in open content. In open source, there is concern about forking—creation of two incompatible versions of one package. Similarly, two completely different dialogues can develop in parallel as part of the same discussion thread. In open source, it is critical that a popular project have a coordinator who provides filtering to ensure that not all proposals go in the code. Project organizers prevent code from becoming an indistinguishable noodle string of undocumented hacks. Similarly, open content sites need to have strong moderators to prevent dialogues from descending into incoherent ranting.

The management of open source projects is not an obscure art arising from the bizarre social mechanisms of technocrats. Rather, each open source project is a specific example of the management of an electronic community. Every successful business has at its core the management of a virtual community. With smart manufacturing management, the community of concern expanded beyond the design and management divisions to cover the entire firm. Just in time manufacturing moved beyond the office to include the factory floor and supplier networks. In Internet commerce, the community of concern now is broad enough to include the customer.

CONCLUSIONS

By tracking, measuring, and analyzing the movements of workers, scientific management attempted to optimize their efficiency. Yet this model was unable to compete with a system that allowed innovation to arise from the shop floor—a system in which managers assumed workers knew their jobs better than the manager.

Scientific management of the consumer is as certain to fail as scientific management of the worker failed. Proprietary software attempts to capture its users. The amount of user data stored in Redmond, Washington, is overshadowed by the vast incompetence of Microsoft to actually serve its customers' needs by analyzing the data. The compilation of user data is not doomed to failure because it is covert—that is an ethical not an economic concern. It is doomed because organizations and managers are not uniquely endowed with wisdom and understanding that surpasses the sum of all wisdom and understanding of those being managed, regardless of the information systems at the managers' disposal or the information pathologies exhibited by the organization.

Today's website designers collect consumer clicks for extensive data collection and analysis, yet often ignore the explicit requests of consumers themselves. This may seem like irrational behavior, but it becomes immediately recognizable when described as market research versus customer service.

Writing on the functioning of human organizations, Hirschman argues that individuals have two basic choices when confronted with organizational conflict: to exit or to become active and outspoken to cause change. In the past, loyalty was a primary determinant of the path chosen. Yet this work is about loyalty to organizations and institutions greater than brand loyalty.

Previously, consumers had little choice but to exit—to change products. Letters to manufacturers suffered the weaknesses of all analog data—they were hard to sort, analyze, and parse. Online consumers, however, generate digital information. Online consumers self-organize into partisan groups, and such groups offer a wealth of real-time information and debate.

The organizations that have thrived in the early Internet economy have listened to their customers. Cisco is legendary for listening to its customers—for having a sales force that channels customer suggestions on product design to the engineers. Cisco's dominance in the router business is the result.

Despite the concentration on social good in the GNU Manifesto, the final point is this: open source provides the ability to take action without the permission of the original software developer. Sustainable open source business models must be based upon an understanding that their business depends upon the ability to be responsible listeners to their customers—the kind strangers who will help sustain their business.

12 | ALTERNATIVE INDUSTRY FUTURES IN THE GLOBAL INTERNET ECONOMY

Martin G. Hyman and Raul L. Katz

INDUSTRY TRENDS AND EVOLUTION

The telecommunications industry is experiencing an unprecedented restructuring. This fundamental discontinuity is characterized by several trends. First and foremost is the horizontal and vertical integration of major carriers in pursuit of economies of scope and scale. Second, an explosive growth in data communications services and IP networking led to acquisition of tier one Internet service providers by telecommunications carriers. Third, both new and incumbent telecommunications operators are proceeding with the deployment of next-generation integrated digital networks (IDNs) that promise dramatic cost reductions, step-function bandwidth increases, and the integration of voice, data, and video. Fourth, telecommunications operators continue to implement global expansion and alliances to satisfy needs of business customers and to capitalize on deregulation of national monopolies. In addition to global partnerships, alliances are also established between carriers and computing companies in pursuit of end-to-end capabilities and network-centric application solutions. Finally, we are witnessing the emergence of wireless data services that, after many unfulfilled promises, will deliver a complement to new end-user device functionality.

As a result of these trends, the competitive landscape is evolving into a tiered environment dominated by large-scale, full-service next-generation carriers, a second tier of scale players, and a third group of niche specialists (see figure 1).

Figure 1 ————————————

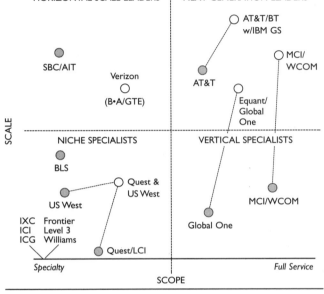

Search for Economies of Scale and Scope

Do these changes signal a new paradigm for the telecommunications industry or are they just part of a transition toward an as yet unknown endgame? Can we determine a developmental pattern that characterizes the dynamics of a "creative destruction" process at work? At a minimum, these events clearly challenge the long-standing traditional industry structure defined around regionally product-centric businesses, even if the final form of the industry is not known at this time. This uncertainty argues for a scenario analysis to determine the most likely outcome.

INDUSTRY SCENARIO FRAMEWORK

We have developed a scenario framework as a tool to test the proposition that a new industry paradigm is emerging. The scenario framework is an important starting point, because it purposefully conditions the view of industry evolution from the future-back, rather than starting incrementally from today's structure. The approach was to describe potential industry scenarios that capture the potential predominant supplier- and customer-demand characteristics that can be hypothesized to drive future industry structure. Therefore, the starting point is a description of scenarios from which are derived the underlying structural dimensions. Specifically, scenarios were defined that reflect the primary distinguishing characteristics of today's industry structure, its future evolution, and the potential discontinuities. Key features were defined for each scenario. Finally, the most sufficient dimensions of difference were derived to allow display and characterization of the potential scenarios along three orthogonal dimensions. Part of the value in determining the major dimensions governing future scenarios was to provide rigorous definition of the orthogonal and fundamental dimensions that describe the solution space.

The starting point was to identify four potential scenarios that describe the current and already apparent industry trends. The first trend is the emergence of integrated and interconnected service providers. These players with regional footprints (i.e., SBC, Verizon, and BellSouth) offer discrete, application-specific solutions without end-to-end capability. Under this industry configuration, end-to-end customer solutions can only be developed by interconnecting both horizontally with other regions and vertically with higher value-added services. Driven by this situation, these players seek to maximize value by controlling the end connection with the customer. This scenario explains the wave of ILEC (incumbent local exchange carrier) consolidation.

The second trend is the emergence of service providers that focus on a particular horizontal component of the value chain (e.g., transport or switching) and offer it end-to-end on a national/global basis (see figure 2). Under this configuration, providers seek to maximize value through economies of scale

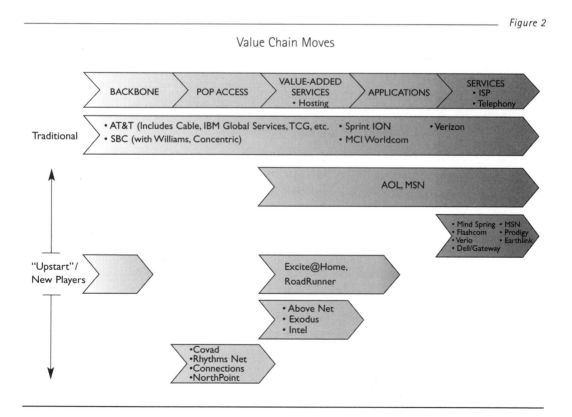

Figure 2

Value Chain Moves

and control over a key element of the value chain. Williams, and Level 3 represent emerging models of this scenario.

Third, and orthogonal to the previous trend, we witness the emergence of providers with national/global footprints offering end-to-end solutions. They vertically integrate their operations to achieve direct control over service consistency, quality of service, service-level agreements, and provisioning. These providers seek to maximize value through economies of scale and control over the total customer value proposition (e.g., major carrier initiatives toward horizontal and vertical integration).

Fourth, and as a particular case of the previous trend, we identify service providers focusing on offering full-service vertical solutions that exploit an existing franchise of customers. Solutions must be interconnected horizontally to reach other franchises. Emerging e-business networks such as WebMD and ANX represent business models that capitalize on this scenario.

These four scenarios are most distinct with respect to their underlying assumption about the dominant character of demand and a recomposition of the industry structure in terms of degree of vertical or horizontal integration or stratification. More specifically, these four scenarios can be analyzed with two key dimensions that could indicate a change in the industry paradigm:

1. Value Proposition: Are customers requiring more complex end-to-end networking solutions, or will interconnected offers be sufficient? Key explanatory factors of this dimension are customer buying behavior, solution complexity, and the ability of off-net solutions to meet customer needs. In particular, the resolution of the value proposition will rest on the demand-side trade-offs between "anywhere connectivity" and closed community of interest security and reliability. Already there are significant signposts of this "on-net versus off-net" tension playing out among competing architectures.

2. Industry Structure: Will the industry be dominated by business models that vertically integrate offers—perhaps balkanized by application or vertical segment—and operations, or will the preeminent dynamic be a move toward distinct horizontally stratified businesses that are powered by the distinct core competencies that are required for success at each layer? Key drivers of this dimension are the basis of industry competition

(e.g., scale versus customer control) and the feasibility of businesses to achieve interoperability of networks and systems through standards. In particular, the interoperability challenge is a derivative of Coase's Law in which the "frictional cost" of resource assembly across the value chain either does (or does not) outweigh the cost of complexity (value of single focus) due to integration (decomposition) of businesses at different layers of the value chain.[1]

Figure 3 depicts the two dimensions schematically.

Figure 3

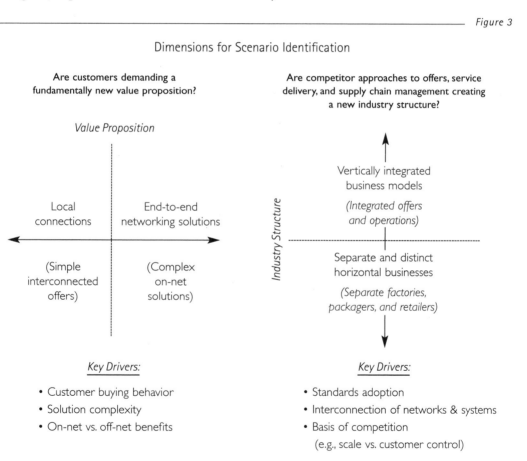

Dimensions for Scenario Identification

Are customers demanding a fundamentally new value proposition?

Value Proposition

Local connections — End-to-end networking solutions

(Simple interconnected offers) — (Complex on-net solutions)

Are competitor approaches to offers, service delivery, and supply chain management creating a new industry structure?

Industry Structure

Vertically integrated business models

(Integrated offers and operations)

Separate and distinct horizontal businesses

(Separate factories, packagers, and retailers)

Key Drivers:

• Customer buying behavior
• Solution complexity
• On-net vs. off-net benefits

Key Drivers:

• Standards adoption
• Interconnection of networks & systems
• Basis of competition
  (e.g., scale vs. customer control)

The combination of these two dimensions allows us to plot the four scenarios reviewed above (figure 4).

Figure 4

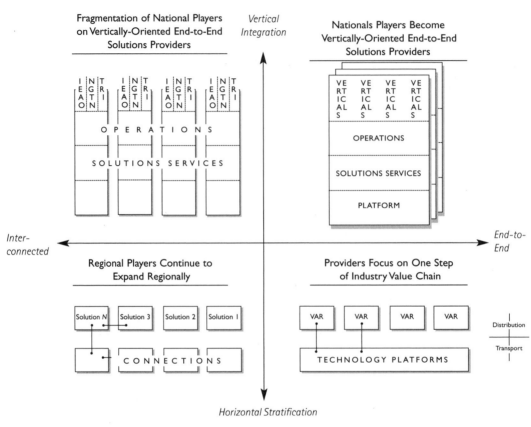

Two-dimensional Scenario Framework

According to this framework, each scenario represents a different outcome along the two dimensions described above.

UNCONVENTIONAL SCENARIOS

The scenarios described by the end-user and supplier dimensions do not yet accommodate some less-conventional thinking about the future of the industry. Specifically, four additional dynamics shaping the future of the industry should be considered.

First, one should consider the emergence of players that capitalize on a new demand model aimed at creating a powerful horizontal solution platform that exhibits superior features when compared to the emerging vertically integrated digital network players. This model possesses clear advantage because of the economies of scale in development costs (e.g., software/platform reuse), and by its nimbleness and speed in responding to the needs of new forms of retail demands. Examples of this model are E*Trade trading network, the Sony gaming network, and the Hyatt reservations network. Level 3 is an example of a carrier that believes the fundamental nature of demand is changing in an unprecedented manner, shifting toward "pure IP" networking solutions that have entirely different demand characteristics—not just architecturally, but in buying process, the buyer, and so on.

Second, exploiting the potential for wired and wireless communities of interest, a different scenario views the "anywhere" need of end-users as preeminent—potentially defined around workflows or e-business communities. This scenario could potentially challenge the "on-net" character of "networks rule" or "platforms rule" by meeting the off-net needs for specific communities defined by trading groups, workgroups, or personal networks. Even among players who are pursuing an apparent strategy of vertical integration, such as AOL/Time Warner, there is a certain ambivalence reflected in parallel initiatives around AOL Anywhere. In a sharp sense, the parallel initiatives toward vertical and horizontal integration, while at the same time pursuing an "off-net anywhere" strategy, reflect contradictory or hedge bets against two different scenarios.

Third, an alternative scenario assumes the creation of regional solutions that establish mass market solution islands in multiple geographic regions as "chips" in the ultimate alliance endgame. Telefónica remains the prototypical example.

Fourth, there is the potential emergence of a mass-market-focused scenario that aims at attaining customer control by means of leveraging a single device. This alternative is best represented by Sony's vision of interconnected end-user devices. This is a completely orthogonal thrust that reflects the long-standing battle between the network and the customer premise for architectural control. The notion that cheap, unlimited bandwidth and storage can in tandem force a future where all of the network architectural issues revolve around delivery of quality-of-service is a radical point of departure.

THIRD-DIMENSION AND NONCONVENTIONAL SCENARIOS

Outlining the four nonconventional scenarios has defined a third dimension of the scenario framework. A third governing dimension characterized as "reach" —consumers versus enterprise—provides the necessary market-focused perspective. In effect we have defined reach as the underlying dynamic that reflects the ultimate preeminence of "offnet anywhere," whether enabled indirectly by technology (device-centric, network everywhere) or new business models (new demand models), or directly driven by mass market demands.

By adding this third dimension, we have developed a "cube" that allows us to plot the four additional scenarios as shown below (Figure 5).

The resulting scenarios framework is quite satisfactory because it accom-

Figure 5

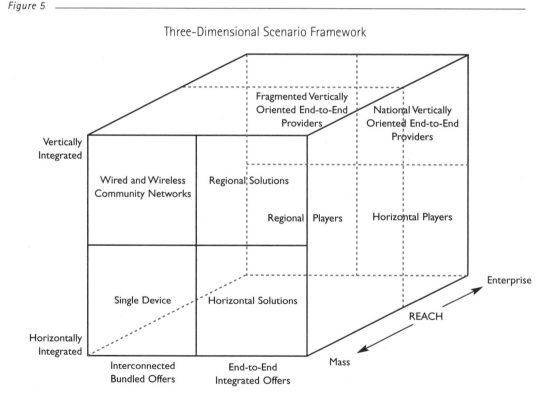

Three-Dimensional Scenario Framework

modates: 1) existing empirical data about emerging business models (the "back face" of the cube), 2) conjectures about less conventional futures (the "front face" of the cube), and 3) fits all of these possible endgame scenarios to a "model" in three dimensions that considers important and relatively orthogonal views of the governing industry dynamics (supplier structure, value proposition, and "market reach").

This framework of scenarios raises two important issues that still need to be explored. First, one clearly should assume a set of dynamic trends that allows for the migration among scenarios. Second, and more important, it raises the issue that, given the uncertainty of outcome, service providers need to craft a business strategy that possesses advantage in one or more of these scenarios and is sustainable in the face of competitors who are working against different endgame visions.

IMPLICATIONS FOR SERVICE PROVIDERS

Each of these scenarios raises a set of strategic implications for service providers.

Horizontal Solutions

The "new demand model" contemplates a discontinuous shift in the model for purchase of communications services. This is hinted at in the notion of network service providers (NSPs) supporting e-business solutions. In a broader manifestation, it could be expanded to include "network-enabled businesses," a notion that Level 3 is promoting. Level 3 uses the example of an e-trade VPN (virtual private network) providing secure, fast, reliable access for customers anywhere, anytime. The theory of the case is premised on the pervasiveness of the Internet in fundamentally changing the business model in many industries.

Winning in this scenario requires a strategy that allows a horizontally focused new-demand platform to have an advantage over megacarriers by virtue of speed and agility in responding to new demand sources that require a "certified" network supplier.

Regional Solutions

Many of the initiatives by carriers have been U.S.-centric—for example, MCI/ WorldCom and Sprint. The major carrier "network rules" scenario increasingly is being played out globally, however, and it is interesting that newer upstarts (e.g., Level 3, Qwest) are among the leaders.

Perhaps there are alternatives to "bulking up" in the United States that create equal or greater advantage in the endgame. In particular, mass market–driven solutions may have a regional (Europe, NE Asia, Pacific Rim, Latin America, etc.) standard in terms of language, content, and culture. Is there a leapfrog strategy that assembles winning mass market positions in multiple geographies? Given that all mass telecommunications markets are local, focusing on the mass market and creating a regional "integrated mass telecom" company could be a plausible option.

Single Device

Current thinking centers around ONE company that focuses on "THE MARKET"—both consumers and enterprise—with ability to leverage both "hard" and "soft" assets. But another plausible scenario might envision distinct companies, because consumers have a completely different set of needs—increased need for entertainment-based services with more asymmetric information flows, and less need for change of dynamic service provisioning (that is, they have more "stable" needs).

This differentiated set of needs (around offerings) combines nicely with intelligent-edge devices that tend to be more consumer-electronics driven: the Sony vision of iLINK as a standard "plug-n-play" interface, connecting stereo, TV, computer, etc.; the Sony Memory Stick, billed as the "universal media." iLINK and Memory Stick together are suggestive of a scenario in which individual users, through endpoint devices, are the driving force. The network is relegated to a less important place, and the architectural control point is around consumer electronics and content.

Thus, we could imagine a situation in which the critical success factors are intimate customer knowledge, ability to provide superior content (with a local flavor), and the endpoint devices that make it happen. This "world" could evolve separately as consumer-centric and enterprise-centric models.

Wired and Wireless Community Networks

As we focus on the mass market, we can envisage the creation of several integrated community networks. In this scenario, service providers can establish strong ties or create a "virtually bound integrated" company with several niche/specialized content and applications players to focus on local community and interest groups. Some consumer needs tend to be very local in nature—local news, local weather, local suppliers, local events, and so on. Any national or international content will be bundled by sourcing those and creating bundled offers along with local differentiated service. For example, AOL could source local content and partner with wireless providers, device manufacturers, or special wireless applications providers to create a new offering that includes instant messaging platform for the "mobility centric" community/interest group.

CONCLUSIONS

At a normative level, we believe the framework presented above provides the capability to assess direction and rationale for many of the ongoing changes in the telecommunications industry, and an opportunity for firms to assess the likely effects of their own business strategies on their changing competitive environment over time. In that sense, it allows us to validate Schumpeter's basic premise. The framework can not, however, provide us with a view of the ultimate configuration of the industry structure: fragmentation versus integration, horizontal versus vertical integration, device centric or network centric, global versus regional. In a communications industry that is undergoing discontinuous change in structure, successful competitors will have to craft business strategies that hold an advantage in one or more plausible endgames.

CONTRIBUTORS

Lee W. McKnight

Lee W. McKnight is an associate professor of international communications and director of the Edward R. Murrow Center at the Fletcher School of Law and Diplomacy, Tufts University; visiting scholar at the Massachusetts Institute of Technology's Center for Technology, Policy and Industrial Development; founder of the Internet and Telecoms Convergence Consortium, and president of Marengo Research LLC, a consultancy. He received a Ph.D. in 1989 from MIT; an M.A. from the School of Advanced International Studies, Johns Hopkins University, in 1981; and a B.A. magna cum laude from Tufts University in 1978.

Professor McKnight is co-editor of *Internet Economics* (MIT Press, 1997) and *Internet Telephony* (MIT Press, 2001), and co-author of *The Gordian Knot: Political Gridlock on the Information Highway* (MIT Press, 1997); and author and co-author of numerous articles. He is a member of the editorial advisory boards of the *Brazilian Electronic Journal of Economics; INFO: the Journal of Telecommunications, Media, and Information Policy and Strategy;* and the *Journal of Municipal Telecommmunications.*

His current research focuses on international technology policy and innovation, the convergence of the Internet and telecommunications industries, Internet telephony policy, and Internet bandwidth markets.

Paul M. Vaaler

Paul M. Vaaler is an assistant professor of International Business at the Fletcher School of Law and Diplomacy, Tufts University. He completed his Ph.D. studies in strategic management at the University of Minnesota's Carlson School of

Management in 1996. He has a J.D. from the Harvard Law School; an M.A. in philosophy, politics, and economics from Oxford University, where he studied as a Rhodes Scholar; and a B.A. in history from Carleton College. At the Fletcher School, Professor Vaaler teaches and publishes in the strategy and international business fields, with particular emphases in comparative aspects of technology management and management in newly privatized industries. His current research interests include global product innovation and risk assessment, product pioneering advantages and disadvantages, business strategy in newly privatized enterprises, and the role of culture and ethics in international negotiation. In addition to this volume, he is co-editor of the forthcoming *Financial Innovations and the Welfare of Nations* (Kluwer Academic Press, 2001). Professor Vaaler is a lawyer with experience in public and private practice and has been a special consultant to the U.S. Federal Trade Commission's Bureau of Economics. He also serves as the director of the Fletcher School's Hitachi Center for Technology and International Affairs.

Raul L. Katz

Raul L. Katz is a vice president and partner with Booz·Allen & Hamilton's Communications, Media and Technology Practice, specializing in business strategy, consumer and industrial marketing, and the management of telecommunications companies. He has worked extensively in the assessment of domestic and international markets for telecommunications services and equipment. His clients have included U.S.-based local exchange and long distance carriers as well as value-added networks and multinational telecommunication equipment and computer manufacturers. He has managed projects in the areas of demand forecasting, competitive analysis, market entry strategy, and new product development for offerings such as broadband services, fiber optics, voice processing equipment, general purpose computing, workstations, applications software, information services, interactive television, and electronic data interchange.

Mr. Katz received his Ph.D. in management science and political science (1985) and an M.S. in communications technology and policy (1981) from the Massachusetts Institute of Technology. He also holds a Licence in history (1979) and a Maîtrise in political science (1980) from the University of Paris-

Sorbonne, as well as a Licence (1979) and a Maîtrise with honors (1980) in communication sciences from the University of Paris.

He is the author of *The Information Society: An International Perspective,* (Praeger, 1988) which focused on deregulation trends in the worldwide telecommunications industry. He has published articles in *Telecommunications Policy* and *The Information Society* and lectures on deregulation and privatization of international telecommunications, information systems planning, the economic impact of information systems, and the use of decision support systems.

William J. Baumol

William J. Baumol is professor of economics and director of the C. V. Starr Center for Applied Economics at New York University and senior research economist and professor emeritus at Princeton University. Born in New York City, he received his education at the College of the City of New York and the University of London. He has been president of the American Economic Association and three other professional economics societies, is an elected member of the National Academy of Sciences and the American Philosophical Society, and is the recipient of nine honorary degrees. Professor Baumol has written extensively on industrial organization, regulation of industry, and the theory of the firm, and frequently acts as consultant to government and private firms in a wide variety of industries. He is author of some 30 books and numerous professional articles.

Jean Camp

Jean Camp is an assistant professor at the Kennedy School of Government, a senior member of the IEEE, and an elected member of the board of directors of CPSR. She has a background in EE, CS, and public policy. Professor Camp's core interest is in the interaction of technology, society, and the economy. This interest that led Professor Camp from graduate electrical engineering research in North Carolina to the Department of Engineering and Public Policy at Carnegie Mellon, and has remained her core research interest at Sandia National Laboratories, and at the Kennedy School. Her expertise is in Internet commerce and design for values. She is the author of *Trust and Risk in Internet Commerce* (MIT Press, 2000), and more than 30 peer-reviewed publications on technical issues of social importance (e.g., privacy, reliability) and social issues with critical technical elements (e.g., content selection).

Leslie Helm

Leslie Helm has covered technology in Japan and the United States for national magazines and newspapers for the past 18 years. He worked as Tokyo correspondent for *Business Week* from 1982 and later became Bureau Chief of *Business Week*'s Boston bureau. In 1990 he returned to Japan as Tokyo correspondent for the *Los Angeles Times*. Since 1993 he has worked in Seattle covering Microsoft and the development of the Internet. Helm is on leave from the *Los Angeles Times* to study the Internet in Japan on a fellowship from the Abe Foundation.

Jill Hills

Jill Hills is a professor of telecommunications policy at the University of Westminster and co-director of the International Institute for Regulators in Telecommunications. Previously she held the post of professor of international political economy at City University in London. Her interests are in international communications, particularly the relationship between international and domestic markets, and in the regulation of telecommunications and broadcasting in the United States, Europe, Africa, and the Far East. She has published widely on telecommunications and broadcasting, and currently is researching a two-volume study of the battle for control of world communications since the 1860s.

Martin G. Hyman

Martin G. Hyman is a vice president and partner in the Communications, Media and Technology Practice of Booz·Allen & Hamilton, Inc. and possesses more than 20 years of experience in consulting for the telecommunications industry. He has led a wide range of assignments in product development and marketing strategy, business development, strategic planning, and cost restructuring. Before joining Booz·Allen in 1987, Mr. Hyman was a vice president of business development and planning for US Sprint with responsibility for development of its five-year strategic plan and management of its corporate acquisition/strategic alliance programs.

Mr. Hyman holds an M.S. in operations research from the Stanford School of Engineering and a B.S. in operations research from the Columbia School of Engineering.

William H. Lehr

William H. Lehr is an economist and industry consultant, a research affiliate and consultant to the Massachusetts Institute of Technology Internet Telephony Consortium (MIT ITC), an associate research scholar on the faculty of Columbia University's Graduate School of Business, and a research associate at the Columbia Institute of Tele-Information. His fields of specialization and research include industrial organization, political economy, and regulation, especially as these apply to information technology industries. He teaches courses in microeconomics and competitive strategy, including courses on the media, telecommunications, and Internet economics, and has published articles on topics that include the effects of industry structure on the quality of telecommunications infrastructure, the economics of standardization, and Internet pricing. Currently, he is engaged in research on the effects of computer investment on productivity and organizational structure and on Internet industry structure and pricing mechanisms. The latter work is undertaken in conjunction with the NUT ITC, an academic/industry consortium devoted to research on issues related to the convergence of Internet and telecommunications infrastructure. In addition to his academic research, Mr. Lehr provides litigation, economic, and business analysis consulting services for firms in the information technology industries.

Mr. Lehr holds a Ph.D. in economics from Stanford (1992), an M.B.A. from the Wharton Graduate School (1985), and M.S.E. (1984), B.S. (1979) and B.A. (1979) degrees from the University of Pennsylvania.

Terrence P. McGarty

Terrence P. McGarty is chairman of the Telmarc Group, LLC, a company he founded in 1984, which invests in and manages several high-tech startup ventures. Currently, he is chairman and CEO of Zephyr Telecommunications, an international record carrier, and managing director of CROSSCONNECT, a venture capital company.

Mr. McGarty has been active in the telecommunications industry for more than 30 years. Until 1992, he was a senior vice president at NYNEX and the chief operating officer of NYNEX Mobile, a cellular carrier. He was the first head of R&D for NYNEX, during which time he conceived and developed one of the first multimedia communications systems and the first network management system using the manager of managers concepts. Mr. McGarty also spent five years as group president at Warner Communications and six years in the satellite communications business as a division director and general manager of COMSAT's first nonregulated businesses. In his early career, he was a faculty and research staff member at the Massachusetts Institute of Technology, where he was involved in research in communications and imaging systems, as well as microeconomic policy development.

He holds a Ph.D. from MIT in electrical engineering and studied medicine in the joint Harvard/MIT program. He is the author of four books on topics that include random process theory, business planning, and telecommunications policy, and author of more than 75 professional papers in areas that include telecommunications, law, radiology, and medical imaging.

Maria Michalis

Maria Michalis is a research fellow in telecommunications regulatory policy at the University of Westminster. She has published articles on digital television, local access technologies, and EU convergence policies. In 1999 she held a BT short-term fellowship and currently is funded by the European Commission Jean Monnet project. She specializes in European communications policy.

Walter T. Molano

Walter T. Molano is head of economic and financial research at BCR Securities, Inc., responsible for all macroeconomic, financial, and corporate research. The emphasis is on Argentina, Brazil, Mexico, Chile, Ecuador, Colombia, Peru, and Venezuela. He issues a series of publications, including a daily fax on emerging markets, monthly reports, and individual country reports. Before joining BCP Securities, he was the director of economic and financial research at Warburg Dillon Read, a subsidiary of UBS AG. In 1995–1996, he was a senior economist and vice president for Latin America at CS First Boston. Mr. Molano completed his Ph.D. at Duke University and was the recipient of the Duke Endowment Fellowship, SSRC Fellowship, and Tinker Foundation Grant. He holds an M.B.A., an M.A. in international relations, a certificate in international law, and is a 1983 graduate of the U.S. Naval Academy. He is the author of *The Logic of Privatization: The Case of Telecommunications in the Southern Cone of Latin America,* published by Greenwood Publishing Group, and has given presentations on privatization at various universities and conferences. He was ranked in the Gold Medal Category during the 1998 Latin Finance Research Olympics and as a top economist for Venezuela in 1997. Mr. Molano is a member of the Council of Foreign Relations, Latin American Advisory Council, and a faculty fellow at the Yale School of Management.

Peter Pekar, Jr.

Peter Pekar is a recognized expert in the area of strategic alliances. His experience comes from both an academic and consultant perspective and from hands-on experience as an operating manager of numerous successful alliances. Since 1993, he has been a senior advisor to the management consulting firm of Booz•Allen & Hamilton, Inc. in the area of strategic alliances. His work at there covers client assignments and research in the United States, Asia, Europe, and Latin America. Along with his duties at Booz•Allen & Hamilton, he is a visiting professor at the London Business School, where he teaches a M.B.A. course on strategic alliances for graduate students and holds alliance seminars for senior executives. He received a Ph.D. in business and economics from Illinois Institute of Technology's Stuart School of Business and an M.A. in mathematics from the University of Illinois-Urbana.

Professor Pekar is co-author with John Harbison, a Booz·Allen partner, of three publications on strategic alliances that have been widely distributed. Their book, *Smart Alliances: A Practical Guide to Repeatable Success,* was published by Jossey-Bass in 1998.

NOTES

Chapter 1

1. For a summary of the papers, presentations, and discussion offered during the March 1999 symposium, see Peter Cukor, Raul Katz, Lee McKnight, Paul Vaaler, "Telecoms in Transition," *Fletcher Forum* (Spring 2000).
2. Joseph A. Schumpeter, "The creative response in economic history." In *Essays on Entrepreneurs, Innovations, Business Cycles, and the Evolution of Capitalism,* R. V. Clemence, ed. (New Brunswick: Transaction Publishers, 1997).
3. Joseph A. Schumpeter, *Capitalism, Socialism and Democracy* (London: Allen & Irwin, 1943) p. 31.

Chapter 2

1. Of course, growth is also the result of investment in human capital and investment in plants and equipment. But given the enormous poverty and the very low savings of the pre-Industrial Revolution economies, it is clear that only the spate of inventions that underlay the revolution made possible the huge investments in human and physical capital that occurred thereafter. In that sense, innovation can be taken as the primary engine of the growth process.
2. Some writers on innovation use the term "spillovers" in a more restricted sense to refer, for example, to direct gains of knowledge by customers of the industry that supplies the R&D in question (see, e.g., Grilliches [1979]). Such use of the term is, of course, entirely legitimate. Here, however, the term is taken as synonymous with total external effects. It represents *all* the social benefits of innovation that do not accrue as private benefits to the inventor or to those who invested in or otherwise contributed to it. This connotation is clearly required by the issue under discussion—the disincentive to innovation activity resulting from the difference between its social and private reward.
3. A reader has argued that this conclusion is unrealistic because innovations *do* benefit workers. That is, of course, correct. But, by definition, zero externalities means that no such benefits go to the workers. This implies that zero

externalities cannot occur in the world of reality—that it is an unattainable goal. The question that remains is whether that imaginary goal, if it could somehow be achieved, could be accepted as optimal. The answer of this paper, emphatically, is that it would not be optimal, contrary to what might be inferred from the literature. Though it would increase the number of beneficial innovations, it would, tautologically, preclude any of the benefits from going to persons other than the innovators. Romer puts the matter very clearly: "This pattern of industrialization without wage gains is what it would take to ensure that the industrialist captures all of the benefits he creates when he introduces machinery. . . . [this] cannot be a historically accurate description of the process of development in industrial countries, for if it were, unskilled labor would still earn what it earned prior to the industrial revolution." (Romer, 1994, p. 29).

4. As I have previously written and emphasized, this pricing rule is necessary but not sufficient for economic efficiency or protection of the public interest. In addition to (1), these goals require either effective competition or regulation in the final-product markets to ensure that the final-product prices yield no monopoly profits and no other efficiency-undermining distortions. For a summary of the discussion and references, see Baumol, Ordover, and Willig (1997, pp. 147–48).

5. See Baumol, Ordover, and Willig (1997, pp. 145–63, footnote).

Chapter 3

1. Frank Rich, "Journal: We All Pass Go. They Collect $200," in *New York Times,* June 3, 2000.

2. For a fuller discussion of what Chairman Greenspan said, what he meant, and the economic forces at work in the markets today, see Robert J. Schiller, *Irrational Exuberance* (Princeton: Princeton University Press, 2000).

3. This section of the chapter is based on several of my "On Technology" columns for *Mass High Tech,* www.boston.com/mht. The tendency of markets toward excess is a well-known characteristic and is not an infrequent occurrence. That regulatory and self-regulatory mechanisms can mitigate this tendency is one of the strongest arguments for public oversight of economic activities. See Charles Kindleberger's aforementioned classic, *Manias, Panics, and Crashes,* for more on this and other financial crises over the centuries.

4. An earlier version of this chapter entitled "Internet Business Models: Wake

Up and Smell the Coffee or Business as Usual?" was presented at the Third International Conference on Technology Policy and Innovation at the University of Texas-Austin, August 30–September 2, 1999. The author is grateful for the helpful feedback from Manuel Heitor and other participants at the conference.

5. If that is what one is seeking, many pundits offer free advice, which is worth at least as much as one is paying for their insights.

6. For recent work on the concept of "disruptive technologies" and their effects on incumbent and new entrant businesses, see Clayton M. Christenson, *The Innovator's Dilemma* (New York: HarperBusiness, 2000).

7. We make our case for an open communications infrastructure policy model in W. Russell Neuman, Lee McKnight, and Richard Jay Solomon, *The Gordian Knot: Political Gridlock on the Information Highway* (Cambridge: MIT Press, 1997; paperback, 1999).

8. I first developed this analogy for my presentation at the Kent College of Law Symposium on Network Convergence, Illinois Institute of Technology, May 2–3, 1998, refined it for my presentation at MIT's Symposium on Internet Commerce, December 1998, and then wrote it up in my column in *Mass High Tech,* January 1999, www.boston.com/mht; all were entitled "Romans, Barbarians, and Internet Commerce."

9. L. Jean Camp, who writes on open source software issues in this book, has also written on managing trust and risk issues in the Internet. See L. Jean Camp, *Trust and Risk in Internet Commerce* (Cambridge: MIT Press, 2000). For further information on how to design systems for maintaining security and transacting business on the Internet, see G. Winfield Treese and Lawrence C. Stewart, *Designing Systems for Internet Commerce* (New York: Addison-Wesley, 1998).

10. The current version of the Internet Protocol is IPv4, or version 4. The next, which is being rolled out as of this writing after years of delays and debates on whether it was really necessary to upgrade the Internet Protocol, is IPv6, or version 6. IPv6's principal virtues are its larger address space and improved security features. To make things more confusing for non-techies, IPv6 is sometimes referred to as IPng—"Internet Protocol for next generation." For more information on the technical specifications and properties of IP, see www.ietf.org.

11. The concept of a bearer service was developed by David Clark and other participants in the National Research Council's landmark study of the

implications of the Internet. See *Computer Science and Telecommunications Board, National Research Council, Realizing the Information Future* (Washington, D.C.: National Academy Press, 1994).

12. Annabelle Gawer analyzes how businesses develop strategies to manage and promote platform technologies that enable innovation in interrelated areas. Examples of such innovations in the information technology arena include Intel's microprocessors, Microsoft's operating systems—and the Internet. See Annabelle Gawer, "The Organization of Platform Leadership: An Empirical Investigation of Intel's Management Processes Aimed at Fostering Complementary Innovation by Third Parties" (Ph.D. diss., Massachusetts Institute of Technology, Sloan School of Management, 2000), http://itel.mit.edu. On the concept of general purpose technologies from an economic perspective, see Elhanan Helpman, ed., *General Purpose Technologies and Economic Growth* (Cambridge: MIT Press, 1998).

13. There are, of course, significant legal implications in information aggregation through the Internet, which typically is thought to be simply an issue of copyright law or information management. For an examination of some of the subtleties involved, see Thomas Lee and Lee McKnight, "Internet Data Management: Policy Barriers to an Intermediated Electronic Market in Data," a paper presented at the 27th Annual TPRC, September 1999, www.tprc.org.

14. The MIT/Tufts Workshop on Internet Service Quality Economics was held December 2–3, 1999, with the support of the U.S. National Science Foundation, Directorate for Computer and Information Sciences and Engineering; U.S. Defense Advanced Projects Research Agency, Information Technology Office; and the Embassy of France, Scientific and Technical Affairs Office. The workshop addressed the most recent advances in Internet standards, business practices, and economic theory for advanced Internet services.

15. For an analysis of optical network costs and performance, see Pedro Ferreira and Beatrice Cossa, "Testing the Scalability of DWDM Networks," presented at the Fourth International Conference on Technology Policy and Innovation, Curitiba, Brazil, August 28–31, 2000. The paper may be found at http://itel.mit.edu.

16. For example, Genuity, one of the largest U.S. backbone network operators, had revenues of $750 million and losses of $750 million in 1999. Nevertheless, Genuity succeeded in an IPO in 2000 and raised several billion dollars in equity.

17. The business shelves of bookstores, real and virtual, are crowded with books offering assured success and pat insights into the changes unfolding in the Internet economy. Even if the author argues here that it is not so simple, he also confesses to having contributed to some degree to this euphoric Internet environment, as a scholar and teacher, as well as a consultant and adviser to start-up Internet and incumbent firms. For more information on the author's research and work with MIT's Internet and Telecoms Convergence Consortium, see http://itel.mit.edu. This chapter represents the author's views, which are not necessarily shared by any of the institutions with which he is affiliated. Any errors of fact or omission are the author's responsibility.

18. Rather, there is a new channel for advertising goods and services. The use of targeted marketing on the Internet, which could be argued to be uniquely suited for personal tracking—and the resultant risks to personal privacy and security—is an important topic, but it is beyond the scope of this chapter.

19. Bailey, op. cit.

20. See W. Russell Neuman, Lee McKnight, and Richard Jay Solomon, *The Gordian Knot: Political Gridlock on the Information Highway* (Cambridge: MIT Press, 1997, 1999), as well as the author's August 1999 column on open access in *Mass High Tech*. See www.boston.com/mht.

21. Ibid.

22. This chapter draws from several of the author's monthly "On Technology" columns for the weekly business newspaper, *Mass High Tech*. See www. boston.com/mht, and look for back issues, for the second week of the month..

23. A tip of the cap to the inspiring and thoughtful first class (2001) in the Fletcher School of Law and Diplomacy at Tufts University's innovative (we think so!) new Global Master of Arts Program, for which the author is currently teaching a combined residency/on-line course entitled "International Technology: The Internet as a Global Innovation Engine." Their individual and collective insight has contributed to this chapter in many ways. See www.gmap.fletcher.tufts.edu for more information.

Chapter 4

1. David Charles, *Technology and Competition in the International Telecommunications Industry* (London: Pinter Publishers, 1989), 11–16.

2. This chapter builds on the work developed in Walter Molano, *The Logic of Privatization: The Case of Telecommunications in the Southern Cone of Latin America* (Westport: Greenwood Press, 1997).

3. Henry British Lins de Barros, *Historia da Industria da Telecomunicacoes no Brasil* (Rio de Janeiro: Associacaco Brasileira de Telecomunicacoes, 1989), 5.

4. Molano, 84–85.

5. Molano, 50–51.

6. Graciela Perez Montero Gotusso, "Uruguay," in *Telecommunications in Latin America,* ed. Eli Noam (New York: Oxford University Press, 1998), 157–60.

7. Hector Mairal, "The Argentine Telephone Privatization" in *Implementing Reforms in the Telecommunications Sector,* ed. Bjorn Wellenius and Paul Stern (Washington, D.C.: The World Bank, 1994), 161–75.

8. Jose Ricardo Melo, "Liberalization and Privatization in Chile" in *Implementing Reforms in the Telecommunications Sector,* ed. Bjorn Wellenius and Paul Stern (Washington, D.C.: The World Bank, 1994), 145–55.

9. Michael Dowley, *Strategic Investments in Innovation: The Telecommunications Equipment Industry, 1975-1986* (New York: Garlord Publishing, 1992), 24–27.

10. Michael Hobday, *Telecommunications in Developing Countries: The Challenges from Brazil* (London: Routledge, 1990), 12–13.

11. Peter Lindert, "Response to the Debt Crisis" in *The International Debt Crisis in Historical Perspective,* ed. Barry Eichengreen and Peter Lindert (Cambridge: MIT Press, 1991) 229–31.

12. Antonio Jose Botelho, "Brazil" in *Telecommunications in Latin America,* ed. Eli Noam (New York: Oxford University Press, 1998), 229–37.

13. Instituto de Pesquisa Economica Aplicada, *O Brasil No Fim do Seculo* (Rio de Janeiro: IPEA, 1994), 245–50.

14. Charles Cooper, *Technology and Innovation in the International Economy* (New York: UN University Press, 1994), 55.

15. Eli Noam, ed., *Telecommunications in Latin America* (New York: Oxford University Press, 1998), xii.

16. Alejandra Herrera, *La Revolucion Tecnologica y la Telefonía Argentina* (Buenos Aires: Legasa, 1992.), 26–33.

17. Molano, 29.

18. Pierre Guislain, *The Privatization Challenge* (Washington, D.C.: The World Bank, 1997), 209–11.

19. Ahmed Galal, "Chile," in *Does Privatization Matter?* ed. Ahmed Galal and Mary Shirley (Washington, D.C.: The World Bank, 1994), 51.

Chapter 5

1. U.S. regulatory theorists include Coase (1960), Marcus (1985), Peltzman (1976), Posner (1974), Stigler (1962, 1971), Wilson (1980). Regulatory theorists from the U.K. include Beesley (1981, 1983), Davies and Davies (1984), Baldwin and Cave (1999), Foster (1992), Littlechild (1983).

2. Recently, FCC Commissioner Michael K. Powell has complained of the commission chairman's willingness to alter the commission agenda to meet President Clinton's goals (Powell, 2000): U.K. Chancellor of the Exchequer Gordon Brown made public a meeting with the director general of Oftel, David Edmonds, to press for lower local call tariffs (Teather, 2000a).

3. The BBC is self-regulated by its board of governors, appointed by the Crown, and the Home Office under obligations set out in a Royal Charter and Agreement (Scannell and Cardiff, 1991).

4. Consolidation of the British ITV network of regional broadcasters has been limited by two rules. First, according to the 1996 Broadcasting Act, no single ITV company can control more than 15 percent of audience share. Second, following a number of undertakings to the Office of Fair Trading in 1994, no single ITV company can have more than 25 percent of national television advertising revenues.

5. ITV is a federation of regional broadcasters funded by advertising. It offers national coverage through fifteen licensees broadcasting in fourteen regions, each regulated as a public service broadcaster.

6. List of abbreviations used:

ADSL	Asymmetric Digital Subscriber Line
BBC	British Broadcasting Corporation [UK]
DCMS	Department for Culture, Media and Sport [UK]
DG III	Directorate general responsible for industry [European Commission]
DG IV	Directorate general responsible for competition [European Commission]
DG X	Directorate general responsible for culture and audiovisual [European Commission]
DG XIII	Directorate general responsible for information society and telecommunications [European Commission]
DG XV	Directorate general responsible for the internal market [European Commission]

Note that, under the Presidency of Romano Prodi, the European Commission's Directorates General have been restructured.

DSL	Digital Subscriber Line
DTI	Department of Trade and Industry [UK]
FCC	Federal Communications Commission [USA]
ISDN	Integrated Services Digital Network
ISP	Internet Service Provider
ITAP	Information Technology Advisory Panel [UK]
ITC	Independent Television Commission [UK]
ITV	independent television [UK]
OECD	Organization for Economic Co-operation and Development
OFT	Office of Fair Trading [UK]
Oftel	Office of Telecommunications [UK]
VDSL	Very high-speed Digital Subscriber Line

7. Mercury (a consortium consisting of Cable and Wireless Communications (CWC), Barclays Bank, and British Petroleum) was licensed in 1982 and began offering services in the City of London, the financial and business center, in 1983. The British government adopted the so-called duopoly policy limiting competition in the fixed network to BT and Mercury until 1991. CWC subsequently bought out the other investors in Mercury.

8. In April 1997, CWC was formed from a merger between Mercury Communications and three cable companies (Nynex Cablecomms, Bell Cablemedia and Videotron). Further consolidation in the British cable market is underway. In May 2000, NTL confirmed its plan to complete, subject to regulatory approval, the acquisition of CWC Consumer Co. The new group will be the largest domestic broadband company and will compete against BT and BSkyB in telecommunications and pay-TV.

9. Because of their dependence for content on the satellite broadcaster and BSkyB's pricing and bundling practices, the cable companies had appealed unsuccessfully to the Office of Fair Trading on the grounds of restraint of trade (OFT, 1996). Only in 2000 did the Independent Television Commission begin to enforce unbundling of BSkyB channels.

10. The Bangemann report, drawn up by a group of large-scale industrialists, saw the information society as built on private solutions. It called for full liberalization of European telecommunications and the acceleration of the single market in communications.

11. Some EU member states have already adopted local loop unbundling (Austria, Denmark, Finland, Germany, and the Netherlands).

12. ADSL (Asymmetric DSL) uses a special modem in the home and another at

the telephone exchange. It is an asymmetric technique in which the transmission speeds are different in each direction. The upstream user-to-network channel operates at up to 64kbit/s and the downstream network-to-user channel operates at up to 9Mbit/s. In contrast, a basic ISDN connection offers up to 128kbit/s (2B64). Other systems, such as VDSL (very high-speed DSL) offer rates of up to 52Mbit/s downstream but operate only over short distances (up to 1.3km).

13. Lunney v. Prodigy Services Company Opinion, Court of Appeals of New York. Alexander G. Lunney, appellant v. Prodigy Services Company, respondent, et al., defendants. 99 N.Y. Int. 0165. December 2, 1999. 2 No 164. available on <http://caselaw.findlaw.com/scripts/getcase.pl?court=ny&vol=i99&involv=0165>

14. Open claims more than 450,000 people have registered for e-mail, and it is estimated that the service could reach three million users by the end of 2000 (Teather, 2000b).

15. The BCC's Internet involvement started in late 1996 with its commercial arm, BBC Worldwide, launching a website (beeb.com). Subsequently, the public-service site (bbc.co.uk) was launched, funded solely by the license fee (no advertising revenue). BBC Online, with high-quality content, is one of Europe's most popular Internet sites. In 1999, following recommendations of a government committee, BBC America was set up on commercial lines.

Chapter 6

1. *Kibo no Kuni no Exodus* (*Exodus in the Hopeful Country*) by Ryu Murakami, serialized in *Bungei Shunju*, beginning October 1998.

2. See the writings of Jon Katz in *Wired Magazine*. Technorealists like Andrew Shapiro are less optimistic but predict similar social impacts as a result of the Internet.

3. Howard Rheingold, *The Virtual Community: Homesteading on the Electronic Frontier* (Reading, Mass.: Addison-Wesley Publishing, 1993).

4. Richard J. Samuels, *Rich Nation, Strong Army: National Security and the Technological Transformation of Japan* (Ithaca: Cornell University Press, 1994).

5. Chalmers Johnson, *MITI and the Japanese Miracle: The Growth of Industrial Policy, 1925-1975* (Stanford: Stanford University Press, 1982).

6. Joseph A. Schumpeter, *Capitalism, Socialism and Democracy* (Harper & Row, third ed., 1962), p. 84.

7. Robert E. Cole and Dimitry Rtischev, "Social and Structural Barriers to the IT Revolution, as Seen from High-Tech Industries." Keynote address at NIME International Symposium 1999 (www.nime.ac.jp/conf99).

8. Marie Anchordoguy, "Japan Software Industry: A Failure of Institutions?" *Research Policy,* March 2000, pp. 391–408.

9. Lonny E. Carlile and Mark C. Tilton, *Is Japan Really Changing Its Ways?* (Washington D.C.: Brookings Institution, 1998), p. 5.

10. *Intanetto Hakusho* (Internet White Book) '99. Impress Corp., Internet Association of Japan, Access Media International, 1999, p. 29

11. Ibid.

12. Ibid. p. 168.

13. Members of the network included Tokyo University, Kyoto University, Tohoku University, Hitachi, Fujitsu, NEC, and Nippon Telegraph and Telephone Co. The Ministry of Education paid for the system. Jeffrey Shapard, "Islands in the (Data) Stream: The Influence of Language and Character Codes on Electronic Insularism and Isolation in Japan," *Working Paper Series,* Center for Global Communications (Glocom), International University of Japan, February 1992, p. 11.

14. Open Systems Interconnection.

15. Shapard, p. 11.

16. Bob Johnston, "Wiring Japan," *Wired Magazine,* 2.02, February 1994.

17. Izumi Aizu, interview, December 1999.

18. Burgess Laird, "Japanese Government Policies for the Development of an Advanced Info-Communications Infrastructure," conference paper, *Cyber Japan: Technology, Policy & Society,* Library of Congress, May 31, 1996, p. 37.

19. Izumi Aizu, "Building Japan's Information Infrastructure: Create New User Demand Through Innovation That Brings 'Increasing Return,'" *Nihon Keizai Shimbun,* April 16, 1993.

20. Ibid.

21. Laird, p. 59.

22. "Real-Internet Consortium (RIC)—Terabit Router," Report ATIP99.07, Asian Technology Information Program (ATIP) 1999.

23. See www.ietf.org for more information.

24. "Mobile Communications/Computing in Japan," Report ATIP, January 2000.

25. "Ministries Seek Standard for Info-tech Construction," *Nikkei Weekly,* November 8, 1999, p. 5.

26. William Ouchi, *Theory Z: How American Business Can Meet the Japanese Challenge* (Perseus Books, 1981).

27. Cole and Rtischev, "Social and Structural Barriers to the IT Revolution, as Seen from High-Tech Industries."

28. Hiroyuki Itami, "The Human-Capitalism of the Japanese Firm As an Integrated System," in *Business Enterprise in Japan,* ed. Kenichi Imai and Ryutaro Komiya (Cambridge: MIT Press, 1994), p. 73.

29. Ibid. p. 83.

30. Motoshige Ito, "Interfirm Relations and Long-Term Continuous Trading," Imai and Komiya, p. 105.

31. W. Carl Kester, "Governance, Contracting, and Investment Horizons: A Look at Japan and Germany," in *Studies in International Corporate Finance and Governance Systems: A comparison of the U.S., Japan, and Europe,* ed. Donald H. Chew (Oxford University Press 1997), p. 227.

32. Gene Bylinsky, "For Sale: Japanese Plants in the U.S.," *Fortune,* Feb. 2, 2000, p. 240.

33. Tim Clark, editor of *Japan Internet Reports,* has frequently made this observation.

34. "Digital Window Tribes Get Up and Leave," *Nikkei Business,* December 20, 1999, p. 26.

35. MPT White Paper 1999, p. 169.

36. Industry interviews, November 1999.

37. Ibid.

38. Samuels.

39. Schumpeter, p. 90.

40. Ibid. p. 87.

41. "Mobile Communications/Computing in Japan," *Asian Technology Information Program Report #00.008,* February 14, 2000, p.5.

42. Voytek Siewierski, NTT Docomo, interview, January 2000. Also see "Mobile Communications/Computing in Japan," ATIP/Japan, January 2000.

43. Asano Ayu, "Mobile Nation," *Look Japan,* October 1999, p. 7.

44. "Introducing Low Fixed Rates in Communications," *Nikkei Business,* June 28, 1999, p. 32.

45. "Traders to Peddle Steel Online," *Nikkei Weekly,* January 24, 2000, p. 11.

46. Rebecca Knight and Mariko Sanchanta, "Masayoshi Son: The right touch at Softbank," *Financial Times,* February 22, 2000.

47. "Internet Wars" *Economisuto,* January 11, 2000, p. 58.

48. "Sony's plan stirs up Internet-banking race," *Nikkei Weekly,* December 13, 1999, p. 1.

49. "E-commerce set to explode in Japan," *Nikkei Weekly,* January 24, 2000, p. 11.

50. Interview in *Nihon Keizai Shimbun,* January 8, 2000, p. 9.

51. "Internet Wars," *Economisuto,* January 11, 2000.

52. "Principal quits over Web criticism," *Yomiuri Shimbun,* September 6, 1999.

Chapter 7

1. Descriptive and statistical analyses of data on strategic alliances of nearly 800 firms in the United States and abroad provide the empirical basis for this chapter. In 1987 we began this research by sending out a 50-question survey to CEOs of Fortune 500 firms, covering alliances formed during the period 1983 to 1987. We received 157 (31.4 percent return rate), of which approximately half (75) were completed by firm CEOs, presidents, or COOs; the rest were returned by chief strategists or operating executives in charge of alliances. The questionnaire was developed with the help of a number of senior executives from alliance-building firms, and was beta-tested and revised before being mailed. Responding firms came from a variety of industries including consumer products, drugs and health care, electronics and computers, environmental, manufacturing, and natural resources and energy. The only condition we imposed for inclusion in the survey was that the firm had to be in at least one alliance for one year—in an operating alliance, not in planning or implementation stages. We supplemented the written survey with 50 field and phone interviews with firms such as HP, American Motors, Ford, and Beatrice Foods. The survey and field interviews combined raised the number of firm responses to approximately 200 firms and approximately 500 alliance relationships.

We asked respondent firms to indicate the principal industry served and provide a self-assessment of alliance performance. Performance measures included firm and alliance sale/revenue size, average alliance investment, international sales, research and development, new product development, business diversity, average alliance return on investment, types of alliance, alliance number, and alliance success ratings. We also inquired about important alliance issues facing the firms. Respondents also evaluated their firm's alliance formulation methodology and its key practices, including identification, evaluation, negotiation, and implementation processes associated with alliances.

A new survey was sent to *Business Week*'s top 1000 firms in 1993. The initial survey was expanded to 59 questions, covering the period 1988 to 1992. Again the key condition was that a firm had to be in at least one alliance for one year. Categories of industries surveyed were expanded to include aerospace and defense, biotech, transportation, entertainment, telecommunications., and more. We conducted 80 supplemental field and phone interviews with firms such as Hexcel, Lockheed, and Quaker Oats. Our total number of usable responses totaled 283 and covered nearly 1,800 alliances. Analysis of this second set of data confirmed results noted in the first survey. For example, in both the first and second survey we uncovered clear positive relationships between alliance experience and alliance performance measured as return on investment.

In 1996 we sent a third survey to 300 non-U.S. firms containing 89 questions. The aim in this survey was to test the robustness of our previous findings with a sample of exclusively non-U.S. firms. We received 60 responses covering 1,000 non-U.S. alliances, and obtained results consistent with our previous two surveys.

Follow-on surveys in 1997 and 1998 provided further evidence of the robustness of findings from our earlier surveys. In 1997 we sent out three surveys. Two were targeted at a select group of firms from which we were trying to gather specific data on alliance skills and implementation approaches. They were completed in 1997, covering institutionalization of alliance skills within an organization and integration and implementations of a strategic alliance. Both studies involved approximately 40 firms. A third study involved examining 1,300 firms to gain insight on their growth trajectory. This study was a combination of in-house analysis and survey work at Booz·Allen & Hamilton.

In 1998 we updated our global database with a 69-question survey about alliances directed to 300 European CEOs. We received 75 responses. Based on this information, we sent an 89-question survey to the CEOs of the top 1,000 U.S. and top 1,000 European firms about their alliance efforts. We received 235 responses that covered much of the same ground of earlier surveys but also expanded the efforts into new territory. Our most recent survey was conducted in conjunction with the Association for Growth. We developed a survey to compare alliance attitudes, efforts, and performance of small and mid-size firms with information in our database on large firms. We also look at the issues of alliances as an alternative to venture capital, IPOs, and debt-financing. As of spring 2000, our alliance database contains information on more than 1,000 U.S. and non-U.S. firms and more than 10,000 alliances. We have held more than 200 interviews with these firms to share and verify the results.

2. The bibliographic reference section of this chapter provides a list of recent commentary and analysis of interorganizational models important to the historical development of alternative "allianced-enterprise" structures.

Chapter 8

1. Robert Goldstein and Kim Hoan Vu provided valuable research assistance on this chapter. Financial support for this research, provided by the Fletcher School of Law & Diplomacy's Hitachi Center for Technology & International Affairs, is gratefully acknowledged.

Chapter 9

1. Vinton G. Cerf, "Core Protocols," in *Internet System Handbook,* eds. Daniel C. Lynch and Marshall T. Rose (Reading, Mass.: Addison-Wesley, 1993), 84–85.
2. Ibid, 117–18.

Chapter 10

1. Source: *Boardwatch Magazine, Directory of Internet Service Providers,* 11th Edition. See boardwatch.internet.com/isp/summer99/backbones. html.
2. Source: Table 19.3 in *Trends in Telephone Service,* Federal Communications Commission, Washington, D.C., March 2000. These are counts for the number of carriers that pay into the telecommunications relay service fund.
3. Source: Table 1.2 in the *Statistics of Communications Common Carriers 1998/1999,* Federal Communications Commission, Washington, D.C., December 1999.
4. I am referring to the model for an IP bearer service market outlined in Clark (1995) and the National Research Council (1994) report.
5. Large commercial customers are more complex because they are more heterogeneous and because they face a larger array of outside options. Examining the behavior of large commercial customers requires consideration of their needs for intranet services and their decisions to self-provision, which

means that one must examine interactions between equipment vendors and service providers. Because all of the challenges or opportunities present in residential (or small business) Internet service markets are present in commercial markets as well, focusing on the former provides a good starting point.

6. For example, in many countries the PTT provides both long-distance and local telephone services and Internet access.

7. For example, in the United States, there are local IAPs that rely on local telephone carriers to deliver traffic to their POP and from their POP to the ISP that provides them with Internet backbone services. The ISP may lease its transport facilities from interexchange carriers.

8. We ignore the possibility of separate contracting arrangements between the end-user and other stages in the value chain (e.g., separate service contracting for IAP and ISP services) on the grounds that such relationships seem unlikely for residential consumers. Large commercial customers are more likely to consider this a viable option because they consider private networks and use of the PSTN as substitutes. The largest corporations are likely to have complex pricing agreements with players at all levels in the value chain.

9. As noted earlier, we will focus on the model of providing service to residential consumers to simplify the discussion. Service to commercial customers is inherently more complex and heterogeneous because they have a larger array of needs and a wider selection of outside options for meeting those needs.

10. Typically, backbone providers peer with other backbone providers using "bill and keep," in which they agree to terminate each other's traffic at no cost. Larger ISPs may decline to peer with lower-level regional ISPs and require them to pay capacity- or usage-sensitive transport fees.

11. In the future, however, it may include other types of local access providers, such as community TV providers (cable) using cable modems, or wireless providers (e.g., PCS, mobile cellular, spread spectrum, etc.).

12. That is, local access markets are very local—local access plant that does not pass a home does not offer a viable substitute, whereas in long distance services, switches in San Francisco and San Jose can offer competing long distance services.

13. An expectation of repeated future interactions can give rise to implicit contracts.

14. Horizontal integration increases market share. The principal motivations for horizontal integration are (1) scale and scope economies; (2) to extend or protect market power (monopoly—over buyers; monopsony—over suppliers).

15. This may include reductions in the costs of managing risk (i.e., insurance) as when an upstream supplier sells into diverse downstream markets subject to uncorrelated demand shocks. This reduces diversifiable risk in the form of demand uncertainty (analogous to investing in a market portfolio rather than a single stock).

16. Co-specialized assets are assets that are more valuable when used together in a coordinated way. The classic example is a coal mine and the rail facilities that serve that coal mine. Independent ownership of these assets can result in excessive bargaining costs as each player tries to "hold-up" the other.

17. Srinagesh and Gong argue that a competitive market for an undifferentiated bearer service may be unsustainable because of the existence of substantial sunk costs, the likelihood of excess capacity, and aggressive "Bertrand-like" price competition that would prohibit cost recovery. According to Srinagesh and Gong, resolving this dilemma will require that upstream suppliers of bearer services integrate forward to differentiate themselves or use long-term contracts to shift the risk of cost recovery toward downstream customers. Kavassalis, Lee, and Bailey (1997) disagree with this assessment, arguing that the bearer service market need not be a commodity because service providers will be able to successfully differentiate their bearer services. These issues will be discussed at greater length below.

18. For example, ITel software company may have to integrate backward to produce board-level product if no supplier can be found to provide. Or, upstream suppliers may need to integrate forward to develop new distribution channels for new product.

19. Firm may vertically integrate to acquire additional skills and expertise, especially in technologically complex environments.

20. Public review of mergers by the U.S. Department of Justice focus on the likely effect of the merger on competition. For horizontal mergers, the focus is on post-merger market concentration. The analysis of vertical mergers is inherently more complex.

21. If the target market is already competitive, then prices should not exceed economic costs. Moreover, the firm with market power should be able to extract its monopoly rents without forward (backward) integration by pric-

ing its goods at monopoly levels. Vertical integration to establish market power over a previously competitive market is often difficult unless the entering firm is able to force the exit of competitors and erect barriers that will prevent re-entry.

22. For example, an upstream provider of a bottleneck facility (e.g., local access services in telephone) may seek to integrate downstream to avoid price regulations intended to constrain monopoly power over the bottleneck facility.

23. For example, if the upstream supplier has substantial sunk investments in sunk capacity, it may seek to integrate forward to deter competition that could destroy the quasi-rents associated with this sunk capacity.

24. Today we have standalone IAPs (e.g., TIAC), IAPs that are vertically integrated with ISPs but do not own wide area transport facilities (e.g., UUNET), and IAPs that vertically integrated with facilities-based ISPs (e.g., MCI).

25. It is likely that the returns to scale for network management first decrease significantly (i.e., very small networks are easy to manage, but quickly become more difficult as they grow larger—extreme example, no problem with single computer becomes big problem with network of two computers), then increase over some range, and then eventually decrease again (i.e., it is possible for a network to be too large).

26. Technological advances have been reducing network costs in absolute terms and have facilitated the development of more scalable and modular technologies, which reduces the effects of increasing returns to scale.

27. A large network may choose to deny interconnection or offer interconnection at higher prices or of inferior quality to a smaller network to lessen the competitive threat posed by the smaller network. Because of the importance of network externalities, manipulation of interconnection policies to exploit, protect, or enhance the market power of a dominant incumbent will remain an important concern for procompetitive regulatory authorities.

28. Currently, large backbone carriers exchange traffic using "bill and keep" arrangements. These presume that the costs of termination are minimal or that traffic is balanced. This raises the interesting question of who should be allowed to peer with whom, which is ultimately a question of what smaller networks should pay for universal termination services. Currently, a number of large backbone carriers refuse to peer with smaller networks and charge those networks capacity- and usage-sensitive interconnection fees for transport services.

29. If customers switch to cable modems, the copper plant in the ground will become available for other uses.

30. Facilities-based providers could deter reseller competition by colluding to set the wholesale price for bearer services too high. First, such a strategy would violate antitrust law. Second, while such a strategy may be collectively profitable, it would be privately rational for an individual facilities-provider to defect and offer wholesale bearer services to resellers.

31. In order of increasing entry barriers, the markets may be ordered as: IAP, ISP, WAT, LAT. Facilities-based entry is more capital intensive and LAT entry is the most capital intensive. Moreover, the LAT market is relatively small for the capital investment and is most likely to exhibit natural monopoly characteristics.

32. Were the RBOCs to suddenly become the dominant internet access providers, squeezing out existing IAPs, regulatory authorities could be moved to impose additional regulatory restraints. Similarly, cable TV providers might hesitate to provide telephone service competition (if ITel takes off) for fear of becoming subject to telephone regulation (subject to equal access provisions, required to contribute to universal service, etc.).

33. That is, IAP-ISP-LAT-WAT firms.

34. That is, IAP and IAP-ISP firms that do not own facilities, but act as either pure or facilities-based resellers of underlying transport services.

35. That is, are local access facilities a natural monopoly?

36. The existence of excess capacity to support a facilities-resale market does not preclude congestion problems. I am presuming that usage pricing or admission control procedures will be adopted to address congestion problems such as wasteful use of the Internet. What is necessary is that at any point in time there will be a carrier willing to lease local or long-distance transport services to retail-only resellers.

37. In the near term, this is not true for international service along certain routes; however, international capacity should be expanded rapidly.

Chapter 11

1. Transmission Control Protocol/Internet Protocol. TCP/IP is a protocol *suite* (or *stack,* because it involves more than one protocol) endorsed by the U.S. Department of Defense in 1978 as a data communications standard. It was specified as the required protocol on Arpanet and Milnet by the U.S. Office of the Secretary of Defense in 1983. TCP\IP is a very popular data commu-

nications protocol, because it is available for most operating systems and hardware platforms and enables all these computers to communicate (UNIX workstations; PCs running MS-DOS, Windows, or OS/2; Apple Macintoshes, IBM Mainframes; DEC Minicomputers, etc). TCP\IP is the protocol that reliably connects the networks that, connected, are the Internet.

2. A proxy is a piece of software that sits between a network user and the network to provide a measure of privacy by routing all network requests through a filter that masks the actual characteristics of the user to the network and yet returns the information sought by the user.

3. One of the current debates on the Internet concerns the use of "cookies." Cookies are small pieces of text that certain websites leave on the local hard drive of the internet user. The text of the cookie can contain information about where the user has been and what he or she has done on the Internet.

4. "[I]t is clear that the development and widespread deployment of cryptography that can be used to deny government access to information represents a challenge to the balance of power between the government and the individual. Historically, all governments under circumstances that further the common good, have asserted the right to compromise the privacy of individuals. . . . [U]nbreakable cryptography for confidentiality provides the individual with the ability to frustrate assertions of that right." National Research Council, *Cryptography's Role in Securing the Information Society,* ch. 2 (May 30, 1996) sect; 8.1.3.

Chapter 12
1. See R. Coase (1937), "The Nature of the Firm," *Economica* 4(3), 144.

REFERENCES

Chapter 2

Aghion, Philippe, and Peter Howitt. *Endogenous Growth Theory.* Cambridge, Mass.: MIT Press, 1998.

Baumol, William J. "Having Your Cake: How to Preserve Universal-Service Cross Subsidies While Facilitating Competitive Entry." *Yale Journal on Regulation* 16, no. 1 (Winter 1999): 1–17.

———. "On Distribution, Lump-Sum Transfers and Innovation Spillovers." *Economic Events, Ideas and Policies: The 1960s and After.* Washington, D.C.: The Brookings Institution, 2000 (forthcoming).

———. Janusz A. Ordover, and Robert D. Willig. "Parity Pricing and Its Critics: A Necessary Condition for Efficiency in the Provision of Bottleneck Services to Competitors." *Yale Journal on Regulation* 14, no. 1 (1997): 145–63.

Grilliches, Zvi. "Issues in Assessing the Contribution of Research and Development to Productivity Growth." *Bell Journal of Economics* 10 (1979): 92–116.

Maddison, Angus. *Monitoring the World Economy, 1820-1992.* Paris: Organization for Economic Cooperation and Development, 1995.

Mohnen, Pierre. *The Relationship Between R&D and Productivity Growth in Canada and Other Industrial Countries.* Ottawa: Canada Communications Group, 1992.

Nadiri, M. I. "Innovations and Technological Spillovers." New York University, 1991, unpublished.

National Science Board. *Science and Engineering Indicators, 1996.* Washington, D.C.: U.S. Government Printing Office, 1996, NSB 96-21, p. 84.

Nordhaus, William D. *Invention, Growth and Welfare.* Cambridge, Mass.: MIT Press, 1969.

Romer, Paul. "New Goods, Old Theory and the Welfare Costs of Trade Restrictions." *Journal of Development Economics* 43 (1994): 5-38.

Solow, Robert M. "A Contribution to the Theory of Economic Growth." *Quarterly Journal of Economics* 70 (1956): 65–94.

U.S. Bureau of the Census. *Historical Statistics of the United States, Colonial Times to 1970, Part I.* Washington, D.C.: U.S. Government Printing Office, 1975.

———. *Statistical Abstract of the United States, 1997,* 118th ed. Washington, D.C.: U.S. Government Printing Office, 1998.

Willig, Robert D. "The Theory of Network Access Pricing." In *Issues in Public Utility Regulation,* H. M. Trebbing, ed. Vol. 109, 1979.

Wolff, Edward N. "Spillovers, Linkages and Technical Change." *Economic Systems Research* 9 (1997): 9–23.

Chapter 3

Bailey, Joseph P. "Aggregation and Intermediation in Electronic Commerce" Ph.D. diss., Technology, Management, and Policy Program, MIT, 1998.

Branscomb, Lewis M., and James H. Keller. *Investing in Innovation: Creating a Research and Innovation Policy That Works*. Cambridge: MIT Press, 1998.

Bronson, Po. "Is Anyone in Silicon Valley Still Making Things?" in *The Wall Street Journal*, August 16, 1999, p. A14.

Browning, E. S. "Tech Lovers Begin to Fret About the "V" Word: Valuation. Is There Rationale That Can Justify Lofty Stock Prices?" in *The Wall Street Journal*, March 23, 2000, p. C1.

Camp, L. Jean. *Trust and Risk in Internet Commerce*. Cambridge: MIT Press, 2000.

Gawer, Annabelle. "The Organization of Platform Leadership: An Empirical Investigation of Intel's Management Processes Aimed at Fostering Complementary Innovation by Third Parties." Ph.D. diss., Massachusetts Institute of Technology, Sloan School of Management, 2000.

Kindleberger, Charles P. *Manias, Panics, and Crashes: A History of Financial Crises*. New York: Basic Books, revised edition, 1989.

McKnight, Lee W. and Joseph P. Bailey. "Global Internet Economics," in *Brazilian Electronic Journal of Economics*, 1997.

———. "Introduction to Internet Economics." *In Internet Economics*, ed. L. McKnight and J. Bailey. Cambridge: MIT Press, 1997,1998.

Nelson, Richard B. ed., *National Innovation Systems*. New York: Oxford University Press, 1993.

Rogers, Everett. *Diffusion of Innovations*. New York: New York: Free Press, 4th edition, 1995.

Schumpeter, Joseph A. *Capitalism, Socialism, and Democracy*. New York: HarperCollins, 1984.

——— . *Essays: On Entrepreneurs, Innovations, Business Cycles, and the Evolution of Capitalism*. Somerset, N.J.: Transaction Publishers, 1989.

Schwartz, Evan. *Digital Darwinism: 7 Breakthrough Strategies for Surviving in the Cutthroat Web Economy*. New York: Broadway Books, 1999.

Shapiro, Carl, and Hal R. Varian, *Information Rules: A Strategic Guide to the Network Economy*. Boston: Harvard Business School Press, 1998.

Treese, Winfield and Lawrence C. Stewart. *Designing Systems for Internet Commerce*. New York: Addison-Wesley, 1998.

Chapter 5

Akdeniz, Yaman [Director of Cyber-Rights and Cyber-Liberties, UK] (2000). "The Internet, as a global medium is thought to be the land of free speech and democracy," *The Guardian,* 27 April.

Baldwin, R., and M. Cave (1999). *Understanding Regulation: Theory, Strategy and Practice.* Oxford and New York: Oxford University Press.

Bangemann High Level Group on the Information Society (1994). *Europe and the Global Information Society: Recommendations to the European Council,* 26 May [Bangemann Report].

Bauer, J. M. (1997). "Market power, innovation, and efficiency in telecommunications: Schumpeter reconsidered," *Journal of Economic Issues* 32(2): 557–65.

Beesley, M. (1981). "The liberalisation of British telecom," *Economic Affairs,* October, pp. 19–27.

———— , and S. Littlechild, (1983) "Privatisation: Principles, problems and priorities," *Lloyd's Bank Review,* July, pp. 1–20.

BIPA [British Internet Publishers' Alliance] (1999). BIPA submission to the Davies Review Panel, London: BIPA.

Broadcast, 6 August 1999.

Bruce, R. R., J. P. Cunard, M. D. Director (1986). *From Telecommunications to Electronic Services.* Austin, Boston, Seattle, St. Paul: Butterworths.

Coase, R. (1960). "The problem of social cost," *Journal of Law & Economics* 3: 1–44; reprinted in R. Coase (1990), "The problem of social cost," *The Firm, the Market and the Law.* Chicago: University of Chicago Press, pp. 95–185.

Commission Directive 95/51/EC of 18 October 1995 amending Directive 90/388/EEC with regard to the abolition of the restrictions on the use of cable television networks for the provision of already liberalized telecommunications services, OJ L256/49, 26 October 1995.

Commission Directive 95/47/EC of the European Parliament and of the Council of 24 October 1995 on the use of standards for the transmission of television signals, OJ L281/51, 23 November 1995.

Commission Notice concerning the status of voice communications on Internet under Community law and, in particular, pursuant to Directive 90/388/EC, OJ C6, 10 January 1998.

Davies, G., and J. Davies (1984). "The revolution in monopoly theory," *Lloyd's Bank Review,* July, pp. 38–52.

DTI [Department of Trade and Industry—UK] (1999). *Regulating Communications: The Way Ahead.* Results of the Consultation on the Convergence Green Paper. London: DTI.

Dudman, J. (2000). "BT hit by US threat over DSL," *Communications Week International,* 17 April.

European Commission (1994). *Strategy Options to Strengthen the European Programme Industry in the Context of the Audiovisual Policy of the European Union*, COM(94)96 final, Brussels.

——— (1997). *Green Paper on the Convergence of the Telecommunications, Media and Information Technology Sectors, and the Implications for Regulation. Towards an Information Society Approach*, COM(97)623 final, 3 December, Brussels.

——— (1999a). *The Convergence of the Telecommunications, Media and Information Technology Sectors, and the Implications for Regulation. Results of the Public Consultation on the Green Paper* [COM(97)623]. *Communication to the European Parliament, the Council, the Economic and Social Committee and the Committee of the Regions.* COM(99)108 final, 10 March.

——— (1999b). *Towards a New Framework for Electronic Communications Services: Infrastructure, Transmission and Access Services—The 1999 Communications Review*, COM(1999)539 final, 9 November 1999.

——— (2000). *Commission Recommendation on Unbundled Access to the Local Loop*, COM(2000)1059 final, 26 April 2000.

Foster, C. D. (1992). *Privatisation, Public Ownership and the Regulation of Natural Monopoly.* Oxford and Cambridge: Blackwell.

Goodwin, P. (1998). *Television under the Tories. Broadcasting Policy 1979-1997.* London: British Film Institute.

Groom, B., and P. T. Larsen (2000). "Byers may scrap media and telecoms regulators," *Financial Times,* 12 May.

Harding, J., and P. T. Larsen (1999). "Carlton-United deal may transform ITV," *Financial Times,* November, pp. 27–28.

Harris, R. A., and S. M. Milkis (1991). "Regulatory regimes, social regulation, and prospects for deregulation," in *Public Policy and Economic Institutions,* M. Dubnick and A. Gitelson, eds. London and Greenwich, Conn.: JAI Press.

Hills, J. (1986). *Deregulating Telecommunications: Competition and Control in the United States, Japan and Britain.* London: Frances Pinter.

——— (1998). "Liberalisation, regulation and development," *Gazette* 60(6): 459–76.

———, and M. Michalis (1997a). "Digital television and regulatory issues. The British case," *Communications & Strategies,* no. 27, 3rd quarter, pp. 75–101.

———, and M. Michalis (1997b). "Technological convergence: Regulatory competition. The British case of digital television," *Policy Studies* 19(3/4): 219–37.

———, with S. Papathanassopoulos (1991). *The Democracy Gap: The Politics of Information Technologies in the United States and Europe.* New York and Westport: Greenwood Press.

Information Technology Advisory Panel [ITAP-UK] (1982). *Cable Systems: A Report by the ITAP.* London: The Stationery Office.

Littlechild, S. [Department of Industry, UK] (1983). *Regulation of British Telecommunications Profitability: Report to the Secretary of State.* London: Department of Industry.

Lunney v. Prodigy Services Company Opinion, Court of Appeals of New York. Alexander G. Lunney, appellant v. Prodigy Services Company, respondent, et al., defendants. 99 N.Y. Int. 0165. December 2, 1999. 2 No 164. available on http://caselaw.findlaw.com/scripts/getcase.pl?court=ny&vol=i99&involv =0165

Maitland, I. (1985). "The limits of business self-regulation," *California Management Review* 27, pp. 132–45.

Marcus, A. (1985). "Business demand for regulation: An exploration of the Stigler Hypothesis," *Research in Corporate Social Performance and Policy* 7, pp. 25–46.

Michalis, M. (1999). "Access issues: Operational Support Systems and regulation," *Telecommunications Policy* 23(6): 481–93.

OECD [Organization for Economic Co-operation and Development] (1998a). *Traffic Exchange: Developments and Policy,* DSTI/ICCP/TISP (98)1/Final, Paris: OECD.

—— (1998b). *Cross-Ownership and Convergence: Policy Issues, Working Party on Telecommunication and Information Services Policies,* DSTI/ICCP/TISP (98)3/Final, Paris: OECD.

OFT [Office of Fair Trading, UK] (Dec. 1996). *The Director General's Review of BskyB's Position in the Wholesale Pay TV Market.* London: OFT.

Oftel (August 1995). Beyond the telephone, the television and the PC –I A Consultative Document on the regulation of broadband switched mass-market services (and their substitutes) delivered by telecommunication systems. London: Oftel.

—— (July 1999a). *Access to bandwidth: Proposals for action—Consultation.* London: Oftel.

—— (November 1999b). *Access to bandwidth: Delivering competition for the Information Age.* London: Oftel.

Peltzman, G. (1976). "Towards a more general theory of regulation," *Journal of Law and Economics* 14: 109–48.

Posner, R. (1974). "Theories of economic regulation," *Bell Journal of Economics* 5: 335–56.

Powell, M. (2000). "FCC Commissioner Michael K. Powell Criticizes apparent Politicization of Commission Business," 18 April, available from http://www.fcc.gov/Speeches/Powell/Statements/2000/stmkp006.html

Public Network Europe, November 1999.

Quirk, P. J. (1981). *Industry Influence in Federal Regulatory Agencies.* Princeton: Princeton University Press.

Rufford, N. (2000). "MI5 builds new centre to read e-mails on the net," *The Sunday Times,* 30 April.

Scannell, P., and D. Cardiff (1991). *A Social History of British Broadcasting: Vol. One, 1922-1939, Serving the Nation.* London: Basil Blackwell.

Schumpeter, J. A. (1943). *Capitalism, Socialism and Democracy.* London: Allen & Unwin.

—— (1949). Foreword to 1949 edition, *Capitalism, Socialism and Democracy.* London: Allen & Unwin.

Stigler, G. (1971). "The theory of economic regulation," *Bell Journal of Economics* 2: 3–21.

——, and C. Friedland (1962). "What can regulators regulate? The case of electricity," *The Journal of Law and Economics* V (October): 147–67.

Teather, D. (2000a). "BT hurt by Brown effect," *The Guardian,* 17 February.

—— (2000b). "Open will outdo Freeserve, say experts," *The Guardian,* 24 February.

Telecommunications Markets (1994), no. 244, 14 April.

The Economist (8 May 1999), "The BBC: Online and in a mess."

Tracey, M. (1998). *The Decline and Fall of Public Service Broadcasting.* Oxford: Oxford University Press.

Wilson, J. Q. (ed.) (1980). *The Politics of Regulation.* New York: Basic Books.

Chapter 7

Anderson, Paul, Griffiths, and Tim Laseter. "Strategic Sourcing: A Competitive Imperative." New York: Booz•Allen & Hamilton, 1993.

Badaracco Jr., Joseph. *The Knowledge Link: How Firms Compete Through Strategic Alliances.* Boston: Harvard Business School Press, 1991.

Bleeke, Joel, and David Ernst. *Collaborating to Compete.* New York: John Wiley & Sons, 1993.

Chan, Peng and Anna Wong. "Global Strategic Alliances and Organizational Learning." *Leadership & Organizational Journal* 15, no. 4 (1994).

Coned, David, Peter la Place, and Kenneth Wexler. *The Partnership and Alliances Audit.* Switzerland: Strategic Direction Publishers Ltd, Switzerland, 1994.

Contractor, Farok. "A Generalized Theorem for Joint Venture and Licensing Negotiations." *Journal of International Business Studies* 16, no. 2, pp. 23–50 (1985).

De La Sierra, Margaret Cauley. *Managing Global Alliances: Key Steps for Successful Collaboration.* New York: Addison-Wesley, 1995.

Dunning, John H. *Alliance Capitalism and Global Business.* New York: Routledge, 1997.

Freidheim, Cyrus. "The Global Corporation." Presented to World Economic Forum, Davos, Switzerland. Booz•Allen & Hamilton, New York, 1993.

Friedland, Jonathan. "Strategic Alliances." *Far Eastern Review* 157, no. 19, May 12, p. 56 (1994).

Gibson, David, and Everett Rogers. *R&D Collaboration on Trial: The Microelectronics and Computer Technology Corporation.* Boston: Harvard Business School Press, 1994. (Chapters 1 and 2.)

Gomes-Casseres, Benjamin. *The Alliance Revolution: The New Shape of Business* Rivalry, Cambridge: Harvard University Press, 1996.

Gullander, Stefan. "Joint Ventures and Corporate Strategy." *Columbia Journal of World Business* 11, no. 1, p. 104 (1976).

Habib, Ghazi. "Measures of Manifest Conflict in International JVs." *Academy of Management Journal* 30, no. 4, pp. 808–816 (1987).

Hamel, Gary. "Competition for Competence and Inter-Partner Learning within International Strategic Alliance." *Strategic Management Journal* 12, pp. 83–103 (1991).

Harbison, John, and Peter Pekar. "A Practical Guide to Alliances: Leapfrogging the Learning Curve." Booz•Allen & Hamilton, New York, NY, 1994.

———. "Cross-Border Alliances in the Age of Collaboration." Booz•Allen & Hamilton, New York, NY, 1997.

———. "Institutionalizing Alliance Skills: Secrets of Repeatable Success." Booz•Allen & Hamilton, New York, NY, 1997.

———. "Strategic Management: Dinosaur or Differentiator?" Booz•Allen & Hamilton, New York, NY, 1997.

Harrigan, Kathryn. "Joint Ventures and Global Strategies." *Columbia Journal of World Business* 19, no. 2, pp. 7–16 (1984).

———. *Strategies for Joint Ventures.* Lexington, Mass: Lexington Books, 1985.

Hennart, Jean-Francois. "A Transaction Costs: Theory of Equity Joint Ventures." *Strategic Management Journal* 9, no. 4, pp. 361–374 (1988).

Killing, J. Peter. "How to Make a Global Joint Venture Work." *Harvard Business Review* 60, no. 3, pp. 120–127 (1982).

Koh, Jeongsuk, and Venkatraman, "JV Formations and Stock Market Reactions: An Assessment in the Information Technology Sector." *Academy of Management Journal* 34, no. 4, pp. 869–892 (1991).

Moore, James F. *The Death of Competition: Leadership and Strategy in the Age of Business Ecosystems.* New York: Harper Business, 1996.

Newman, William, "Launching a Viable JV." *California Management Review* 35, no. 1, pp. 68–80 (1992).

Osburn, Richard, and Christopher Baughn. "Forms of Interorganizational Governance for Multinational Alliances." *Academy of Management Journal* 33, no. 3, pp. 503–519 September (1990).

Reich, Robert, and Eric Mankin. "Joint Ventures with Japan Give Away Our Future." *Harvard Business Review* 64, no. 2, pp. 78–86, 1986.

Rigby, Darrell, and Robin Buchanan. "Putting More Strategy into Strategic Alliance." *Directors & Boards* 18, no. 2, pp. 14–19 (1994).

Rowe, Frederick. "Antitrust of European Acquisitions and Joint Ventures in the United States." *Law and Policy in International Business* 12, no. 2, pp. 335–368 (1980).

Sullivan, Jeremiah, and Peterson, Richard, Kameda, Naoki, et al. "The Relationship Between Conflict Resolution Approaches and Trust: A Cross-Cultural Study." *Academy of Management Journal* 24, no. 4, pp. 803–815 (1981).

Teece, David. "Profiting from Technological Innovation: Implications for Integration, Collaboration, Licensing and Public Policy." *Research Policy* 15, no. 6, pp. 285–305 (1986).

Tyebee, Tyzoon, "A Topology of JVs: Japanese Strategies in the U.S." *California Management Review* 31, no. 1, pp. 75–86 (1988).

Chapter 8

Acs, Z., and F. Fitzroy. 1994. "A constitution for privatizing large eastern enterprises." *Economics in Transition,* vol. 2, pp. 83–94.

Aggarwal, R., and J. Harper. 2000. "Privatization and valuation in transition economies." In *Financial Innovations and the Dynamics of Emerging Markets.* Edited by L. Jacque and P. Vaaler. Boston: Kluwer Academic Publishing, in press.

———. 1998. "Equity valuation and the Czech voucher privatization auctions." Working Paper. Boca Raton: Florida Atlantic University.

Barberis, N., M. Boycko, A. Shleifer, and R. Vishny. 1996. "How does privatization work? Evidence from Russian shops." *Journal of Political Economy,* vol. 104, pp. 764–90.

Bias, B., and E. Perotti. 1997. "Machiavellian underpricing." Working Paper. University of Amsterdam and Universite de Toulouse.

Black, B., R. Kraakman, and J. Hay. 1996. "Corporate law from scratch." In *Corporate Governance in Central Europe and Russia.* Volume 2: *Insiders and the State* (World Bank Ceu Privatization Project). Edited by R. Frydman, C. Gray, and A. Rapaczynski. Central European University Press.

Bolton, P. 1992. "Privatization and the separation of ownership and control: Lessons from Chinese enterprise reform," *Economics in Transition,* Vol. 3. European Bank for Reconstruction and Development, London, England.

Borish, M., and M. Noël. 1996. "Private sector development during transition: The visegrad countries," World Bank Discussion Paper 279, World Bank, Washington, D.C.

Boubarkri, N., and J. Cosset. 1998. "The financial and operating performance of newly privatized firms: Evidence from developing countries." *Journal of Finance,* vol. 53, pp. 1081–110.

Boycko, M., A. Shleifer, and R. Vishny. 1995. *Privatizing Russia.* Cambridge: MIT Press.

Brealy, R., and S. Meyers. 1996. *Principles of Corporate Finance.* New York: McGraw-Hill.

Brigham, E. 1995. *Fundamentals of Financial Management.* Fort Worth: Dryden Press.

Caves, R., and L. Christensen. 1980. "The relative efficiency of public and private firms in a competitive environment: The case of Canadian railroads." *Journal of Political Economy,* vol. 88, pp. 958–76.

Donaldson, D., and D. Wagle. 1995. *Privatization: Principles and Practice,* Lessons of Experience Series, Volume 1. International Finance Corporation, World Bank, Washington, D.C.

D'Souza, J., and W. Megginson. 1999. "The financial and operating performance of newly privatized firms in the 1990s." *Journal of Finance,* vol. 54, pp. 1397–438.

Due, J., and S. Schmidt. 1995. "Progress on privatization in Bulgaria." *Comparative Economic Studies,* vol. 37, pp. 55–77.

Duncan, I., and A. Bollard. 1992. *Corporatization and Privatization: Lessons from New Zealand.* Auckland, New Zealand: Oxford University Press.

Economist. 1997. "Selling out the state," March 22.

Feingenbaum, H., and J. Hennig. 1994. "Political underpinnings of privatization: A typology." *World Politics,* vol. 46, pp. 285–308.

Ferguson, P., and G. Ferguson. 1994. "State or private control?" In *Industrial Economics: Issues and Perspectives,* 2d ed. New York: New York University Press.

Financial Times. 2000. "Attacks mount on deutsche telekoms $46 bn bid," July 25, p. 19.

Fox, I., B. Schrage, and P. Vaaler. 2000. "Privatization and Valuation in Emerging Markets: Financial Approaches and Strategic Implications." In *International Research in the Business Disciplines,* Volume 3. Edited by C. Swanson, A. Alkhafaji, and M. Ryan. Stamford, Conn.: JAI Press. In press.

Galal, A., L. Jones, P. Tandon, and I. Vogelsang. 1994. *Welfare Consequences of Selling Public Enterprises: An Empirical Analysis.* New York: Oxford University Press.

Guislain, P. 1997. *The Privatization Challenge: A Strategic, Legal, and Institutional Analysis of International Experience.* Washington, D.C.: World Bank.

Hart, O., A. Shleifer, and R. Vishny. 1997. "The proper scope of government: Theory and application to prisons." *Quarterly Journal of Economics,* vol. 112, pp. 1127–1161.

Hillion, P., and S. Young. 1996. "The Czechoslovak auction: An empirical investigation." Working Paper, INSEAD, Fontainebleau, France.

Hingorani, A., K. Lehn, and A. Makhija. 1997. "Investor behavior in mass privatization: The case of the Czech voucher scheme." *Journal of Financial Economics,* vol. 44, pp. 349–496.

Holmström, B. 1979. "Moral hazard and observability." *Bell Journal of Economics,* vol. 10, pp. 74–91.

International Finance Corporation. 1999. *Emerging-Market Country Indicators, 1999.* International Finance Corporation, World Bank, Washington, D.C.

Jensen, M., and W. Meckling. 1976. "Theory of the firm: Managerial behavior, agency costs and the ownership structure." *Journal of Financial Economics,* vol. 3, pp. 305–60.

Jones, S., W. Megginson, R. Nash, and J. Netter. 1998. "Share issue privatization as financial means to political and economic ends." *Journal of Financial Economics,* vol. 34, pp. 23–47.

Joskow, P., R. Schmalensee, and N. Tsukanova. 1994. "Competition policy in Russia during and after privatization." *Brookings Papers on Economic Activity,* pp. 301–81.

Kerf, M., and W. Smith. 1996. "Privatizing Africa's Infrastructure: Promise and Challenge." World Bank Technical Paper 337, World Bank, Washington, D.C.

Kikeri, S., J. Nellis, and M. Shirley. 1992. "Privatization: The Lessons of Experience." World Bank, Washington, D.C.

Kogut, B. 1996. "Direct investment, experimentation, and corporate governance in transition economies." In *Corporate Governance in Central Europe and Russia: Volume 1: Banks, Funds and Foreign Investors.* (World Bank Ceu Privatization Project). Edited by R. Frydman, C. Gray, and A. Rapaczynski. Central European University Press.

La Porta, T., and F. Lopez-de-Silanes. 1997. "Benefits of privatization: Evidence from Mexico." Working Paper. World Bank, Washington, D.C.

Lessard, D. 1996. "Incorporating country risk in the valuation of offshore projects." *Journal of Applied Corporate Finance,* Fall, pp. 535–63.

Lhomel, E. 1993. "Les transformations économiques en Roumaine: Premier bilan." *Reflets et Perspectives de la Vie Economique,* vol. 32, pp. 257–68.

Lopez-de-Silanes, F. 1995. "Determinants of privatization prices." NBER Working Paper #5113, National Bureau of Economic Research, Cambridge, Mass.

————. 1996. "Determinants of privatization prices." NBER Working Paper #5494, National Bureau of Economic Research, Cambridge, Mass.

McWilliams, A., and D. Siegel. 1997. "Event studies in management research: Theoretical and empirical issues." *Academy of Management Journal,* vol. 40, pp. 626–57.

Megginson, W. 1998. "From state to market: A survey of empirical studies on privatization." Working Paper. University of Oklahoma, Norman, Okla.

————, and J. Netter. 1999. "From state to market: Survey of empirical studies on privatization." Conference paper, Conference on Global Equity Markets, New York.

————, R. Nash, and M. van Randenborgh. 1994. "The financial and operating performance of newly privatized firms: An international empirical analysis." *Journal of Finance,* vol. 49, pp. 327–36.

Minor, M. 1994. "The demise of expropriation as an instrument of LDC policy, 1980–1992." *Journal of International Business Studies,* vol. 25, pp. 177–88.

OECD. 1995. *Mass Privatization: An Initial Assessment.* Organization for Economic Cooperation and Development, Paris, France.

Perotti, E. 1995. "Credible privatization." *American Economic Review,* vol. 85, pp. 847–59.

Prokopenko, J., ed. 1995. *Management for Privatization: Lessons from Industry and Public Service.* Management Development Series 32, International Labour Organization, Geneva, Switzerland.

Ramamurti, R. 1992. "Why are developing countries privatizing?" *Journal of International Business Studies,* vol. 23, pp. 225–49.

Rozenfelds, J. 1993. "Latvia: Legislation and denationalization of land." *Law Institute Journal,* vol. 67, pp. 358–59.

Shleifer, A., and R. Vishny. 1994. "Politicians and firms." *Quarterly Journal of Economics,* vol. 109, pp. 1313–323.

Stanbury, W. 1994. "The extent of privatization in Canada: 1979–1994." Working Paper. University of British Columbia, Vancouver, Canada.

Trigeorgis, L. 1996. *Real Options.* Cambridge: MIT Press.

Vernon, R. 1988. *The Promise of Privatization: A Challenge for U.S. Policy.* Council on Foreign Relations, New York, N.Y.

Vickers, J., and G. Yarrow. 1988. *Privatization: An Economic Analysis.* Cambridge: MIT Press.

Vincent, A. 1995. "Enterprises et holdings publics fédéraux: Restructurations et privatisations, 1992–1995," *Courrier Hebdomaire du CRISP1488-1489.* Centre de Recherche et d'Information Socio-Politiques, Brussels, Belgium.

Vuylsteke, C. 1988. "Techniques of Privatization of State-Owned Enterprises. Vol. 1: Methods and Implementation." World Bank Technical Paper 88, Washington, D.C.

Waelde, T., and A. Kolo. 1999. "Renegotiating previous governments' privatization deals: The 1997 UK windfall tax on utilities and international law." *Northwestern Journal of International Law & Business,* vol. 19, pp. 405–24.

Williamson, O. 1975. *Markets and Hierarchies: Analysis and Antitrust Implications: A Study in the Economics of Internal Organization.* New York: Free Press.

———. 1985. *The Economic Institutions of Capitalism: Firms, Markets, Relational Contracting.* New York: Free Press.

Yarrow, G. 1986. "Privatization in theory and practice." *Economic Policy,* vol. 2, pp. 324–77.

Yergin, D., and J. Stanislaw. 1998. *The Commanding Heights: The Battle Between Government and the Marketplace That Is Remaking the Modern World.* New York: Touchstone-Simon & Schuster.

Chapter 10

Clark, D. "Interoperation, Open Interfaces, and Protocol Architecture," mimeo, Laboratory of Computer Science, Massachusetts Institute of Technology, 1995.

Coase, R. "The Nature of the Firm." *Economica* 4, no. 3 (1937).

Grossman, S., and O. Hart. "The Costs and Benefits of Ownership: A Theory of Vertical and Lateral Integration." *Journal of Political Economy* 94: 691–719 (1986).

Katz, M. "Vertical Contractual Relations." In *Handbook of Industrial Organization.* Vol. 1, edited by R. Schmalensee and R. Willig. Elsevier Science Publishers B.V., 1989.

Kavassalis, P., T. Lee, and J. Bailey. "Sustaining a vertically disintegrated network through a bearer service market." Draft mimeo, September 1997.

Krattenmaker, T., and S. Salop. "Anticompetitive Exclusion: Raising Rivals' Costs to Achieve Power over Price." *Yale Law Journal* 96(2): 209–23 (December 1986).

National Research Council. *Realizing the Information Future and Beyond.* Washington, D.C.: National Academy Press, 1994.

Perry, M. "Vertical Integration: Determinants and Effects." In *Handbook of Industrial*

Organization. Vol. 1, edited by R. Schmalensee and R. Willig. Elsevier Science Publishers B.V., 1989.

Riordan, M., and S. Salop. "Evaluating Vertical Mergers: A Post-Chicago Approach." 63 *Antitrust L.J.* 513 (Winter 1995).

Srinagesh, P., and J. Gong. "The Economics of Layered Networks." In *Internet Economics,* edited by L. McKnight and J. Bailey. Cambridge: MIT Press, 1996.

Williamson, O. *Markets and Hierarchies: Analysis and Antitrust Implications.* New York: The Free Press, 1987.

Chapter 11

Camp, J., and R. Tsang, "Universal service in a ubiquitous digital network." *INET* 99, The Annual Meeting of the Internet Society. San Jose, Calif., 1999.

Clark. "Explicit Allocation for Best Effort Packet Delivery Service." The Telecommunications Policy Research Conference. Solomons Islands Md., 1996.

Dibona, C., S. Ockman, and M. Stone, eds. *Open Sources: Voices from the Open Source Revolution.* Cambridge, Mass.: O'Reilly, 1999.

Galbraith, J. K. *The Affluent Society. 40th Anniversary Edition.* Boston: Houghton Mifflin, 1998.

Hagel, J., and A. Armstrong. *Net Gain: Expanding Markets Through Virtual Communities.* Boston: Harvard Business School Press, 1997.

Hirschman, A. O. *Exit, Voice, and Loyalty: Responses to Decline in Firms, Organizations, and States.* Cambridge: Harvard University Press, 1970.

Horn, S. *Cyberville: Clicks, Culture, and the Creation of an Online Town.* New York: Warner Books, 1997.

Johnson, D., and H. Nissenbaum. *Computer Ethics and Social Value.* Englewood Cliffs: Prentice Hall, 1995.

Mackie-Mason, and H. Varian. "Pricing the Internet." In *Public Access to the Internet,* ed. Kahin and Keller. Englewood Cliffs: Prentice Hall, 1995.

Mueller, M., and J. R. Schement. "Universal Service from the Bottom Up: A Study of Telephone Penetration in Camden, New Jersey." *The Information Society* 12(3), 273–92, 1996.

Samuelson, P. "Why the anti-circumvention regulations need revision." Association for Computing Machinery, *Communications of the ACM.* New York, September 1999.

Stallman, R. "The GNU Manifesto." http://www.fsf.org/gnu/manifesto.html. Originally written in 1984.

INDEX